YOU ONLY DIE ONCE

YOU ONLY DIE ONCE

How to Make It to the End with No Regrets

JODI WELLMAN, MAPP

VORACIOUS

LITTLE, BROWN AND COMPANY

New York   Boston   London

Voracious / Little, Brown and Company
Hachette Book Group
1290 Avenue of the Americas, New York, NY 10104
voraciousbooks.com

First Edition: May 2024

Voracious is an imprint of Little, Brown and Company, a division of Hachette Book Group, Inc. The Voracious name and logo are trademarks of Hachette Book Group, Inc.

The publisher is not responsible for websites (or their content) that are not owned by the publisher.

The Hachette Speakers Bureau provides a wide range of authors for speaking events. To find out more, go to hachettespeakersbureau.com or email HachetteSpeakers@hbgusa.com.

Little, Brown and Company books may be purchased in bulk for business, educational, or promotional use. For information, please contact your local bookseller or the Hachette Book Group Special Markets Department at special.markets@hbgusa.com.

Illustrations by Jodi Wellman

ISBN 9780316574273
Library of Congress Control Number: 2023949283

Printing 1, 2024

LSC-C

Printed in the United States

This book is dedicated to the Grim Reaper—
as a sign of respect for the inspiration
he is to live an Astonishingly Alive Life.
I see you there, lurking in the shadows, Grim.
Let's make a deal: I'll seize the day, and
you can have the night shift.

CONTENTS

YOU
ONLY
DIE
ONCE

INTRODUCTION: I'M DYING TO MEET YOU!

Hello! I'm Jodi, and as of this moment I have 1,821 Mondays left to live. By the time you're reading this, I might only have 821...or 82...or who knows? I might have bit the biscuit already. I might be in an urn, waiting patiently for The Husband to figure out where to sprinkle me.

But if I am in an urn (shit for me), and if you're reading this (yay for you), that also means that before the Grim Reaper showed up at my doorstep, I had a chance to write this book and chronicle not only my life-long crush on Grim himself (bear with me, I swear that'll make sense soon) but also my passion for living Astonishingly Alive Lives in the stark light of our Inescapable Deaths. And I'm so glad you're along for the ride.

This book is a guide for people who might die someday (whether or not they'd like to admit it). It's reassuring to know you're in the right place, isn't it? More specifically, I'm guessing you're here because you want So Much More Out of Life. Maybe you're feeling like your life is passing you by...like you've been taking it for granted...like you're stuck in autopilot with your productive-but-is-this-all-there-is-surely-this-isn't-all-there-is way of being.

Do any of these bullet points ring a bell to you?

- ☠ You have that niggling sense that you're playing it a little too small, a little too safe...and you believe there's more you can wring out of your life.
- ☠ You want more agency in your life, but you don't know where to find it...because who is ever taught to do *that*?
- ☠ You feel like you've been sleepwalking through your days...and that sleepiness is boring you to tears.

- You're already all about learning + growing + self-actualization, and because it's your oxygen, you need and want so very much more.... I feel you! If you're not green and growing, you're ripe and rotting, right?

- You're curious about a different version of your life that you could be living, a better version ... kind of like Gwyneth Paltrow in *Sliding Doors*.

- In those quiet moments, when it's just you and you wonder, *"Is this all there is?"* ... and I'm here to tell you there is so very much more out there for you.

- You don't want to die with "what could have been" on your mind.... You're ready to move out of the land of regret and into the land of living.

I see you over there, reading this page. I get you. And I'm throwing you a welcome party.

BY WAY OF INTRODUCTION...

You may be wondering, who is this 1,821-Mondays-left woman with a penchant for carpe diem?

I'm a corporate executive who smartened up and became an executive coach and then really smartened up and became a "stop squandering your life" speaker and coach.

I'll elaborate for a bit (so you know you can trust me as we plan the rest of your incredibly alive life together), and then I promise we'll get back to our regularly scheduled programming (i.e., *you*).

- I have twenty-five years of corporate leadership experience ... so I get what it's like to be swept off your feet by the amazingness of a meaningful job that fills you with energy and also to have your soul snuffed out of you by a job that zaps you of even the wee-est bit of joy and energy. I made it out of the rat race alive and kicking!

- I'm a Professional Certified Coach and a Certified Professional Co-Active Coach...which means that I'm basically overqualified with thousands of hours of one-on-one and group coaching. I've spent years coaching C-level big cheese executives, leading CEO peer advisory boards (which is really like herding cats—thank God I like cats), and coaching normal people (like you and me) on how to work well and live even better.

- I have a Master of Applied Positive Psychology (MAPP) from the University of Pennsylvania, where I'm also an Assistant Instructor in the master's program...which means I've studied with the world's top researchers on happiness and what makes life worth living. (More on "WTF is positive psychology" in a bit.) I wrote a 101-page thesis on this You Only Die Once (YODO) topic of using mortality as the spark to live with width and depth (with 324 references—yikes). The science doesn't lie: death really can bring us back to life.

- I created my company—Four Thousand Mondays*—around this mission to wake the fuck up and live like we mean it before we go. I come alive getting to do keynotes, workshops, and coaching programs for people looking to undead their lives and live more on purpose.

Enough résumé, more mission! I'm quite simply hell-bent on helping us all make the most of our time while we're lucky enough to be above ground...to not take life for granted, to not feel like we've squandered our time, to not feel like we lived in any other way than astonishingly. I want us to live regret-free lives we can feel proud of when the plug finally does gets pulled.

WAKE THE FUCK UP TO LIFE

BEFORE YOU DIE!

What a perfect segue to introduce you to my dead mother.

---

* Spoiler alert: we get about 4,000 weeks on the planet. Chop chop!

A QUICK PERSONAL BACK STORY

Losing a parent is almost always shitty, and losing a parent who dies with a litany of regrets in her fifty-eight-year-old soul has its own distinct flavor: pity. Followed by fear.

When my dear sweet mom died, so did her dreams. Cleaning out her apartment revealed folders and drawers and cabinets full of couldas, shouldas, and wouldas: manuscripts, cartoons, business cards, artifacts of small business ideas she lacked the confidence to pull the trigger on.... Her home was a variety pack of Dormant Intentions. Seeing these unmanifested hopes and wishes, I was as gripped by the fear of dying with my own laundry list of "if onlys" as I was by grief over losing the woman who gave me the gift of life (and Teddy, her orange tabby cat, by way of inheritance).

In many ways, I have my mother to thank for waking me up to life, for helping me to course-correct potential regrets in the making. It's because of her that I've become the (self-appointed) Captain of the Regrets Prevention Department, driven to help you avoid your own deathbed "what ifs." Let's not have anyone pity you at the end. Mourn you for years and years? Absolutely. Feel bad for you? We'll have none of that.

After my mom died, in the spirit of living a regret-free life, I got down to the business of Being Successful as a corporate crusader. I thought I could win at the game of life by dominating the job/title/salary step-ladder. But long story short, I came to find that defining success based on approval from the big boss can mean that instead of living the big, beautiful, extravagant life that should come with all those juicy promotions and raises, we start clinging to the little things we can control and/or trying to cope with the pressures of Being Successful and such. Hey, no one's to blame—we do what we can with the skills we have available, right? My skills at that time, as well as my desire for control, were aimed quite squarely at being a Very Vigilant Anorexic. And I was so good at it! Until I wasn't good at it anymore and became a Very Successful Bulimic instead.

I now see how I was tranquilizing myself to avoid the real and raw parts of life, including my increasing disdain for a job that I believed defined me—a career that was inextricably linked with my Being

Successful identity. When one is feeling simultaneously stuck in her job and afraid to die like her mother—chock-full of regrets—one sometimes does things that aren't super productive or life-affirming. So I starved myself and barfed my brains out for a decade.

While you might not have an addiction (oh, I so hope you don't), I'm suspecting you can relate to my then-life of quiet desperation in some way or other. We find ways to cope when we're even the smallest bit dead inside, don't we? It wasn't until I let the thing I had been stuffing down all along—my passion for this mortality-as-a-motivator topic—come alive that I ended up course-correcting my life. Starting the MAPP program and giving myself permission to study this (*ahem*) unusual topic firmly shifted me into the land of the living.

I began counting how many Mondays I had left when I started studying positive psychology. After quantifying (but not dwelling on) how much time I had wasted, and calculating how much time I had left to live with intention, I experienced a slap-in-the-face awakening. I was done with the squandering. I had a purpose, a focus, a passion, a fervor.

Death motivates me to live, but not out of fear. Knowing I'll be dead soon(ish) sparks an intense desire to do this life justice and get to the end of my days without a sliver of regret. (I have 1,821 Friday nights left, if I lead an average life that doesn't involve getting hit by a Mack truck. How can I make the most of them without feeling inordinately hungover on 1,821 Saturday mornings?) I want this special, "live a regret-free life" motivation for you, too.

I want us to poke and prod at the absurdity of it all, the mystery of this shared human experience of racing toward the inevitable finish that we too often avoid talking about. I want you to get inspired to maybe make even one small change in how you're doing this thing called Living to escape the disenchantment of regret, because that's time well spent in a life where time is at a premium. My goal is to not just open your eyes to what you want out of life but to get you figuring out—with tweezer-like specificity—*how* to carpe those diem. Quoting the perennial classic *Mean Girls*, "Get in, loser." We're going to seize your Mondays.

So no matter how vibrantly alive or walking dead you're finding yourself today...no matter how autopilot-y you're feeling...no matter how skittish you're feeling about this living and dying thing, know that I've

MY CURIOUS COIN

I keep a tarnished coin close by with the sole purpose of reminding me that I'm going to be dead soon. I say those exact words, too, every time I stumble across the coin, whether it's in my top left desk drawer, in the little pocket of my purse where I keep my lipstick, or on the front table where we keep the keys. "I'm going to be dead soon," I solemnly whisper while touching the coin. It's a tad dramatic. To further alarm you, if that's even possible, the coin has a rather ominous-looking skeleton engraved beside the Latin term "memento mori," which translates to the most profoundly motivating words that have blown the doors of my life wide open: Remember you must die. This practice of remembering I will die recalibrates my experience of being alive. Peeking at a coin sounds deceptively simple, doesn't it? And yet it nudges me to live. It helps me prioritize what matters. And we're going to get you memento-mori-nudged, too.

made it through the wringer and found life on the other side of fear/apathy/squanderousness. All it took was a perspective shift on my own mortality.

And here is where we bond, you and me. This is where we forge our lifelong friendship because of what we both have in common: We're both totally temporary. Perishable. Finite. If I were feeling flippant, I'd say we're beautiful corpses-in-the-making, careening wildly toward utter oblivion (i.e., Our Inescapable Deaths).

Now that we're all chummy, should we skip-walk down the sidewalk together on our way to the ice cream parlor? Talk some more about our mortality over waffle cones with the Reaper? Before we go for our double scoops, however, I'd like to make sense of a few things . . . unscare you, if I may. I'd like to reassure you that my role as the Grim Reaper's cheerleader is not to be funereal.* This "rah-rah Reaper" dialogue is in service of us living lives that feel nothing short of astonishingly alive.

---

* That really is a word! As you might've guessed, it means "Having the mournful, somber character appropriate to a funeral." Not what we're after.

You: Can't we do the "astonishingly alive" thing without inviting the Grim
   Reaper out for ice cream with us?
Me: Great question! But the answer's a hard no.

WHY WE NEED TO INVITE THE REAPER
OUT FOR ICE CREAM WITH US

LET'S NOT ASK WHAT
FLAVOR THIS IS, OKAY?

MINE   YOURS   GRIM'S

We love the idea of "living like we mean it," don't we? We drink our coffee
out of "seize the day" mugs, we nod in earnest agreement that "you only
live once," and we want quite fiercely to "HAKUNA MATATA" (yes, in all
caps). Oh, we have such good intentions to make the most of our precious
time!

And yet.

We tend to take our lives for granted, don't we? We think we'll have
time to the things we long to do... "later." We slip into autopilot in a
hurry—we've got shit to do, after all—so we go through the motions, and
all of a sudden another month has flown by. We're so often left feeling
like we've missed out on our lives.

So what can we do with this oft-thwarted desire to Really Live Before
We Die?

We befriend the Grim Reaper is what we do. Paradoxically, chum-
ming up with Grim is the thing that can wake us up and breathe even
more life into our lives. Reminding ourselves of our inevitable, no-way-
out-alive, possibly imminent (but hopefully not immediate) death—well,
in my experience, that tends to snap people to attention.

Reflecting on our mortality may be anxiety inducing for most of us, but contemplating death is ultimately a life-affirming practice: it jolts us to fully participate in our lives with urgency, priority, and meaning—and I *know* we all want more of that. It shifts us into deliberate and delicious action, which is what makes the difference between a deathbed experience full of satisfied "I killed this life!" memories...and a bunch of wistful "coulda shoulda wouldas."

I know what you're thinking: it could be viewed as macabre (gasp!), this willingness to dabble in death. But fear not, we won't be loitering in the morgue. No, we're going to be crafty and strategic about using our relationship with the Reaper to our advantage—using the soul and science of positive psychology (a topic I know a thing or two about) to help us thoughtfully edit our lives and live on purpose.

WAIT—WHAT IS "POSITIVE PSYCHOLOGY" AGAIN?

Positive psychology is the scientific study of what makes life worth living... the study of what we're doing when we're not frittering life away. Dr. Martin Seligman—the Father of All Things Positive Psychology—issued a plea in 1999 as then-president of the American Psychological Association "to steer psychology away from the darkness and toward light." This practice fabulously asks: Why not focus on mental *wellness* instead of illness? Positive psychology has been basking in the light of human potential and well-being ever since.

Marty founded the Master of Applied Positive Psychology (MAPP) program at the University of Pennsylvania. In pursuit of my MAPP degree in 2019, Marty became my teacher and opened my eyes to existential positive psychology...the study of how life and death are intertwined. Positive psychology (with a delightfully morbid twist) changed my life, and I want it to do the same for you, too. Everything we delve into in these pages together will be informed by this science of flourishing. Languishing, no. Flourishing, yes.

NORMALIZING OUR DESIRES TO LIVE LIVELIER LIVES

Working with clients over the years, I've noticed a few recurring themes. Oh, the dilemmas we face associated with being alive! Maybe you've gotten a little lazy in life because it's easier to stick your head in the sand than confront the thought of your own mortality and actually do something about it (more on that later). Maybe you've been filling your days with meaningless tasks and appointments because you've lost the plot on the difference between living a busy life and living a life of consequence (more on that later, too). Maybe you're bored and you don't know how to unbore your life (more, as you suspected, on that later). Maybe some of my bullet points earlier on in this introduction sounded eerily true for you.

You're not alone in your hopes for more—from your life, from yourself. You're not alone in fearing you might not live up to your Potential (yes, with a capital *P*), that you'll arrive at your deathbed with more regrets than satisfactions, that you'll always be tripping over the thought of *what might have been*. You're not alone in your fear of living a Squander-Filled Life—instead of the Squander-Free one we're clamoring for. You're not alone in wanting to feel even more alive than you do today—even if you aren't sure how to make that happen just yet.

Fear not, I'm here to guide you.

THE ITINERARY FOR OUR PAGE-BY-PAGE ADVENTURE

We're going on an expedition together in these pages (It's not too grandiose to call it an odyssey, is it?*) and oh, how we like road maps!

> YOU: What do I need to pack? Do I need to bring my own blow-dryer?
> ME: All you need is an open mind and a notebook. I strongly recommend your favorite beverage to sip on along the way (no judgment if that beverage is a venti vanilla foam half-caf matcha latte milkshake or a whole shaker of cosmopolitans; cold-pressed juices don't cut it for me either).

Here's the road map:

- ☠ **We are going to start with a pre-mortem**—a pulse check about how your life is going for you today and where you might want it to go

---

* No, it's not too grandiose! And we're here for some grandiosity, aren't we?

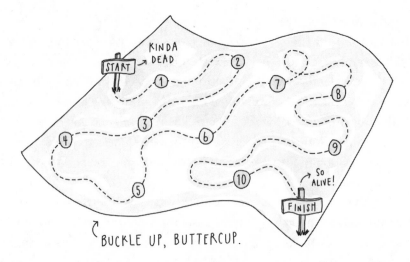

BUCKLE UP, BUTTERCUP.

tomorrow. We'll diagnose the dead zones and get you primed to feel decidedly more alive.

☠ **We'll then dig up the proverbial grave of death**—getting you centered on the life-changing role memento mori ("remembering you must die") can play in your life, why we usually head for the hills when we talk about death, and how we can learn from what people who have looked death in the eye have to teach us. We'll also unearth your life-deadening habits and laser in on your regrets-in-the-making as fodder for how you'd love to live the rest of your Mondays.

☠ **Then comes the living part**—where you'll get to come up for air:

☠ We'll talk about how we can make your life wider by stuffing it full of all the vitality we can jam in...all the amusement, all the experiences, all the pleasure, all the kinds of chocolate (yes, even milk chocolate, you purists, you). Imagine getting to the end and lamenting that you didn't get to go on just one more roller coaster ride? Or that you didn't visit your buddy in Missoula? Or that you didn't quit work twenty minutes earlier each day to enjoy almost seven extra hours a month to do Anything Other Than Work*? Or that you didn't feel...alive enough? We shall stratospherically widen your life with vitality.

---

* Unless you love your work more than anything, in which case I will not hold you back from working up even more of a storm. Bring on your work monsoon! (And the rest of us will talk about leaving work twenty minutes earlier.)

☻ Because a well-lived life can't all be fun and games, we won't just widen your life—we'll deepen it, too. We'll plunge the depths of meaning...getting you centered on your purpose, how to design a life that feels whole and harmonious, how to live a life that feels like it matters and is full of the things you care about. We'll go deep on themes of connection, giving, spirituality, awe, reflection, challenge, and how deep-seated appreciation can arise from the realization that your existence is precious and fleeting.

☻ **We'll wrap up with a paint-by-numbers approach to taking action / lighting your life on fire and with a postmortem**—the giant "so now what" about all that we'll have discussed. I don't know if you're like me, but I hate feeling full of dreams and ideas and epiphanies, without being sure of WTF To Do with any of them. It's like going to a fabulous brainstorming session and then stumbling out uncertain of what's next...wondering if all your great ideas are just going to get buried in your coffin with you someday. I will not let you leave this book with thoughtfully answered rhetorical questions and inklings of dreams that go nowhere! We'll get you action-planning specific steps to live with width and depth, to follow through on a life that takes your breath away...before the Grim Reaper actually does take your breath away.

☻ Watch for little sidebars sprinkled along the way, like way-finding signs on our little quest:

 "Coaching Chestnuts": picture these as words o' wisdom from a coach—moi—sitting on your shoulder.

 "Positive Psychology Interludes": smart yet unboring nuggets from the science of happiness.

BEFORE WE GO ANY FURTHER: A BRIEF BUT IMPORTANT DEATHLY DISCLAIMER

While you'll often find me making light of the topic of death, any discussion herein isn't meant to dismiss the cocktail of emotions that can bubble up when we talk about it—especially if you've experienced a loss lately. Let's notice and appreciate the possible feelings of fear, grief, anxiety, and denial as you flip through these pages. Like any good paradox, we can use these complicated emotions to our advantage as we shape more full-bodied lives for ourselves. Your discomfort might be the very thing that motivates you to edit your Mondays-in-the-making—like rekindling friendships you've let dwindle, taking better care of your body, filling and emptying and refilling your bucket list, leading that neighborhood cleanup, and eating more legumes. (It so often comes down to legumes, guys. If you read up on Blue Zones—places in the world where oodles of residents manage to live to one hundred and beyond—what do they have in common? Legumes.) No one said that grappling with the awareness of your pending demise would be easy, but *not* grappling with it is like asking to be buried alive.

THE BINDING CONTRACT YOU SHOULD PROBABLY SIGN BEFORE WE BEGIN THIS BOOK ODYSSEY TOGETHER

(Or, said differently so that the lawyers in the room don't get all hot and bothered: the non-legally-binding-yet-morally-compelling pinky-swear agreement that it's going to take to create a "life that's getting lived around here.") Repeat after me:

- ☠ **I Will Give Two Shits** *(not just one, but two).* How astonishing your life will be is pretty much proportional to the amount of effort you put into it. Engaging in the ideas and exercises in these pages is a great demonstration of giving two shits. You might be tempted to pick and choose the exercises that work for you and pass over the ones you don't want to do. You're all grown up, so you can absolutely do that . . . but I challenge you to try it all. The very thing you think "nah" to might be the very thing you kind of need to do. Are you committed to the two-shits kind of life you deserve?
- ☠ **I Will Feel Feelings.** Reflecting on your life, let alone your death, can excavate some pretty meaningful thoughts and emotions. Our job is to get curious about them along the way. Don't let discomfort stop you from moving forward. Everything you want is on the other side of the

fear fence. Are you willing to try it all out and see what emerges, to feel your feelings (instead of eating them *sigh*)?

- **Life Will Get in the Way.** You will get busy, and you might think things like "FML, I can't get a grip on getting dinner on the table on a Tuesday night, let alone read a chapter about liking my life a little bit better." *There, there.* You can pace yourself in this book. You can do it in your own time. Are you willing to be self-compassionate as you aim to get this puppy read before you die?

- **Passion Requires Risk.** No one ever figured out their passions and interests from the couch. You have to get out there and try things on for size, get bit by the bug, see what takes your breath away. You have to be willing to participate in your life. I'm deliberate about the phrase "participate in your life," by the way—because this is about showing up ready to play, not sitting on the sidelines hoping for passion to find us or for time to magically appear in our schedules to get to do the things we long to do. Are you willing to pursue passion, even if—no, when—it feels scary?*

- **I Will Take Others' Input in Stride.** People can get weirded out when someone close to them starts to make themselves better, because it represents some sort of change for all parties involved. If you start playing the flute again and hiking and taking online courses and watching less TV and cooking with way less bacon fat, don't be surprised if some of the people you thought would be supportive of your little Alive Project aren't so... supportive and alive themselves. Your job is to focus on elevating *your* life experience right now, and if listening to less-than-encouraging friends, sisters, stepdads, or bosses is bringing you down, then tune them out as best as you can, and keep on keeping on. Are you game to take others' opinions with a grain of salt?

- **I Will Take MY OWN Input in Stride.** Oh right, your own voice! That always kind, encouraging, and loving voice you talk to yourself with!† It's normal to feel uncomfortable and even disappointed about

---

* Fun fact! "Passion" is rooted in both Greek and Latin words for "suffering." And that is why we give two shits—for the cause.
† *Yeah right.*

how you maybe haven't been "living like you're dying" (as Garth Brooks croons/advises) up until now. Let's press the mute button on that self-judging voice, shall we? You're here. You're already making progress.

- ☠ **I Give Myself Permission to Dream.** Here is your permission slip to imagine all sorts of futures, careers, ways of being, schedules, hobbies, and versions of your life. If you let the voice that says, "Yeah, but that's not practical," or "I can't afford that," or "They'll think that's silly" pipe up in your head, you'll prick a hole in your balloon before you even try to blow it up. Give yourself a chance to imagine something cool. You don't have to execute on every idea, but will you allow yourself to dream *big*?

- ☠ **I Will Find the Fun in This. Not just fun—unbridled fun...** The willing-to-laugh-at-yourself-and-the-ridiculousness-of-life kind of fun. Growth isn't always smooth, so if we can't make fun of it...we'd better all throw in the towel right quick. You're okay to laugh at the absurdity of it all, right?

At this point it's your job to explicitly commit to these seven (totally unbinding) points. Please sign your name—in blood if you're up for it:

_____	_Jodi Wellman_
Your Signature	My Signature

This is so exciting! We're going to get you to pay fierce attention to your dreams and hopes—to care for them, nurture them, honor them. Through these pages together, we're going to help you live with astonishing aliveness in stark juxtaposition to the finality of death.

I want us to die happy, especially because we only

do it once. I want us to live lives remarkably free of regret, just as tarnished as my memento mori coin: worn, beautifully weathered, valued, and fully spent.

Life's short; this show sure as shit isn't going to go on forever. Let's make this a party on death row! Now, did you order extra fudge, sprinkles, and a cherry on top? Because we're going for the full sundae.

CHAPTER 1

THE PRE-MORTEM: THIS THING CALLED YOUR LIFE

Dearly Pre-Deceased, we are gathered here today to dissect the life you're living, in an effort to maximize your time left on the planet. Think of this pre-mortem as the most fun autopsy you'll ever have the pleasure of experiencing.

> YOU, looking understandably trepidatious: Remind me what a pre-mortem is again? And will I smell like formaldehyde after?
> ME: I love you already.

We are going to get you looking at your life in a deep and thoughtful way in the pages of this chapter. We are going to get you reflecting on the parts and pieces of your life that range on the Spectrum of Aliveness from feeling luminously alive to undeniably anesthetized (i.e., the total fucking living dead). We are going to get you clear on what's energizing you, what's draining you, and what parts of your life might already be decomposing (*insert wide-eyed emoji here*).

 In the words of the iconic Maya Angelou (who we can't not love; RIP), "Do the best you can until you know better. Then when you know better, do better." That's the point of this pre-mortem: we're going to get you knowing yourself better, so you can ~~do~~ *be* yourself better.

If we were together in person, this chapter would be like the first Discovery session in our coaching relationship—the deep dive into All Things You. So let's pretend we're sitting together on ridiculously comfortable cushy chairs, mimosas in hand, getting curious about your life: the way it looks today and the way you'd like it to look tomorrow if you were asked the right questions...and if you were given permission and encouragement to live it that way...*and* if you were reminded about your limited amount of time to live said life.

Wait, what? Limited time? (Here is where we'd order another round of mimosas.)

You already knew you were reading a book with a "morbid twist," what with this cover and all, although you might not know what the twist is about and just how twisted it's going to get. Allow me to reassure you that it's going to get *appropriately* twisty. Together, we are going to get in touch with your mortality, so you can live the life I'm pretty entirely sure you want: the life that feels undeniably alive, plugged in, on purpose, inspired, and full of moments that take your breath away...moments that *you* will make happen.

Does the life you live now feel taken for granted, overly routinized, hollow, one-dimensional (like you're living a cardboard cutout of your life), and—let's say this last one in a whisper-voice because it's so true it hurts—*boring*? Pack your bags; we're about to depart from the status quo.

While I'll be asking you eleventy thousand questions in this chapter, in service of envisioning the life you'd love to live more of, I know that little action-oriented you over there is going to be chomping at the bit to Transform, Today. Can I gently encourage you to be patient and kind with yourself, and take our conversations here in stride before blowing up your life by quitting your job and moving to Bali?* We're going to get you contemplating a few possibilities of how to undead your life...but not in a crack the whip, "*Get 'er done, Sparky*," kind of way...in more of an "It's okay to let a seedling of an idea (perhaps even a couple?) take root, and then we'll work together on watering it and sunning it and

_____

* Oh dear God, I will not be insisting that you blow up your life! (But I have heard that Bali is fabulous?)

whispering sweet nothings to it and growing it throughout the rest of this book" kind of way.

I'll be with you every step of this odyssey adventure. Because that's what this is—the start of an adventurous discovery about *you*—and we all know adventures lead to giant treasure chests.*

So do you feel it? That slightly smothering sensation? That's the warm, mimosa-fueled bear hug of a welcome I'm giving you in this nowhere-near-morbid pre-mortem. (If, however, you are feeling a full-on smothering pressure in your chest, call 911 because that's not me hugging you; that's you having a cardiac event. Please don't die before you even finish chapter 1, because that would be a real shame—and also, no one will be giving you your money back for the book.)

The first step to kicking off the rest of your "living like you mean it" life is, as the title of this chapter suggests, to take stock of your life and the things that need a-fixin' before you can comfortably contemplate a one-way ticket to the afterlife. Forgive me if I go ahead and assume that somewhere on your bucket list is a bullet point labeled "die happy." If so, you are in the right place—so high five to you for being interested in making the very most of your remaining days.

YOU: What does that even mean, to *live like I mean it*?
ME: I was hoping you'd ask.

LIVING LIKE YOU MEAN IT VS. LIVING LIKE YOU'RE A WEE BIT DEAD INSIDE

"Living Like We Mean It" looks like ...	"Living a Wee Bit Dead Inside" looks like ...
The pursuit of astonishing aliveness...living lives we'd be proud to look back on without the faintest whiff of regret on our eventual deathbeds. Living like we mean it summons up the courage to start things over—like jobs, friendships, marriages, partnerships, the towns we live in, hairdos—even (especially) when it's out of our comfort zones to do so.	Living in that comfort zone that's so undeniably and ironically uncomfortable...working at jobs we merely tolerate *(been there)*, lamenting our unused vacation time *(done that)*, thinking we'll start knitting again or work up to doing ten pushups or really learning to speak French once and for all—but without a plan to actually do any of it as the pages of the calendar flip by.

---

* Either that or pilfering pirates...but we'll remain cautiously optimistic.

"Living Like We Mean It" looks like ...	"Living a Wee Bit Dead Inside" looks like ...
Playing to win ... like putting your name in the ring for that juicy promotion, signing up for Toastmasters, entering the race, taking risks of any kind or size, giving things that matter *all*—not a self-protective fraction—of our effort.	**Playing not to lose** ... which looks like succumbing to the play-it-safe mentality of "I'd better not put myself out there; Tom's got a better chance of getting the gig anyways." (Tom is going to be your nemesis for the rest of these pages, FYI.)
Playing till the buzzer ... playing full out right until the end. The end of what? The game, the Q3 strategy, the recital, the assignment, the two weeks' notice period, the relationship, The Life.	**Playing till the going gets tough** ... quitting early because it's hard or inconvenient or we are afraid of looking like an ass.
Adopting a healthy attitude toward failure ... like knowing how to dust ourselves off and learn from our inevitable cock-ups.	**Believing that failure is a shameful indictment of our deeply flawed character** ... which will keep us shrink-wrapped versions of our amazing selves until the day we die.
A life full of variety ... what with it being the spice of life and all. This looks like a willingness to shake shit up every now and then and try the squid ink pasta.	**Anchored by routines and habits** ... that make our weeks feel like they're passing us by in an "every day is the same" kind of blur.
Saying yes to life ... like last-minute concert-in-the-park invitations; yes, to the butterfly-inducing dreams like selling our stuff on Etsy; yes, to our friend's not-easy-to-get-to wedding in Turks and Caicos; yes, to things that aren't always convenient but almost always lead to a vitally alive existence.	**Riddled with a lot of nos** ... and sofa time and what-ifs and regrets-in-the-making.
A conscious reprioritization of what really matters in life ... a deliberate reshuffling of how we spend our time, attention, and energy.	**A conspicuous absence of intention** ... that characterizes a dead-inside life (i.e., floating down the lazy river of life). Many clients I have worked with lament letting their lives happen *to them,* letting their careers, for example, unfold in ways that leave them wondering, "How did I end up here, working for Tom after all these years?" It can be easy to fall asleep at the switch of life.
The epitome of positive psychology ... doing what it takes to flourish and live a life worth living. This also looks like knowing it's within our control to go after this version of a life that lights us up from the inside out.	**The antithesis of positive psychology** ... being okay to just "get by" and settle or, worse, feeling like empowerless victims who are destined to be stuck in the raw sewage of life until we die—and maybe even in death, too.

After reading through the compare 'n' contrast chart above, were you leaning off to the Living Like You Mean It side or more toward Living Like You're a Wee Bit Dead Inside? Maybe there was one glaring Dead Inside section that made you feel feelings—and not of the "I love this about me!" sort? That's okay. You're not alone. The first step toward living in a state of aliveness is to astutely note your observations about where you're already Living Like You Mean It vs. You're a Wee Bit Dead Inside.

I find it helps to normalize our Dead Inside snafus and tendencies in life (so...the entire right side of the chart). We have such good intentions to live like we mean it, to live these full and rich lives, and then all too often we let the rest of life get in the way. We get busy...reports need writing and the tires need rotating. We get tired...kids wake us up at three thirty in the morning and by Friday evening we just want to stay in, ideally in a horizontal position with a remote control in hand. We get scared...intimidated to jostle the routines and rhythms of our narrow but comfortingly predictable lives. How many of us have slacked off with our bodies, our relationships, our goals, our hobbies, our joie de vivre? How many of us feel rather clumsy at living? How many of us have slipped into a lifestyle unbecoming of someone fortunate enough to still be alive? Taking life for granted because that's just what we do?

Okay, so here is where I'm going to answer my own question, about how many of us have phoned it in with our lives, so to speak: All of Us. We do this because that's what people do. Some of us slack off with our lives more than others, sure, but this is a judgment-free-zone kind of book, and I don't care if you're Queen or King of the Living Dead...I just want you to know there's hope. We can stop the squandering. We can undead our lives.

And so now your pre-mortem shall continue with a "How's your life going?" provocation.

YOUR LADDER OF LIFE

Let's do a quick well-being pulse check. This cute little ladder[1] offers an easy way to subjectively evaluate your life.

The top of the ladder represents the best possible life for you. The bottom of the ladder represents the worst possible life for you.

1. On which rung of the ladder would you say you're standing right now, at this very moment?
2. On which rung do you think you'll stand about five years from now?

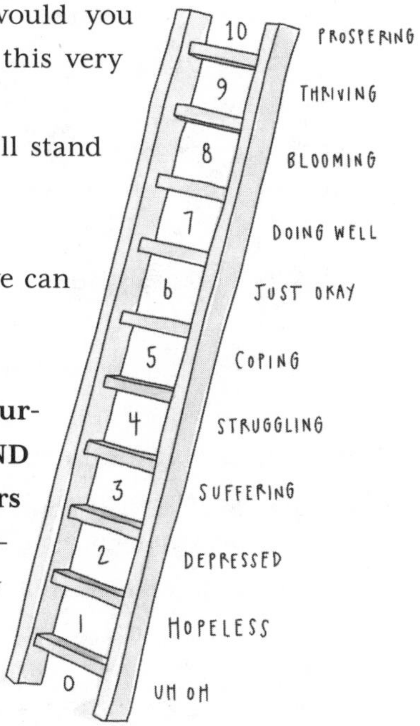
10
PROSPERING
9
THRIVING
8
BLOOMING
7
DOING WELL
6
JUST OKAY
5
COPING
4
STRUGGLING
3
SUFFERING
2
DEPRESSED
1
HOPELESS
0
UH OH

There are three life-ladder zones we can fall into:

- **If you have poor ratings of your current life situation (4 and below) AND negative views of the next five years (4 and below),** you're in the "Suffering" category, and unfortunately your well-being is at high risk. Folks who are struggling are more likely to experience physical pain, stress, sadness, worry, and anger. If this is you, I am so glad you're here. Well-being TLC is on the menu.
- **If you have moderate views of your current life situation OR moderate or negative views of your future (between 5 and 6),** you're in what's known as the "Struggling" category, and your well-being is moderate or up and down. Chances are you experience more daily stress and concern about money than the "Thrivers" above you on the ladder and need more than double the number of sick days. Researchers[2] say you are less likely to eat healthy foods and are more likely to smoke.
- **If you have positive views of your present life situation (7 and above) and the next five years (8 and above),** you're "Thriving." Yay, you! Your well-being is strong, consistent, and progressing. Thriving people report more happiness, interest, enjoyment, and respect in life. What's fascinating is that Thrivers also tend to be *strivers*—consistently interested in maximizing their life satisfaction, pursuing an even greater degree of self-actualization over the years of their lives. They don't just get to the thriving rungs and put their feet up for a smoke break. Many of the clients I work with are sitting above 7 on the ladder

already, acutely interested in ascending to the Very Next Rung, Please and Thanks. Just as there are "lifelong learners" out there, there are "lifelong livers"* who want to see what life's like beyond the top of the ladder. The good news is there's an unlimited number of rungs on this ladder, so there's no need to stop at 10.

The 2023 World Happiness Report[3] noted that the US average life evaluation was 6.89, while the global average was 5.54. Forty-four percent of Americans are Suffering or Struggling (6 or below), while 56 percent are Thriving (7 and above).

We're all striving for the thriving zone, right? Whether you're suffering, struggling, or thriving as of this moment, positive psychology science is clear that we're all teeming with eagerness and agency to climb up the ladder, even if it's an eighth of a rung at a time. Let's do a postmortem pause for a moment to dig into this worthwhile interlude.

Positive Psychology Interlude: Happiness is a talent we work at, not an inborn trait. We have more control than we think to move the needle on our subjective life satisfaction. We have agency! We have the power!

Researchers[4] have demonstrated it's possible to take purposeful steps to *get* happier and to *stay* happier in our lives. Many of us think happiness is all about genetic endowment—that we're preordained for a life of happiness or sheer and utter gloominess because our parents were Miss Congeniality or Mr. Curmudgeon. DNA absolutely impacts our happiness constitution, so our cheery mom and morose dad's genes *will* impact us, but not in a way we can't work past.

Circumstances in life—like if we have a debilitating illness or if we're born into a certain socioeconomic class—they also impact our happiness, but to a lesser extent than we might think.

With my sincerest apologies for bursting any excuse bubbles—that we can't blame our unastonishing lives on genetics or extenuating circumstances—let me tell you about how it's our time to shine. It turns out, the

---

* No, not the organ; people who live.

intentional actions we take to boost our happiness and well-being have monumental effects on our satisfaction with life. This breakdown of the "how of happiness" is sometimes referred to as the "happiness pie"; it has been hotly debated how big each slice of pie is between genetics, circumstance, and intentional action, but the DIY intentional action slice has been allocated as much as 40 percent of the pie. That is, your pursuit of happiness can be the thing that creates actual happiness. Almost like how practicing yoga incrementally makes you a better yogi—you're not going to wake up one day in a 'grammable crow pose without putting in the hours, just as you won't one day wake up happy without putting in the pursuit.

So how big can you make your intentional action slice of pie? What deliberate activities are you participating in to get happy? It's pretty much up to us to make our own happiness. Luckily, it's not that hard once we (a) accept that we're in the driver's seat of our lives and (b) work through the inertia and/or fear that prohibits Living with a capital *L* (and of course a capital *H* for Happiness too).

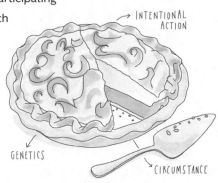

MY "DEAD INSIDE" STAPLER STORY

Personally, I needed to learn the "we're baking our own happiness pies" lesson the hard way.

Fully disenchanted by my job back in 2011, I found myself stapling inconsequential pages together, trying not to staple my own face to spice up the day. When the stapler ran out of staples, as staplers do from time to time, I distinctly recall what happened next: I carefully loaded a pristine row of two hundred staples into the stapler, thinking (out loud) with solemnity, "I'd better not still be here by the time I have to reload this stapler." The challenge was on. I beamed with optimism—it felt good to declare something so definitive with a two-hundred-staple deadline. It's ~~funny~~ unfunny how we latch onto the little things when we're scared stiff of change, isn't it?

Fast-forward to about a year later, promoted to new levels of executive unhappiness, stapling more pointless pages together. You have a hint of what's coming next—my stapler had the nerve to run out of staples. I felt like I had been drop-kicked, only I was the one doing the drop-kicking. I whispered softly to my filing cabinet, "I'd better not still be here by the time I have to reload this stapler again." Deja vu, in this moment, felt more like a lethal boomerang.

And then I promptly and unproudly did nothing about it. As they say, a dream without a plan is just a wish accompanied by a lot of sauvignon blanc.

This isn't a tale of "hanging in there" (like those posters of a kitten dangling precariously on a branch) or of "hanging in there" at work with blind hope as your strategy. This is really a tale of regret. (We're totally going to get into these bad boys down the road in chapter 6, FYI.) I had a deep desire for things to be better in my career, but I was too busy, scared, and stuck to make a change.

And then I felt worse about myself every time I let two hundred staples pass me by, ultimately spending three years of my life certain it was so much better on the other side of fear but paralyzingly unsure how to get there.

In 2014, I finally summoned up the courage to take my future into my own hands. I buckled down with one-day-at-a-time bravery. I worked with a career coach to figure out my "career WTF" questions, registered for a year-long coach certification program, and plugged my nose before jumping into the deep end of the pool as an entrepreneur. I made the career change I knew I needed to make if I wanted to feel my pulse ever again.

I like to think I learned my lesson—that it's just not enough to let good intentions and hope for more get me where I want to go—but I keep the stapler close to keep me honest. (I took it with me when I left for greener pastures, and I keep it in my top-right desk drawer.) It represents the need to take action and to not settle, even for a single staple. I learned, and continue to remind myself, to live the life I've imagined by actually doing something about it, not just waiting for it to happen to me, not waiting to be saved, not waiting to be put out of my misery.

Have you ever felt disenchanted by your job? Never mind, I already know the answer. Statistically[5] speaking, fewer than a third of us are engaged at work. Half of us are disengaged (sleepwalking through our days), and about 17 percent of us are what's known as "actively disengaged" (i.e., spewing vitriol on Glassdoor and stabbing Tom the boss's tires at 4:00 a.m.). I tell you my stapler story to not only relate to you but to provide hope. Living like we mean it means busting out of the trappings of success, of fear, of uncertainty. The dead-inside version of ourselves settles, tolerates, waits to be saved. No, nope, and nada. If I lived to tell the tale by forging a new career path forward, so can you. We can dig into that hefty intentional action piece of the happiness pie. We can do so very much better while we're still above ground, with however many Mondays we have left.

On that note—how have we not pulled out your calculator yet?

YOUR LIFE CALCULATOR EXERCISE

Do you know how many Mondays you have left? Oh, and I do mean in total—in the life you're living right now.

We're going to wax philosophic in the next chapter about why counting your Mondays should become even more important than counting your money, but for now let's just get your calculator out and follow these instructions:

- ☻ Take the number 81 (if female), 76 (if male), or 79 (if you don't identify with either) and subtract your age.
- ☻ Take that number and add 1, because reading this book has to get you some kind of life credit, yes?

- ☻ Multiply that number by 52 weeks. That's your total number of Mondays to go.*
- ☻ *How does this number make you feel? Does it seem like a lot or an alarming not-a-lot?*

Feeling frisky? Want to calculate your total number of working Mondays left?

- ☻ Take the number of years left that you plan to work.
- ☻ Multiply that number by however many weeks you plan to work each year (backing out weeks for vacation, holidays, PTO). That's your total number of employed Mondays left.
- ☻ *That's barely enough Mondays to love or too many Mondays to dread. Which one is it for you—not enough or a suffocating amount too many? Might now be the time to go looking for a new gig where your remaining number of Mondays feels like an exciting prospect instead of a death sentence? Before two hundred more staples pass you by?*

Feeling zealous? Contemplate what else you have left in your waning number of Mondays.

- ☻ **How many big vacations do you have left?** Many people take one giant vacation every few years, for example. Assuming you're spry enough to travel until you're seventy (fingers crossed), how many jumbo jets will you fly in before you die? A fifty-five-year-old woman I worked with recently went white when she realized she'd likely only get five more stamps in her passport. She immediately booked the trip to Montenegro she had been delaying until "someday."
- ☻ **How many visits with family and friends who live far away?** If your mom lives in Tucson and you get there two or three times a year, how many more of her pot roast dinners do you think you'll down before she goes? Does this perspective make you want to visit more often? (It's perfectly okay if the answer is "Hell no, thank you.")

---

* You might want to make a note of this countdown number along with today's date, just in case I (absolutely) ask you to update the number in upcoming chapters (many times).

- **How many big promotions are left in your career?** Or big accounts won, if, for example, you reel in a biggie every couple of years or so? It dawned on a leader I worked with that he had just one or two more acquisitions left in him before he retired. It helped him reframe his priorities and motivated him to buy another amazing business "before I cash in my chips," he joked.

- **How many more "hobby highlights" are in store for you?** If you run marathons every other year, how many more are realistic to fit in before your knees blow out? If you restore old cars once every couple of years, how many might you have left to drive? An author I know did the math and realized she had time for five more books. She had ideas for twenty, so this sharpened her focus on the stories she longed to tell. Jack Canfield (Yes! The cocreator of the Chicken Soup for the Soul empire!) recently interviewed me, and in our conversation he recalled a time being asked, "Imagine you had to give only ten more speeches. What would you talk about? And why are you waiting?" This woke him up to laser focus on what he needed—not just wanted—to say.

- **How many years do you have left with your kids while they are still in the house?*** How many summer vacations or spring breaks do you have left until they have zero interest in traveling with you, let alone watching movies on the couch with you on a Saturday night? Might this inspire you to Make Something Special with the vacations and breaks you do have left—with or without oodles of cash? One of my clients gets her kids to complete a fun survey about things they'd like to do over the holidays, within a really modest budget. After the time off, she compiles a "memory movie" with videos and pictures to commemorate the visit to the lake, the popsicle-eating contest, and all the fun 'n' frugal things they delighted in over their time off together.

We get about four thousand Mondays in our lifetime, on average. If you're about halfway through your life, you might have about two thousand to go until your life calls it quits. How do you want to spend those finite days?

---

* I know this sounds like a trick question, because Timmy is likely to hunker down in your basement until he's thirty-eight.

How about you whip out your notebook or journal to mull over the following questions:

- ☠ What impact does seeing the number of weeks you have left have on you?
- ☠ Does seeing your Monday number ignite a sense of urgency?
- ☠ What does it feel like to contemplate your temporariness?
- ☠ Does your number of Mondays-to-go feel like fodder for an existential crisis?
- ☠ How many career Mondays do you have left—and is this good news or daunting news?
- ☠ How many promotions or Big Career Moves are likely in store for you? What are you waiting for to get started on making the next one happen?
- ☠ Approximately how many big trips are on your horizon? Where do you want to go?
- ☠ How many family visits and holidays might you have left? Should you plan a bonus one soon?
- ☠ How many friend visits and excursions do you think are in the pipeline? Can you revive the group chat and coordinate a weekend?
- ☠ What kinds of hobby milestones are at hand for you? How will you celebrate?

Thinking of your answers to these questions, jot down actions you might want to take (or further contemplate taking!). You don't have to make any commitments right now. The goal is to create a laundry list that becomes a short list that becomes an inspiring life to-do list. Save this for later; we're going to use it again.

Reflecting on your impermanence can spike your perceived value of being alive. If you knew you were going to live forever, for example, your life would be entirely unprecious, wouldn't it? You'd take everything for granted because that's what people who live for eternity do. It's hard to savor a trip to the Maldives when you know you can revisit it 5,750,000+ more times. It's hard to motivate yourself to apply for that role at your dream company when you know you can throw your name in the ring at any of your next several billion careers. It's hard to appreciate the value of a meaningful friendship when you know you'll have 85,345,950+ more friends. It's hard to cherish life when you're invincible. So, reality check: you're not invincible! You're a slowly rotting corpse-in-the-making! No really: you and your cells are decaying at an imperceptible yet indisputable rate as a direct cause of the terminal disease* we all have called Life. So maybe let your finite number of weeks act as a motivator to live like you mean it?

WOULD YOU RECOMMEND YOUR LIFE?

Here's an unexpected way to look at your life in our pre-mortem: I'm sure you've heard of the Net Promoter Score (NPS)—the gold standard in customer experience metrics and also a guaranteed way to put you to sleep if we keep talking about it—so instead of giving you a boring lesson on NPS, I'm just going to cut to the chase. One of the two questions in an NPS survey is called The Ultimate Question, and it goes like this:

How likely is it that you would recommend [Service X / Organization Y / Product Z] to a friend or colleague?

You've likely filled out surveys with this question before. You've had to think hard if you'd recommend your local Target to a friend . . . if you'd recommend your doctor to a neighbor . . . if you'd recommend wherever you get waxed to a colleague in desperate need of a bushwhacking. You've had to quantify this recommendation on a scale of 0–10 (where 10 means *"I'd absolutely and gleefully recommend the Brazilian wax to that new gal in HR!"* and 0 means *"I'm currently litigating my waxologist, and I'm not at liberty to comment"*).

If you were sent a survey about your life, how would you answer this bastardized NPS question?

How likely is it that you would recommend your exact life to a friend or colleague? On a scale of 0–10, how likely are you to recommend that another human being live the EXACT life you've lived, right down to the minutest detail?

---

* Life, the disease, is actually an STD—I wanted to share that in case you, like me, find it amusing.

Let's use a graphic to help you out:

HOW LIKELY ARE YOU TO RECOMMEND YOUR EXACT LIFE TO SOMEONE ELSE?

BEST LIFE AWARD!

0 1 2 3 4 5 6 7 8 9 10

TOTAL TRAIN WRECK OF A LIFE | OH JEEZ | HALF GREAT, HALF CRAP | GOOD STUFF | FREAKING ASTONISHING!

So where are you on the scale?

- Is the goal to get to a 10? Maybe, but not necessarily. *(Perfection is pretty, but I'm lucid enough to know it's a mirage.)* Let's not add to the omnipresent pressure to LIVE LIFE PERFECTLY *(yes, in yelling caps)* . . . so maybe 10 isn't realistic (unless you're already at a 9.4, and who am I to stop you from leveling up?).

- If you're in the "recommend" category (over 5 or so), how does your number make you feel? Are you giving yourself a thumbs-up in the mirror, or is that voice of sneaking suspicion telling you, *"You could be 'living it up' more than you are today"*? Only you know if that voice is the incessant sound of self-judgment or the gentle nudge of your best self, encouraging you to live with more guts and gusto. What might it take to notch yourself a half point up on the NPS-of-life scale?

- If you're in the "not recommend my life" category (under 5 or so), you likely have a few circumstantial things going on (e.g., fifth divorce, bankruptcy, maybe you really were in a train wreck). What's one small way to live life from today onward that makes you feel incrementally alive? What can you do today to start nudging your life toward the 5+ zone, so you can answer differently the next time you're surveyed about your life?

The good news is that you have a choice about how you live from this moment on. Choosing an *internal locus of control*—the belief that you have the power to control events and outcomes through your own behavior, a.k.a. *agency*—has been shown by researchers[6] to significantly predict subjective well-being and self-confidence. This sits in contrast to the *external locus of control*, which has us believing that our lives happen *to* us...that we're sad 'n' sorry Victims of Circumstance...that we have good reason (i.e., excuses) to rain check the lives we want to be living.

To be clear: circumstances can suck. Cars will break down, debts will mount, hearts will be broken, pink slips will be issued, ants will show up at the picnic. Circumstances throw wrenches in our best-laid plans—because that's the deal with getting to be alive—and yet we aren't doomed by them.

One of my clients sprained her ankles (yes, ankles *plural*—don't ask) right before a family reunion ski trip. But instead of canceling and staying at home to cry onto her crutches, she set herself up by the fireside with a hot chocolate / hot toddy bar and made sure to get quality visiting time with as many cousins and nieces and nephews as possible...something she'd never have done if she was out on the slopes, skiing her heart out.

We'll talk more in these pages about how we often overestimate what we think it takes to be happy—more specifically, how we think we need to *be* rich to *live* a rich life—and how we underestimate the impact that mini moments of joy have on our perceptions of happiness and well-being. We might not be able to afford a fifty-dollar visit to the yarn store when our student loans are breathing down our necks, for example; financial circumstances are real. But we can design a happy life regardless. We can plan for pleasure with a low-to-no budget, like making a twenty-minute lunch break feel special with a walk outside around the office park, listening to our favorite podcast that makes us laugh, returning to work with a spring in our step. We don't need deep pockets to have a deep (and wide) life; thankfully many of the best things in life really are free.

Even if your life has been an unrecommendable shit show thus far (i.e., minus 17 on the Would You Recommend Your Life Scale), our goal is to get you comfortable and confident to step forward into a totally recommendable life from today onward: one in which you run the show of every single Monday you have left, in which it's in your control to identify the things that light your life up and uncover a sense of purpose that adds meaning to your days. But first...

DIAGNOSING THE DEAD ZONES: THE "ASTONISHINGLY ALIVE" ASSESSMENT

We're entering the Big Enchilada phase of your pre-mortem, right here, right now. A quick bit of context before you make your way through this sixty-eight-question experience: You know how business school grads are programmed to chant Peter Drucker's "you can't manage what you can't measure" adage? In unison? We shall take a page from that playbook, minus the brainwashing. You can't live an astonishingly alive life if you can't pinpoint and address the dead zones, so we're here to do just that . . . identify the domains of your life that might be drained of life.

Because I'm not a total downer, I'll also ask you to notice the pockets of your life that feel bountifully alive, because they're usually spots of sunshine worth maximizing.

So brace yourself for an onslaught of questions about every nook and cranny related to your well-being. It's all for a good cause . . . so please get comfy, refresh your beverage, keep an open mind, and try not to overthink the answers; they will be a reflection of where you're at today, which could be different from where you might be tomorrow—so go with your first instinct.

		5 ☺	4	3	2	1 ☹	
1	Being happy is of tantamount importance to me.						Being happy is nice but not necessary. Like bubble baths.
2	I think my personal well-being is off the charts, in a good way.						My personal well-being isn't feeling so well these days.
3	My work is a source of unbridled joy in my life.						My work is an evil, black hole that sucks the soul out of me.
4	I'm totally engaged at work.						I am trying to sink the ship at work.
5	I get to contribute great stuff at work that I'm proud of.						If I'm being honest, I don't really add much value at work. (Shh.)

		5 😊	4	3	2	1 ☹	
6	I feel like I'm really valued at work, and people let me know I matter there.						They don't value me at work; it would take them several days to notice if I died.
7	I'm definitely treated fairly at work.						Fairness schmairness.
8	I have a general plan/idea in mind for what's ahead in my career.						My career path is nonexistent.
9	I'm a time management master (and this assessment had better not take more than 6.5 minutes).						Time. What is time? It's so elusive. I don't have a handle on it because it cannot be tamed.
10	I get to use my strengths—the things I know I'm good at—regularly in my life.						I'm sure I have strengths (deep down in there), but I never get to apply them.
11	I'm often in a state of flow—in the zone, where I get gleefully and productively lost in my work.						I feel lost *about* many of the things I do, but I'm never lost *in* those things—especially with glee.
12	I make sure I'm always learning new things. Learning and growing are like oxygen to me.						I haven't grown or learned anything since I was eleven.
13	I have so much more to learn!						I know enough stuff.
14	I am a master or expert in something—a skill, talent, or technique.						I'm a master of nonmastery, maybe.
15	My to-do list is a source of pride that I'm always on top of. Want to see it?						I have so many things to do, but they rarely make it to a list, let alone a list that gets tackled.
16	I'm on top of all the big-picture tasks and projects in my life—like a will, life insurance, etc.						All my big-picture tasks are swept under various carpets.
17	I feel like a success story because I've achieved many of my goals.						I feel like a sob story because achievement and I aren't synonymous.

		5 😊	4	3	2	1 😞	
18	I celebrate the progress I make toward my goals, each step of the way toward the gold star.						I don't structure my goals in such a way to celebrate much along the way. No gold stars here.
19	I'm supersatisfied with the physical environment (places and spaces) I spend time in.						My home / office / physical environment leaves much to be desired.
20	My closet / basement / office / drawers / etc. would make Marie Kondo (the *Tidying Up* guru) proud. So organized.						My closet / basement / office / drawers / whatever stresses me out.
21	I make enough money to breathe easy, knowing my basics are covered.						Woefully . . . not . . . enough . . . money . . . *(hyperventilating)*.
22	I rest assured knowing that I have a plan for my finances, like a budget and retirement plan.						My finances are even more disorganized than my to-do list . . . There is zero budget or plan.
23	I feel the warmth and support of being connected to others in my life.						I'm not saying I'm a hermit, but I have zero human connections in life.
24	My relationship with my significant other makes my life so much better.						My relationship with my significant other is highly problematic.
25	I have a physical, intimate relationship that's as invigorating as I want it to be.						My yearly doctor's visit is as intimate as I get.
26	Love is in my life; I feel loved, I give love, and more than just on Valentine's Day and birthdays.						Love, as they say, isn't making my world go 'round.
27	I get to interact socially with friends, family, etc. regularly throughout the week.						I never see people intentionally. Animals, yes. People, no.

		5 😊	4	3	2	1 ☹	
28	I'm never lonely.						Loneliness is my state of being.
29	I feel like I totally belong to the communities I am a part of.						"Belonging" isn't a word I'd ever use to describe how I feel.
30	The people in my social circles are happy, especially the ones I spend the most time with.						All the people I know are miserable.
31	My social circle is full of people who I think are positive influences in my life.						My social circle is full of people who I think are total derelicts.
32	I'm the king/queen of physical fitness. Hail to SoulCycle!						150 minutes per week of moderate activity *plus* resistance training? You're kidding. 150 minutes of Netflix, sure.
33	I'm almost always in a state of movement—standing, walking, taking the stairs, you name it.						I am almost always in a state of inertia—sitting, taking the escalator, parking close to the door, etc.
34	I'm also the king/queen of healthy eating. Hail to kale!						Kale = Barf.
35	I'm so in tune with how what I eat makes me feel—physically, energetically, mentally . . .						I don't tend to notice a relationship between my diet and how I feel in any way.
36	My health is a serious priority: I have regular doctor's visits and take such good care of myself.						Of all the priorities in life, my health doesn't make the list.
37	You'll usually find me outside, connecting with nature and the gift of vitamin D that the sun provides.						I go outside only when a fire alarm is pulled and it's dangerous to remain indoors.
38	I get 7–9 hours of refreshing sleep every night.						Insomnia is the most predictable part of my life.
39	I feel really well-rested.						I feel haggard and exhausted.

		5 😊	4	3	2	1 ☹	
40	I am acutely in tune with how energetic I'm feeling, aware of what adds to and detracts from my energy levels.						I'm shockingly unaware of how my energy ebbs and flows, or even if it ebbs and flows at all.
41	I actively make choices to maximize/turbocharge my energy.						I'm not making choices in the best interest of feeling energetic.
42	I look after myself diligently; prioritizing self-care (like grooming, massages, alone time, etc.) is a big deal in my life.						I never make time to look after myself; even this survey feels indulgent.
43	I'm really comfortable with the physical image of myself that I present to the world.						I am really uncomfortable with my physical appearance, clothes, you name it.
44	People would describe me as a ray of sunshine, typically full of positive emotions.						People would describe me as a cold November rain, typically exuding negative emotions.
45	My resting face has a genuine smile on it.						Resting bitch face was a phrase coined in my honor.
46	I always have something to look forward to in my life, whether it's big or small.						There's never anything to look forward to in my life, just a lot of garbage to look back on.
47	I plan for and take all the vacation time I am entitled to, every year.						I skip so many vacation days. *Sigh.*
48	I have such an abundance of gratitude for the things in my life—the big and the small.						I'm not thankful for much around here.
49	I can find things to be thankful for in tough situations.						Silver linings are delusions for the weak in challenging times.
50	Kindness is my middle name.						I'm not morally opposed to being kind, but it's not something I'm known for.

		5 😊	4	3	2	1 ☹️	
51	I frequently seek out ways to be giving and generous to others.						I'm definitely not a big giver.
52	I'm crystal clear on the things that make me happy in my life.						I'm super fuzzy on what it takes to make me happy in my life.
53	I organize my life in such a way that I can spend time on the things that make me happy.						I don't plan for or make time for the stuff that might make me happy.
54	I feel like I have a distinct purpose on the planet, like my life has some kind of meaning.						Some days my purpose is to just stay alive until tomorrow morning.
55	I have a vision of how I want my future to look, and it's looking super bright.						I haven't the faintest clue what I want for my future.
56	I find myself stopping frequently to live in the proverbial moment, mindful of what's going on and how I'm feeling.						I'm never living in the moment. All the hours are a blur, including these minutes right now.
57	I stop and savor the good times when they're happening.						I'm distracted during the good times, and I can barely remember them afterward.
58	I'm always reliving my best memories from the past, savoring the little details (like the taste of that gelato in Italy).						It's true that the gelato tasted great in Italy, but I never look back and relive the good stuff in my mind.
59	I believe there's something spiritual out there that's bigger than me.						I don't think there's anything out there on the spiritual front (unless aliens count).
60	I feel a consistent connection to my spiritual beliefs.						I feel consistently *unconnected* to anything spiritual whatsoever.
61	I naturally believe that things will always work out in the end.						I naturally believe that things will always blow up in the end.

		5 😊	4	3	2	1 😟	
62	I see failure as a temporary setback that doesn't define me; it's part of growth.						I see failure as personal, permanent, and damaging. So I'm not a fan.
63	When I mess up, I give myself the same kindness and compassion I'd give to a good friend.						When I mess up, it validates that I'm worthless and unacceptable as I am.
64	I feel like I'm in control of the choices I make in my life.						I feel like I'm settling in my life.
65	I make decisions in accordance with the things I value the most.						I pretty much ignore all the values that matter to me when I make decisions.
66	I'm a confident person, through and through.						I'd admit my self-confidence was severely lacking if I had the confidence to do so.
67	I believe I can make the goals I have for my future actually happen, that I can figure it out.						I believe I can't get any of my ideas off the ground, even the half-baked ones.
68	Brownies are the answer to most of life's problems, when eaten in moderation of course.						Brownies make life incrementally worse.

Making Sense of Your Assessment

Kudos for finishing sixty-eight questions; I hope it was more eye-opening than demoralizing. Here's a rough 'n' ready answer key:

- ☠ Questions 1–2 (and 68) offer a general life overview
- ☠ Questions 3–22 pertain to your Productive Life
- ☠ Questions 23–31 refer to your Social Life
- ☠ Questions 32–43 are about your Physical Life
- ☠ Questions 44–67 relate to your Inner Life

1. Highlight your lowest-scoring questions and choose whether you'd like to *do* anything about those aspects of your life . . . all in the

interest of liking your life *just a little bit more* than you do today. No life scores perfect 5s in all areas. But what could your life be like if you moved one of your 1s to a 2, or a 2 to a 3?

#	QUESTIONS I SCORED THE LOWEST	DO I WANT TO DO ANYTHING ABOUT THIS RIGHT NOW?	IF YES, WHAT IS ONE THING I COULD DO IN THE NEXT MONTH?

2. Highlight some of your highest-scoring questions and reflect accordingly...

#	QUESTIONS I SCORED THE HIGHEST	WHY DO I THINK I SCORED SO HIGH?	HOW CAN I USE THIS TO HELP IMPROVE MY LOWER SCORES?

3. What categories were particularly high vs. low (Productive, Social, Physical, Inner Lives)? Are there any thematic ah-ha's that emerge for you?
4. Go eat a brownie.*

DISCLAIMER TIME

Before we go any further in your pre-mortem, I want to answer an important question that you've asked (maybe for a friend?). We need to set the record straight as we continue along this adventure together.

---

* You might want to make a big ole batch of brownies to get you through copious Thought-Provoking Life Assessments in these pages.

YOU: An astonishing, live-like-you-mean-it life sounds great but also potentially exhausting. I don't think I have enough Adderall to live like that full-time?

ME: You are so right! I need to issue a little disclaimer or two. (Also, do we need to get you some help with the Adderall thing or no?)

The Astonishing Life Disclaimer #1

You might want a life full of thrills, or you might want a rather Zen existence. I don't judge what you want; I just want to help you get it. The conversation we're having here in these pages and chapters is not about overhauling your life in grand, sweeping gestures—unless you want and/ or need that. Do you want that? Need that? Or are small gestures more sustainable for you?

I talk a lot about vitality—our wish to feel very much alive in the shadow of inevitable death—but I *won't* talk about inundating ourselves with intense stimulation in an effort to remedy the blandness of boredom. Becoming thrill-seeking daredevils might be a tad too extreme (wearing a YOLO T-shirt while rock climbing without a rope, for example), whereas making subtle tweaks to breathe more oxygen into our lives (maybe wearing that YOLO T-shirt while taking perfectly safe rock-climbing lessons) might be more sustainable for the rest of us. Pressure abounds to LIVE LIFE TO ITS FULLEST (again with the all caps), and for most of us, those words emblazoned on mugs, tea cozies, and all over Instagram feel less like encouragement and more like a directive that often ends in judgment. This book is meant to inspire even the smallest of tweaks to appreciate and get more out of our lives, not make us feel like we're living wrong. Let's consider this a discussion about what we *could* do, not what we *should* do. Life is the possibility of more possibility.

→ THE YODO SHIRT IS WAY BETTER.

Coaching Chestnut! Beware the "Should." Any time you hear the word *should* come out of your mouth, you'll want to slap yourself in the face. It usually means you're on the verge of succumbing to a rule or rigid standard that's rooted in obligation or someone else's interests. The thought or phrase "I should _____" should (ha ha) cause you to pause and question. Start noticing when *should*, *must*, and *ought* start bossing you around inside your head, and interrogate reality with a question like, "Do I *really* need to help Yolanda move this weekend?" (Can we all just agree to never help anyone move or to never ask anyone for help with a move, unless we're eighteen and moving into a dorm?) The idea is to replace the "should" mindset with a "could" mindset to broaden our perspectives and spur unorthodox thinking. "I *could* help Yolanda move her California king mattress down the stairs, but I'd rather use that time to work on my screenplay." "I *could* volunteer for the DEI initiative at the office, and even though I'm swamped, it totally aligns with my values…so I'm going to do it." *Could* carries an air of possibility to it—chock-full of agency. Oh! The *a* word! *Agency* packs a well-being punch because as humans we love autonomy and the freedom to choose things. Most of us need to choose *no* more often, at least when it comes to the things that make us feel dead inside.

The Astonishing Life Disclaimer #2

My encouragement to live an astonishing life is so not meant to sound like an admonishment for living lives that seem ostensibly…*vanilla*. Some of us prefer vanilla ice cream and aren't interested in two scoops of chocolate chip cookie dough, and that's perfectly acceptable (*especially if it's Ben and Jerry's vanilla*). The encouragement here is to live life even more vitally and on purpose—relative to our own needs and preferences. After contemplating the diminishing time we have left, we might be inspired to have more vanilla ice cream because it brings us such simple pleasure. We might feel inspired to become healthier versions of ourselves and consequently have less ice cream. Or we might be inspired to take our good old-fashioned vanilla and put a cherry on top. Some clients I work with want super full calendars with social events galore and experiences up the wazoo. Just as many want quieter lives with a more meticulously edited approach to the finer parts of life that bring them joy. I relate to wanting an intentional life experience that's not necessarily about the volume of more...It's more about the *quality* of more. (Remind me to tell you one day about the oversized *"All we ever wanted was everything"* hot pink neon sign The Husband and I had made for our bedroom. Despite that "more is more" garishness, as a homebody introvert, I love a quiet life with simple, mindful pleasures. "Everything" is fabulously relative.)

THE POWER OF KNOWING WHAT MAKES YOU HAPPY (OH, AND ALIVE)

And now we shall take a different turn in your pre-mortem. After the romping endeavor of diagnosing your dead-as-a-doornail zones, let's add some levity to this giant "Getting to Know Yourself so You Can Live Fully before You Die" project. Let's get you thinking about the things that light you up.

Here's the weird truth: most of us are out of touch with what makes us happy...woefully ignorant about the things that light the flames in our furnaces. It's hard to live fully if we're not cognizant of what makes a fabulously full life for ourselves, isn't it?

This is so not rocket science, though. It's basic stuff, and yet so many of us underestimate the direct relationship between *doing* the things that makes us happy and actually *being* happy.

I see this so often—many clients, typically women who assume strong caregiving roles, have lost the plot about what it takes to make themselves happy. They've been so focused on the care, feeding, and happiness of other people that they don't even really know what their favorite color is anymore. If this is you, that's okay. We'll get you back in touch.*

I also see clients with a list of things they love to do, long to do, used to like to do...like it's someone else's life. A life they *used to* like and live. A life they hope to live again one day. The good news is that with a little awareness, intention, and action, we have the ability to infuse so much more of the pleasing stuff into our days, weeks, months, and years.

---

* When in doubt, pick black.

I'll give you an example. I'm thinking of a client who was busy busy busy—you know, like many of us who use that as our automatic response when someone asks how we are: "Busy!" She was feeling flat, empty, and bored in life. When she completed this list of things that made her happy (the one you are going to do in a minute), it occurred to her that she had at least ten different ways to like her life more that wouldn't take a prohibitive amount of effort, time, or cash. She noted that she loved '80s music, so she made a playlist that had all of her favorite big hair tunes (a lot of Bon Jovi and Cindi Lauper). She realized that she missed walking alone at lunch, so she started doing that (while listening to her playlist, no doubt). She picked up a fiction book to read before bed, instead of the usual business books—because she remembered how much she loved getting lost in stories when she was growing up. She called an old friend from college who she knew would make her laugh and resurrect great memories. She added Thai food into the takeout rotation again, because she forgot how much she really did like hot & sour shrimp soup. And what did all this do for her? It plugged her into a renewable energy source of happiness. She had been depriving herself of simple things that would bring her joy—totally unintentionally—and by getting reconnected to them, she felt exponentially more alive.

Just as you did with the Astonishingly Alive assessment, get comfortable with a pen and paper / fresh new document on your laptop / however you record your brilliant ideas. Because you will be writing about things that make you happy, I encourage you to sit in a place you love ... maybe in your favorite lounge chair, the window seat at your favorite coffee shop, the bench by the lake ... whatever floats your boat. Fill in the following blanks:

☐ I love these activities (e.g., hiking, skeet shooting, browsing at bookstores, napping, art shows, daydreaming, Brazilian jujitsu, etc.):

_____

_____

☐ I love spending time with the following people:

_____

_____

☐ I love doing these things when I'm alone:

_____

_____

☐ I love these locations (e.g., my hometown, grand hotel lobbies, being by the pool, the Adirondack Mountains, the tub, etc.):

_____

_____

☐ I love these travel destinations:

_____

_____

☐ I love to eat:

_____

_____

☐ I love to drink:

_____

_____

☐ I love these desserts:

_____

_____

☐ I love these colors:

_____

_____

☐ I love these songs/bands:

_____

_____

☐ I love these books:

_____

_____

☐ I love these movies:

_____

_____

☐ I love these hobbies:

_____

_____

☐ I love these times of day:

_____

_____

☐ I love these flowers:

_____

_____

☐ I love these smells:

_____

_____

☐ I love these sights:

_____

_____

☐ I love these things to touch:

_____

_____

☐ I love these sounds:

_____

_____

☐ I love work when:

_____

_____

☐ I love accomplishing the following things:

_____

_____

☐ I love looking after myself by:

_____

_____

☐ I love a great day when:

_____

_____

☐ I love myself when:

_____

_____

☐ I also love:

_____

_____

Reflection time

What was it like to complete this list? Some people whip off dozens of ideas for each bullet point, and others liken this exercise to pulling teeth. If your answers came slowly (or not at all!), add to this list as ideas occur to you in the days and weeks to come—because that's what'll happen. When your radar is up for "ways to be happy," you'll start noticing the answers are out there, often right in front of you. The intention right now is to simply get in tune with what makes your heart sing, magnifies your spirit, and makes your heart skip a beat.

How often are you enjoying the things you put on your list? You might be stuffing your life full of known joys already (like one of my clients, who has fresh flowers delivered to herself once a week), or you might be starving yourself of the simple pleasures in life (like my sister, who knew she appreciated a nice mani-cure but didn't indulge in them for decades. She decided when she turned sixty that the time was right to start getting her nails done on the regular... "Fancy is worth it!" she now says).

Of course the idea is to pepper these things into your life in regular intervals, and we'll map this out for

STUFF THAT MAKES ME HAPPY

IN NO PARTICULAR ORDER AT ALL:

☐ PLAYING THE XYLOPHONE
☐ GARDENING
☐ BUYING BOOKS TO MAYBE READ
☐ PEOPLE WATCHING
☐ SPELUNKING
☐ LEARNING TO SPEAK HUNGARIAN
☐ BAKING BROWNIES
☐ NAPPING ON CLEAN SHEETS
☐ BRUNCH WITH BUDDIES
☐ EATING BROWNIES WITH KAHLÚA

you in a later chapter. *These happy things will likely not happen to you; you need to plan to experience them.* One small pleasure at a time is often all it takes to elevate your life experience. (Okay, so I can't not ask, because I'm too impatient to wait until chapter 10...What's one "happy" thing you can do in the next week to boost your experience of being alive?)

THE ALIVEALICIOUS QUESTION

Don't leave your happy chair / coffee shop / park bench just yet! There is a kissing cousin* of this "What Makes You Happy" question, and it provides a one-way ticket to the "living like you mean it" way of life:

"I feel most alive when _____."

Here are a few variations on the deceptively simple question:

1. What makes you feel undeniably alive?
2. What makes you feel so alive you just might burst at the seams when you're doing it?
3. What makes you feel like Liquid Life is coursing through your veins?†
4. What one thing energizes you and makes you feel like life is So Much Better when you're doing it...and maybe even for a period of time afterward?
5. What are the runner-up Alivealicious things on your list? It's perfectly wonderful to have a long list of ways you feel undeniably alive; let's not stop you at just one invigorating thing.

Your answers might identify where the gap exists between your desires to feel like you've shown up to play and that disappointing feeling of "life was left unlived" at the end.

If your "most alive" thing is whitewater rafting, for example, and you live in Kalamazoo, Michigan, well...you're admittedly in a pickle. As the

---

* I really should look up what a kissing cousin is. I'm hoping it's more platonic, less incestuous.

† We all agree that I should trademark "Liquid Life," right?

leader of the Memento Mori Movement, my instinct is to gently encourage you to *immediately pack up all of your belongings and move to the Rogue River in Wyoming*...while another perfectly reasonable option would be to deliberately plan regular vacations to whitewater-rafty places on the planet. I'm here to tell you that *it is not enough* to do the one thing that makes you feel *most* alive once in a blue moon, like going on rafting trips every couple-a-few years. That hurts my heart to imagine for you, in all four thousand beats an hour. And I know you feel that heart hurt, too. We need to get you rafting. This is a matter of life or death (death in this context as the "dying while you're living" kind, which some of us might argue is sadder than the dead-and-gone death).

If your "most alive" thing is a bit more accessible (like one of my clients, who lights up when he's building furniture in his garage), we'll get you challenging the frequency variable. How often are you weaving the baskets that make you feel so alive? How regularly are you going out to ballroom dance? How often are you helping out at the community center that makes you feel so alive and kicking? How often are you redecorating the rooms in your home, if that's what breathes life into you? And here is the zinger: Is that enough for you? If it is, that's amazing! If there might be a way to fit more in, could that make you feel Even More Alive? Maybe you basket weave not just for holiday gifts but on random evenings by the fire? My furniture-making client committed to making one piece a month rather than just three or four coffee tables a year. He's simmering in aliveness in ways he never expected. Put checkmarks next to the Alivealicious things you do often enough to satisfy you. Put stars beside the Alivealicious things you aren't getting to do as often as you'd like; you can decide as we continue our conversation together whether they make the grand priority list.

 Don't ask what the world needs. Ask what makes you come alive, and go do it. Because what the world needs is people who have come alive.

—HOWARD THURMAN

We only get so many Mondays to live. Not every day needs to be carnivalesque (that would be exhausting anyway, and at some point all the clowns would get creepy), but we just might maximize our experience of being alive by identifying what makes us *feel* most energized and *doing* those things more often.

YOU . . . DEAD WHILE ALIVE?

 You know where all of this is culminating, right? No, not death (yet). It's time for a killer Ben Franklin quote: "Some people die at twenty-five and aren't buried until seventy-five." In light of this doozy, I dare you to answer these questions honestly:

- When was the last time you felt like you were living like you meant it, living your life to its fullest and engaging in your alivealicious things?
- When was the last period of your life that you felt astonishingly alive, and not just for a moment at Disneyland?
- If this applies to you, can you pinpoint the time you threw in the proverbial towel of life, as Ben Franklin alludes? How old would you say you were when you became the living dead, even in one category of your life (love, friendships, career, fun, spirituality, health, personal growth, leisure, etc.)?

I know I'm a shit disturber with these questions. But if me disturbing a little bit of your shit helps bring you back to life even a little bit— like finally scheduling that trip to Costa Rica, or putting your phone down to make Play-Doh pasta with your seven-year-old, or starting that business you've been pontificating about for the last decade—then we've scored one for your very much alive life. The Grim Reaper hates it when that happens.

I don't take this life thing lightly (surprise!), because I've lived a long time in the Land of Good Ideas That Don't Get Executed. It's no fun—let's go for coffee if you'd like to share war stories. I decided that I need to get really deliberate with my desire to live a life that I'll be proud of when the plug gets pulled on me (assuming I've lived a ridiculously long life that ends with a gentle slip into a coma at the same exact time as The

Husband). This became evident to me after I refilled my stapler a few times and learned that I needed to take intentional action to Live... *deliberately.*

And I want you to get deliberate with your life, too. You only get one go at this thing called life. You only live once, you only die once,* and the good news is that you get more than one chance to decide how you want your remaining Mondays to be.

TLDR: just because you're breathing doesn't mean you're *living.*

 I'm choosing to assume this quote by Rudy Francisco gives you the same flutter in your stomach that it does for me: "The human heart beats approximately 4,000 times per hour and each pulse, each throb, each palpitation is a trophy engraved with the words 'you are still alive.' You are still alive. Act like it."

Marvel at the miracle of your life—how your heart has been thumping at 35 million beats a year and will continue to do so until you keel over. (I'm at 1.64 billion so far, and with a mom who died prematurely of a bad ticker, I'm grateful for every 100,000-ish beats my heart agrees to eke out each day.) You are here—despite all the bullshit you've surely forged your way through in your spectacle of a lifetime so far—and isn't it fabulous to still have a pulse?

We are fortunate to be alive, with all of our potential years ripe and ready, like a red carpet waiting to be rolled out in front of us. We're going to get you to do this life justice. We're going to get you to live like you have something to lose.

4,000 BEATS PER HOUR

AND COUNTING.

---

* Unless you believe in reincarnation, and if you do, that's so exciting! You're still with me on making the most of *this* life, right? Karma, as they say, is a bitch. Let's make this time around astonishing.

SO NOW WHAT?

You've had quite the interrogation, friend, and I give you credit for holding up under the pressure. You barely cracked!

Kudos to you for being here on this life-crafting mission, to get even more of your zest for life back. Did thinking about your life in context of your waning number of Mondays stir that little voice inside you that says, "It's time to live"? Time to initiate new hobbies, not barely maintain the ones you've put on life support? Time to set those travel plans in motion, going on the best-ever road trips with kitschy diner meals all the way to Charleston? Time to move your body more? Time to get involved with that cause that matters deeply to you? Time to learn a new language? Time to self-care yourself silly? Time to enroll in a class to oxygenate your brain? Time to really connect with a loved one because their time is ticking, too? Only you know what might make you feel truly, astonishingly alive. What hints are emerging from your notes? Speaking of your notes...

Let's get you organized before we move on. Consider your reflections from the pre-mortem exercises:

- Living Like You Mean It vs. Living Like You're a Wee Bit Dead (page 18)
- Your Ladder of Life (page 20)
- Would You Recommend Your Life? (page 29)
- The "Astonishingly Alive" Assessment (page 32)
- The What Makes You Happy List (page 42)
- The Alivealicious Question (page 47)
- Are You Dead at Twenty-Five and Buried at Seventy-Five? (page 49)

After all this assessing and thinking and feeling and musing about your Mondays left in the hopper, how might you answer these questions?

1. What do you want *more of* in your life?
2. What do you want *less of* in your life?
3. What do you want to *change* in your life?
4. What do you need to *detonate* in your life?

Remember that your job right now is simply to take note. Let your observations wash over you, and then revisit them as you make your way through the next chapters. It's fascinating how some things that feel hot today fizzle by tomorrow and how unexpected things might bubble up to the top of your list. So continue to observe yourself like the incredible specimen you  are. Keep your notes handy so when we start to get into the WTFTDN* sections, you're primed to take whatever action you darned well want.

Feeling overwhelmed with your list of Things to Detonate in My Life? Remember that discontentment with where you are today is precisely what's required for you to move in the direction of where you want to be. Change needs a catalyst.

I'm out here wearing a sandwich board for the Grim Reaper, because there is no better catalyst out there than him. He's a self-help master cloaked in disguise. Sure, he has sinister intentions (*he wants us all dead*), but if you stick with me, we'll leverage the gifts he has to offer in his bony, scythe-holding hand. We live daily and die once, so let's live like we mean it until Grim does what he's born to do.

So now that we've wrapped up our pre-mortem, and I've settled the bill for all those mimosas . . . let's get you plotting your life.

---

* What the Fuck to Do Now.

CHAPTER 2

THE ASTONISHINGLY ALIVE ZONES: WHERE WOULD YOU PLOT YOURSELF?

 Man is the only animal who has to be encouraged to live.

—Friedrich Nietzsche

Our goal is to get you personalizing this widening and deepening business, so think of this chapter as a good long look in the mirror before we Get Down to the Business of Planning and Living Your Alive-est Life. Knowing where you stand today and—more importantly—where you want to stand tomorrow is what will position you to craft the best life plan possible.

LOOK WHO'S IN THE MOOD FOR A QUADRANT CHART! (YOU.)

Remember in the introduction when I laid out the road map for our journey together and talked about living wider (the more-experiences, more-travel, more-hobbies, more-pleasures, more-*life* route) and living more deeply (the purpose-driven, meaning-filled path)? Before we can start charting our journey down either road, we first need to figure out what our starting point is, that is, where you currently stand in terms of vitality and meaning in your life at this moment. I'm thinking there could be no better time than now to talk about the Astonishingly Alive Zones. We're ready.

I gave birth to this framework while researching memento mori for my graduate school thesis, and I'm still giddy about it. It illustrates the relationship between the width and depth of our lives, and it depicts where we are, where we want to be, and (sometimes more importantly) where we *don't* want to be.

The metaphoric width (the x-axis) is expressed along a spectrum that refers to our degree of vitality. The continuum ranges from being in a walking coma (not so wide) to "every day is a fiesta!" (latitudinously wide). Key words: life force, pleasure, fun, happiness, experiences, piñatas.

The metaphoric depth (the y-axis) is expressed as the degree to which we find meaning in our lives. The spectrum ranges from feeling cavernously empty (not so deep) to chock-full of any kind of reason for the life we're living (miles deep). Key words: purpose, connection, self-actualization, virtues, do-gooding.

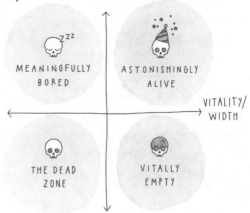

Something spectacular happens when you marry an x- and y-axis together: a love child of quadrants is born!

Here's how my Astonishingly Alive framework plays out:

- ◉ **The Dead Zone:** There's a pulse . . . but it's faint, and it might be a good idea to check where the closest defibrillator is. We're lacking in both vitality and meaning in this zone, and while it ain't pretty, there is hope.
- ◉ **Meaningfully Bored:** Life feels meaningful, sure . . . but sorrily short on zesty splendor. We feel flat, anti-effervescent. No fizz to be found.
- ◉ **Vitally Empty:** So much pleasure! We can have all the fun and eat all the pink popcorn at the circus . . . and still go home feeling empty inside.
- ◉ **Astonishingly Alive:** The hotbed of where life's getting lived . . . with both width and depth. This is the mecca of this little odyssey we're on together.

THE "PLOT THE ENTIRETY OF YOUR LIFE ON A PAGE" EXERCISE

Remember the "pin the tail on the donkey" game from kids' birthday parties? We will not be playing that here.

You will take part in the far more thoughtful Plot the Entirety of Your Life exercise, without blindfolds. Hark back to your Astonishingly Alive assessment from your pre-mortem (page 32) for input if need be.

Step 1: Reflect on your life as of this very moment. How vitality-filled (wide) is it feeling? How meaningful (deep) is it feeling? Put a dot in the corresponding zone on the chart.

Can I encourage you to take out your fine-point pen when drawing this dot? There is a world of difference between being in the lower-left quadrant of the Dead Zone, for example, and the upper-right quadrant. Try to be as precise as possible with where your dot sits today.

Step 2: Imagine it's six months from today. Where do you *want* to be... what zone within what zone? Draw a star to denote where you intend to be.

Step 3: Soul-searching:

- Now that you've plotted away, are you feeling motivated? Equanimous? Curious? Surprised? Despondent? Dead inside?
- How does this "today vs. later" exercise compare to the Ladder of Life (page 20) you plotted yourself on in your pre-mortem?
- Do you have a zone for your "work life" and a zone for your "real life"? That's okay; many people mentally segment work and nonwork. What if you had to meld your lives and come up with one darned dot for today and one single star for six months from now—where would they reside?
- Do you have an "axis of evil" that's bringing you down? Maybe you're doing all right with meaning, but your vitality is zapped. Maybe it's the reverse—fun is being had, but you feel like a hollow shell of a human. Make note of your axis to focus on: width or depth.

- Are you supernosy about where everyone else sits on the Astonishingly Alive model? Of course you are, because even though comparison is a bona fide joy burglar, our propensity to compare ourselves to others in relevant circumstances is part of what makes us human. What we really want to know is, what zone are the Joneses in? Let's go there next, but first...

Step 4: Go eat a brownie.

SURVEY SAYS . . .

Back to comparing where we sit vis-à-vis others.

I love research, and I love it even more when it's my own. I've surveyed thousands of people and continue to get bizarrely enthralled with what the data reveals about us as a species. I'm going to have you work for the results, though.

In this multiple-choice quiz—for which there will be no prizes—what option do you think depicts the actual results of my "How Alive (or Dead) Are You" research?

Option A:
- Meaningfully Bored: 17.3%
- Vitally Empty: 33.2%
- The Dead Zone: 9.1%
- Astonishingly Alive: 16.2%
- Midzone: 11.3%

Option B:
- Meaningfully Bored: 2.9%
- Vitally Empty: 2.9%
- The Dead Zone: 73.5%
- Astonishingly Alive: 2.9%
- Midzone: 2.9%

Option C:
- Meaningfully Bored: 39.3%
- Vitally Empty: 15.1%

- The Dead Zone: 10.1%
- Astonishingly Alive: 7.6%
- Midzone: 28.0%

If you guessed A, we're going to overlook that the percentages didn't even add up to 100. We can't all be mathletes.

If you guessed B, you are the Grim Reaper. Please back up a step.

If you guessed C, high five to you for being correct! You get another brownie.

NOTES AND OBSERVATIONS ON RESEARCH RESULTS

You might have noticed a late entry "Midzone" category, which acts as a bit of a buffer for people who tend to oscillate between zones. I recall a woman whisper-asking me on a break at one of my workshops, "Is it normal that I find myself in all four of the zones, even on a single day?" It *is* normal to find ourselves in all four of the zones, even on a single day.

One of the most startling stats is that more people distinctly identify with the Dead Zone (10.1 percent) than they do with being Astonishingly Alive (7.6 percent). It's true that many of the Midzoners are likely to bleed into the Astonishingly Alive zone from time to time, but the point is clear: one out of ten people waiting in line at the DMV, for example, is walking around lacking in both vitality and meaning...and *less* than one out of ten in that same lineup is feeling positive in both vitality and meaning. The rest of us are looking for more life. Pardon me: some have given up and are like Ben Franklin said—dead at twenty-five and just waiting to be buried at seventy-five. You, on the other hand, are looking for more life in your life (because you didn't make it this many pages in on a whim), and you will be making more.

Most people, clearly, are finding themselves Meaningfully Bored—to the tune of almost 40 percent. These stats held true during *and* after The Plague, in case you were looking to connect dots that really aren't worth connecting. We were just as bored after lockdown as we were during it. These results have had profound implications on the work I do. I will never *not* plug for a deep, meaningful life, but I campaign a little harder for wider, vitality-stuffed lives because I know that's where so many of us are hungry for more.

YOU: So what is the goal? What should we be aiming for—the very top
     right corner of the graph?
ME: You ask such good questions! The answer might surprise you.

Theoretically, yes—we're on this entire adventure together to get to
the Astonishingly Alive zone, so while we're at it, why not max it out and
bust through that top corner? Maximum vitality! Maximum meaning!
Maximum everything! And here is where most people feel the need to
pause, hold onto the handrails, and ask if they can get off the ride for a
quick sec to catch their breath.

I feel the need to remind you, as I did when we climbed aboard
together when you cracked the spine of this book, that living like you
mean it is permissively relative. Your version of the Astonishingly Alive
zone might look very different than Tom's version, which looks different
than your mom's. You living an Astonishingly Alive life and creeping to
the top right corner of the two-by-two chart is entirely defined by what
makes you feel vitally wide and meaningfully deep. So, no "one size fits
all" for Astonishing Aliveness.

For many of us, the trek from your current dot on the page to the
future star looks like a long and laborious journey. Treacherous, even!
And that's really okay. Maybe for you it will feel like a big deal to get
from the Dead Zone just up to the land of Meaningfully Bored. Maybe
it will feel Herculean to go from Vitally Empty to the middle of the
chart, right in that center where the x-axis and y-axis meet. That's a big
fucking deal, and you must be celebrated for any shimmy to the right
and any shimmy upward on this model. Deal? Celebrations for shim-
mying? Ideally, you're getting anywhere net positive on either vitality or
meaning, and then you can worry about breaking into the outer space
of astonishment.

A client of mine from a couple of years ago made a goal to move
from where she had been firmly planted for years—in the inner edges
of the Dead Zone—to the Vitally Empty quadrant. She actively focused
on living with more zest for several months. We had quite the memo-
rable little Zoom party when she achieved her goal; "I'm Vitally Empty!"
she whooped, much to the confusion of her teenage son, who was in
her living room behind her. She then updated her goal to scooch into

the Astonishingly Alive zone, by keeping the pleasure and adding more life-deepening activities. We celebrated that milestone a few months later.

GETTING THE LAY OF THE LAND . . . AND AIMING YOUR COMPASS

It can help to understand the zone you're currently residing in, the zones you want to steer clear of, and the zone you want to extract even more life out of.

As you read through these descriptions, take note of what sounds familiar—things that are so true they hurt, things you're already proud of, things that make you shudder, all of it. Make note of ideas you might want to rope into your mighty action plan to come, too.

Meaningfully Bored (39 percent)

High on purpose . . . low on pleasure (and maybe piña coladas).

If you're in the Meaningfully Bored zone, chapter 8, on vitality, will be the place for you to focus.

Any of these musings sound familiar?

- ☻ "I'm proud of the meaning I've made in my life, but I wonder what a little joie de vivre would feel like, too."
- ☻ "All work and no play makes Jack a dull boy (hopefully not ending up like *The Shining*)."
- ☻ "Other people's weekends are surely more exciting than mine."
- ☻ "I like my comfortable routines but they might be smothering me a bit."
- ☻ "My life could be described as *greige*: a combo of gray and beige."
- ☻ "I think I'm stuck in autopilot, but I don't know how to bust out of it."
- ☻ "I've never been the life of the party, and I wonder what it looks like for an introvert like me to spice things up."
- ☻ "I feel nervous to take risks in a lot of areas of my life these days."
- ☻ "I like the contributions I'm making, and I don't want the fun stuff to get in the way of the deep stuff."

Please know that Aristotle would have tipped his hat to you for living a deep, meaningful life. Happiness, back in Greece about 2,400 years ago, wasn't about (*tsk tsk*) "contentment," but rather living a "virtuous life" aligned with one's values. You've been doing good out there, kid. Now we just need to amplify the vitality in your life, to help infuse interest, novelty, gusto, and good ole R+R into it.

There is room for both pleasure and purpose in an astonishing life. Many Meaning-First clients I work with fear they're mutually exclusive—that adding in more vitality will compromise their Contributions to This World in some way. Taking a midday break to walk by the lake, reading the odd fiction book, lollygagging by a pool for a weekend, eating a sundae for dinner, incorporating sprinklings of spontaneity...these things won't diminish your sense of meaning. Chances are these expansions of your life will serve to further deepen it as well.

If you're feeling Meaningfully Bored, what actions do you think got you into this zone? What stories might you be telling yourself about what adding vitality will "do" to your life? What might you have to gain by "living a little"? Or a lot?

Vitally Empty (15 percent)

Breathless fun followed by tumbleweed blowing across the landscape of one's soul.*

Okay, so you have the vitality part down: you're showing up ready to play, as an active participant in your life. It feels good to savor the flavors of life, doesn't it? The meaning part of life feels like it's missing, though—which looks and feels like a lot of ambrosia salad† (flash) without a lot of meat and potatoes (substance), right?

If you've been feeling Vitally Empty, these comments might sound familiar:

☠ "I love having all this fun, but at the end of the day, these experiences feel empty."

---

* Too dramatic?

† Please tell me you know about this amazing marshmallow salad—the one with coconut, pineapple, and maraschino cherries? Pure vitality, zilcho meaning.

- "I wish the work I did had more purpose."
- "If I'm being honest, I feel shallow."
- "Everyone I know seems to have a purpose to their life or job . . . except for me."
- "Does making meaning mean leaving fun on the table?"
- "I'm pining to do something that matters, but I don't know what that might be."
- "I wonder what it would be like to feel part of something bigger, like a startup or a church or my neighborhood community."
- "This can't be all there is, can it?"
- "I sometimes feel like the happy clown who goes home alone, with a tear slowly streaming down his face."

Imagine the classic fun facade tale—I think of some of my clients with the big shiny jobs who experience the tasting menus, the vintage bottles of wine, safaris in Africa, weekends away on a whim. On the outside they are living large and in charge of all things fun. And those are just the well-to-do ones; I've worked with people with way fewer resources who find ways to outwardly experience the pleasures of life, like one woman who threw epic potluck parties in her community park every single Sunday. A leader I delivered a workshop for didn't have an entertainment budget, but he was hell-bent on making his company a fun place to work. His solution involved a lot of after-hours game nights, karaoke, and cheap beer.

Many of these pleasure seekers—stinking rich or otherwise—undeniably experience the shit out of life. They are off the charts on vitality. But many experience the gnawing feeling that there's more to life, that they're playing in the shallow end. Trust me—many are *just fine* loving life with all the bells and whistles and store-bought zest, and they're okay to limp by for a while with a little less meaning. What they want, what you want, what I want—it can all differ, and I hope you know by now that there's no judgment about what floats your Astonishingly Alive boat. What I offer is that the most fulfilled people out there tend to have a healthy harmony between the width and the depth. Overindexing on vitality might feel astonishing at first, but the sheen wears off as fast as the fancy new car smell starts to fade.

And now, a related word from our sponsor (i.e., the Grim Reaper):

In the spirit of bringing memento mori back into the conversation—because it has been a few (unacceptable) death-free minutes—let's hear what Freud[1] had to say about death and emptiness:

"HI! IT'S ME AGAIN."

"This attitude of ours towards death has a powerful effect on our lives. Life is impoverished, it loses interest, when the highest stakes in the game of living, life itself, may not be risked. It becomes as shallow and empty as, let us say, an American flirtation, in which it is understood from the first that nothing is to happen, as contrasted with the Continental love-affair in which both partners must constantly bear its serious consequences in mind."

An American flirtation sounds fun, but we want the Continental love affair with life, do we not? Remembering that we're perishable can help us step up into the Astonishingly Alive zone rather than splashing around in the Vitally Empty zone.

Rate your current level of meaning/purpose for waking up each day on a scale of 1–10. What would it take to notch it up just half a point? Reflect on the times you felt like you had more meaning in your life. What was different then? Many people are hard on themselves for not having a "big enough" purpose. Are you actually doing meaningful things and judging yourself compared to your neighbor who intercepts human traffickers for a living? How will you know when you're feeling like your life has more meaning?

The Dead Zone (10 percent)

Well. This feels like a rather cadaverous experience of living, does it not?

Worry not, my friend. If you find yourself here, you're definitely not sitting in this zone all alone; many of us feel like life can be both dusty *and* empty, for moments in the day or for far longer stretches. The good news is that there are countless ways to resuscitate yourself. Our goal for you will be to widen your experiences *and* deepen the meaning in your life—likely one axis at a time. You're already on your way toward living like you mean it, just by reading this book. This is a significant sign of life.

See if any of these musings sound familiar:

- "I used to feel truly alive, so I know it's possible to get back to that way of living."
- "Not all the parts of my life feel dead inside, but I could definitely do with some jumper cables with my work and my health."
- "I'm bored, and I don't think I'm living up to my potential."
- "I'm not saying I want to stab myself in the face with boredom, but I sometimes want to stab myself in the face with boredom."
- "I worry that the change it will take to widen and deepen my life will be more than I can handle."
- "I want to be a lively role model for my kids again."
- "I have been swamped with work and family stuff for years, and I want to come up for air to start to feel like things are fun and purposeful again."

One key question worth asking has to do with depression. The National Institute of Mental Health[2] notes that twenty-one million adults in the US experienced at least one major depressive episode in 2021; might it be worth exploring with your doctor or mental health professional if you are clinically depressed? This one step makes the most profoundly positive difference in the lives of so many people I know. I urge you to look into this if you feel hopeless about the future.

Whether you are in the Dead Zone because of depression or if you just took your eye off the ball of life, so to speak, please don't try to overhaul your life in one fell swoop. We'll talk more in our wrap-up chapters about taking one small step at a time...not necessarily quitting your job to move to Finland because they've been crowned the happiest country in the world for so many years in a row.

If you're deadish right now, where are you feeling more stirred on the inside to make a move? Does adding in a vitality-juicing activity sound interesting to you, or would you rather go for depth and explore something meaningful? If you're not sure (because it's true that nothing looks interesting when you're feeling a bit dead), I recommend a life-widening endeavor as a quick-start first step. Boosting your vitality can often lead you down the path toward life-deepening meaning.

The Midzone (28 percent)

Welcome to the catch-all category.

People in this category have life in them—so that's good—and yet there are also spots where they're missing a bit of vitality and meaning. They're not in dire straits, and this is where you'll want to pay attention if you think you might be a Midzoner: you might not have enough "life pain" nagging at you to motivate any important and necessary change. Don't let that lack of a jumbo-sized problem provide the permission to lead a life that's "okay"—a life full of settling, where your motto is "half a loaf of bread is better than no loaf at all." Guys: *We can do so much better than half a loaf of bread.* We are here for the full fucking loaf! Heck, let's make it a fancy baguette, maybe even an artisanal sourdough loaf!

If you've been known to dabble in the Midzone, you might say things like:

- "Sometimes I feel like I have enough vitality but not enough meaning, and sometimes it's the reverse...It's unusual for me to sit fully in either category."
- "I'm kind of a floater; some days are better than others, I suppose."
- "One week I'm feeling alive-ish; then the next week I'm feeling even more averagely alive."
- "Things in my life are generally okay enough."
- "If it's not really broken, I guess I shouldn't fix it."
- "I want more from life, but I don't know how to get it."
- "My friends are mostly Meaningfully Bored; at least some of the time I veer into the Astonishingly Alive category."

The thing about a catch-all category is that there are 950 scenarios as to why someone might land here—all of which are valid. Some clients I work with lead a predominantly Astonishingly Alive zone kind of life, and every now and then they veer off course into Meaningfully Bored, for example. My tax accountant clients get swept up in the yearly tax cycle and acknowledge they will not be having a lot of fun for the first four months of the year (and then thinks get ka-razy!).

Some people spend a fair bit of time in the Vitally Alive category and intentionally deepen their lives every month or so with an activity that feels meaningful, netting them out in the Midzone.

As a coach worth her weight in certifications, I feel compelled to lobby for us to search for something better than the Midzone. Average is okay for bell curves but not for lives worth living. We want the Astonishingly Alive zone! But first, more about bell curves...

Positive Psychology Interlude: Positive Deviance. *Positive* deviance is defined as a departure from the norm—for a good cause, so it won't land you on a watch list with the dodgy deviants your parents told you not to date in high school. It's about exceptional and alternative behavior that veers outside the middling middle of the bell curve.

We don't want to melt in the middle. We want to become deviants of the positive sort! Normal is not going to get us to an astonishing life. Normal is us on autopilot, and that's fine, but we're here to tell "fine" to pack its bags and fuck right off. We must break our rut's rules. We must stray from the well-worn path of the Midzone to live like we mean it.

The
POSITIVE DEVIANCE BELL CURVE

NEGATIVE DEVIANCE

TOTAL WEIRDOS + PEOPLE WHO LIKE TURKEY BACON

BORING NORMAL

＊ POSITIVE ＊ DEVIANCE

EXTRAORDINARY + BENEFICIAL DEPARTURE FROM THE NORM

Astonishingly Alive (8 percent) . . . the Best for Last

Life is a jamboree! It's like taking the second half of this book (you know—the alive parts, instead of the dead parts) and throwing them into a blender with rum and pineapple juice.

If you penciled your dot in this quadrant, you're living with width (full of spicy vitality) and depth (full of meaning umami). Chances are you are eating from the buffet of positive psychology that we've covered together: likely lots of flow, gratitude, psychological richness,* you name it.

It's plausible that you'd think—or maybe even say out loud—the following:

- ☠ "I'm getting down to the business of living!"
- ☠ "I am grateful for the life I have crafted."
- ☠ "I'm feeling invigorated."
- ☠ "I'm in control of so very much in my life, and I actively steer the ship."
- ☠ "I regularly and ruthlessly edit my life to be one that reflects my values."
- ☠ "I'm not perfect at it, but I feel like I experience each moment."
- ☠ "I seek out challenges and love learning how to overcome them, or at least come close."

---

* More on this later. No wait—I can't hold back! Psychological richness is the medley of vitality, meaning, and novelty. It's like chocolate and peanut butter and caramel swirled together.

- ☠ "I try new things all the time."
- ☠ "I usually strike a healthy balance of vitality and meaning."
- ☠ "I love my life!"
- ☠ "I give two shits about how I spend my time."
- ☠ "I want to make the most of my Mondays!"

You might find yourself merrily plunked in the Astonishingly Alive zone, but you're also human—so not every day can or will be magnanimously wide and deep. You might have days where one or both areas feel a little wet-noodley. How might you jolt yourself out of the Vitally Empty and Meaningfully Bored categories on the days you find yourself idling there? What makes your "best practice" list of how to widen and deepen, in a pinch?

If you self-identify as a resident of the Astonishingly Alive zone, we must acknowledge that you're not the type to rest on your life's laurels. You are the mountain climber interested in scaling Maslow's pyramid *allll* the way to the self-actualized top, aren't you? For you, your lifelong project will be one of incremental inching up to the top right corner of the top right corner of the top right corner. We are cheering you on.

HOW ALIVE (OR DEAD) ARE YOU?

Check out some of the questions from my "How Alive (or Dead) Are You?" quiz—which thousands of people have completed at this point. Expect a few reflection questions after reading through them, of course...

How alive do you feel today?
- ☐ Bursting with aliveness
- ☐ Mostly alive, a lot of the time
- ☐ Living but with definite deadness going on
- ☐ Kind of like a corpse

What is your leisure time like?
- ☐ Whirlwind of excitement
- ☐ Depends on the day
- ☐ Leisure time? What is that?
- ☐ Total snoozefest

This is you at work:

- ☐ I'm so totally and utterly engaged!
- ☐ I'm into my work a lot of the time
- ☐ I could take it or leave it. (Leave it, mostly.)
- ☐ I wish I was *anywhere* but here. SOS.
- ☐ N/A...I'm not working

MONDAY MORNING STATUS UPDATE: I'M 100% DEAD INSIDE.

What slogan would most likely be engraved on your tombstone?

- ☐ Carpe Diem
- ☐ All Work No Play
- ☐ All Play and No Purpose
- ☐ All About Purpose

How would the people in your life describe you?

- ☐ Overflowing with vitality and zest
- ☐ Energetic and engaged a lot of the time
- ☐ Alive but kinda lackluster
- ☐ Zapped of life, possibly without blood

What are your thoughts on having a sense of purpose in your life?

- ☐ My life is off the charts full of meaning, purpose, mission...you name it
- ☐ I have purpose in life, but I'm bored
- ☐ I might not have purpose and meaning, but man am I having fun around here!
- ☐ Some days are light on meaning, some are rich with purpose...so they even out
- ☐ My life has no meaning whatsoever; I'm not on any kind of mission, except maybe to the grave

How much joie de vivre (zest for life) is going on for you right now?

- ☐ Off the charts full of vitality! Every day is a carnival!
- ☐ Some days are ho-hum, some feel lively...they even out
- ☐ I have meaning in life but not a lot of vitality
- ☐ There's zilcho pleasure and fun—it's all so very dull

If you kicked the bucket tonight, how would you feel?

- ☐ Satisfied... like I emptied the tank of life!
- ☐ Like I had a lot of fun but my life could have been deeper with meaning
- ☐ Like I had real purpose but didn't participate in my life enough
- ☐ Like I missed out on life, the meaning of life, all of it

Inspect + Reflect

- 💀 How would you have answered these questions?
- 💀 Make notes on the answers that poke you in the ribs, in that way that tells you, "I can do better here, I just know I can."
- 💀 Does it surprise you to learn that only 16.6 percent of people said they would feel fully satisfied with their lives if they met their maker tonight? And that 20 percent of people said they would feel like they missed out on their lives if they died tonight? How does this compare to how you answered the last question? And does this not feel like a global emergency to you, too?

Now that you've plotted "the zone you've been living your life in" on your page, you can see in no uncertain terms what you're dealing with. You definitely can't unsee it. No matter what zone you're in today, it's a great starting point. We're here to Do Something about shifting you over to the right and up to the top.

 As Hunter S. Thompson says,* "Life should not be a journey to the grave with the intention of arriving safely in a pretty and well preserved body, but rather to skid in broadside in a cloud of smoke, thoroughly used up, totally worn out, and loudly proclaiming 'Wow! What a Ride!'"

We bought the ticket... We want the ride, please and thanks. Your ride will now move on to a date with death, so maybe buckle up?

---

* This is my very favorite quote of all time, and I would have it tattooed on myself somewhere if it wasn't so long.

CHAPTER 3

A DATE WITH DEATH: A BRIEF INTRODUCTION TO THE END OF YOUR LIFE

 Though the fact, the physicality, of death destroys us, the idea of death may save us.

—IRVIN YALOM

Now that we've whetted your appetite to feast at the grand buffet of life, let me be the first to welcome you to your date with death!

> YOU: What's a date with death, again? And should I wear my good underwear?
>
> ME: Great q! Allow me to clarify: I would never send you off on a *real* date with the Grim Reaper without some heavy coaching (and pregaming) first; we all know Grim would have you for dinner if things didn't work out. I won't have you dying on my watch. So think of this self-date as a figuratively intimate chance to get to know the Reaper—the redeeming, attractive side of an oft-scorned figure who has more to offer than you might think.*

Am I allowed to declare that this chapter might be my favorite? Or is it like having kids, where you absolutely have a favorite but it's uncouth to

---

* I heartily suggest you take yourself on a date as you read this chapter. Maybe flip through the pages while eating a candlelit dinner for one? Or on the steps of a museum? Maybe the finish line at the race track? Or in a bubble bath? It's your call where you'd like to contemplate the rest of your life.

announce out loud that it's Timmy? No one ever said I had couth; I have a crush on the Grim Reaper, and I'm not ashamed to admit it. Despite his dodgy reputation (killing approximately 6,300 people an hour tends to tarnish one's personal brand), he redeems himself in ways I'm going to tell you all about.

You've just done a lot of heavy lifting in your pre-mortem and zone plotting, so I'm assuming you're primed with ideas and intentions on how to consummate your life. You're also a little vulnerable, I'm guessing, what with the unearthing of a dead zone here and there, it's not easy work to look in the mirror and admit where you've zombied out or gotten lackadaisical about your life. You deserve brownie points (and also an actual brownie—aren't you glad you baked a whole batch already?) for doing that important self-reflective work. You also deserve some context about how your mortality fits into all of this.

You will ultimately (and by "ultimately" I mean by the end of this book) assemble your life wants, wishes, and whims into an action plan, and I'm here to tell you that your plans will be half-assed unless they're underwritten by the Grim Reaper. (By the end of this chapter, you'll know what I mean by that.) (But here's a teaser because I can't resist: your life plans demand a deadline—like death—to be of any consequence at all. Just like that other certainty in life—you know, taxes—you need a deadline to pay them on time, right?*)

The goal of this date, er, chapter, is for you to fully and officially fall in love with the concept of memento mori (remembering that you will die). My wish is for you to turn the pages into the next chapter totally ~~brainwashed~~ sold that the contemplation of death is what will bring you back to life. Even *more* life.

So let's see if all my hard selling on Grim sweeps you off your feet. I'm going to share Six Things Worth Knowing about Death and then a few exercises and ideas to get your juices flowing. If you're feeling interested enough for a meet cute with the Reaper after this chapter, let's talk. But I have a feeling you'll be fangirling just as hard as I do.

---

* Thankfully preparing for an astonishing life is a lot more fun than preparing our taxes.

SIX THINGS WORTH KNOWING ABOUT DEATH

I know this is nerdy to suggest on a date—even one you're on with your-self—but can I suggest you take notes in between the jalapeño poppers and oysters Rockefeller? Pay attention to your thoughts, feelings, questions, and responses to the questions posed about death along the way.

Thing #1 Worth Knowing about Death

The research is fairly conclusive: 100 percent of us will die—yes, even you.

We humans are the only animals that are keenly aware of our eventual extinction.

My mom used to wear lapel buttons on her acid-washed jean jacket when I was a kid (it was the '80s; stop it with the side-eye). The one that stood out to me the most proclaimed, "LIFE SUCKS AND THEN YOU DIE!" in bright orange lettering—launching my early education in mortality awareness. Death appeared to be absolute, but was the life-sucking part necessary? (Other than for people who weren't my bipolar mother, for whom life did suck a lot of the time?) A Buddha-quoting phlebotomist once told me that pain was inevitable, but suffering was optional, after witnessing my near meltdown at a simple blood test. To bastardize the Buddha, death is inevitable... and life-sucking is optional.

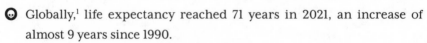

LIFE SUCKS AND THEN YOU DIE!

→ REALLY?

Let's quantify the inevitability:

- ☠ Globally,[1] life expectancy reached 71 years in 2021, an increase of almost 9 years since 1990.
- ☠ Life expectancy at birth for women around the world is 73.8, and for men, it is 68.4.

- Average life length varies widely by country:
  - In the US, the average life expectancy is 79; women live until about 81, and men live until around 76.
  - Hong Kong tops the list with life expectancy averaged at 85, and the Central African Republic bottoms the list at 54 years young.
- Thanks to modern advancements we can expect to live much longer than our ancestors; our global life expectancy[2] increased from less than 30 years to over 71 years over the last two centuries. If it was the year 1825, many of us wouldn't be here reading about death because we'd already be dead.

One of the most disturbing things about death is that it doesn't necessarily occur in age order. It catches most of us by surprise, especially when we're not waiting for it in hospice care.

This chart reveals what we already know to be true: while the likelihood of dying increases as we age, things can go haywire along the way. I have no intention of being a giant buzzkill here and now, but I'd be irresponsibly out to lunch if I didn't flag this fact of life: we all have a shelf life, but some of us are going to spoil faster. Thirteen percent of us are going to die between the ages of fifteen and forty-nine. Said more dramatically, line up ten of your younger-than-forty-nine friends and family and coworkers in your mind; one of those dear souls will die before their fiftieth birthday party.

THE DEATH BY AGE CHART

DEADSVILLE

9% 1% 13% 26% 50%

<5   5-14   15-49   50-69   >70

A full 50 percent of us aren't going to live to see seventy, which means that any deferred plans to "live it up later" should be considered crimes against our own humanity. Waiting for retirement to get into the good parts of life is like gambling with a card shark: good luck with those odds.

And in case you put your calculator away after tallying up your Mondays, I'll do the math for you: 100 percent of us will die at *some* point. So maybe we start living like we mean it now?

Okay, I hear you that this first point doesn't make the Grim Reaper look super desirable, but I promise the next one does.

Thing #2 Worth Knowing about Death

Grim has a real knack for making life seem more valuable. Scarcity can be a good thing.

You might have heard the classic self-improvement nugget about possessing a mindset of scarcity vs. abundance.[3] In most cases, adopting an abundance mindset—that we have or will have all we need—rather than a scarcity mindset, feeling as though or fearing that we don't ever have enough, is arguably a healthier and more productive way to live.[4] Except, however, when it comes to our life spans, where scarcity is our friend.

It's high time we spoke about the concept known as **temporal scarcity**: as a resource becomes scarce, it increases in its perceived value. With temporal scarcity, we reflect on the time we have left when there's an ending on the horizon—like finishing college, or wrapping up a vacation, or the (hopefully vast) expanse of the lives we're living. Framing an event, like the length of our lives, with an expiry date has been shown to make it feel that much more valuable and treasured. Reminders of death translate into in-the-moment reminders of life, that it's a scarce and valuable "asset" worth preserving.

Thinking about the end of an experience can enhance our present enjoyment of it. One study[5] asked college seniors on the cusp of graduating to write about their experience over their four years as students. One group was primed with instructions like "Given how *little* time you have left," while another group's instructions were prefaced with "Given that you have *lots* of time left." Over the two-week intervention, students consistently reminded of how little time they had left experienced heightened subjective well-being and reportedly participated in more college-related activities (More pub crawls?! More flag football?! More streaking across the quad?!). Do you need a reminder that your life is finite to engage in more (metaphoric) keg parties in your remaining time? Does the impending plane trip back to Minnesota spur you to finally really enjoy your last day on the beach in Cabo? Does Labor Day looming finally prompt you to fill the last two weeks of August with Every Summer Activity?

I have worked with countless clients who have relocated for their careers, and what do they do in the weeks before they leave for Phoenix or New Jersey or Munich? They live like tourists in their own city. Their eyes open wide as they realize they've been taking Denver, for example, for granted. "I haven't even been to the art museum," they confess, breathlessly, in a tizzy to jam-pack all they assumed they'd get around to, *one day*. Do you need to explore your own city, as though you had only seven weeks left to enjoy it? What sights would you see? What famous hot dog joints would you visit? Who would you be sure to spend time with before you moved away?

Knowing I only have 1,821-ish Mondays left makes me want to *do something* with that time, with my life, with my flights of fancy, with my pipe dreams. Life becomes valued to the extent we recognize its short-livedness.

Thing #3 Worth Knowing about Death

A daily dose of death is a really good thing. The more Reaper the better.

Memento mori (the Latin phrase that translates to "remember we must die") is so much more than a cool coin to keep in your pocket. It can unexpectedly breathe life back into our lives. Think of death reflection as the firecracker we need to reinvigorate our existence and drive a stake into the heart of our take-it-for-granted mentality.

> YOU: Isn't this act of "remembering we must die" macabre?
> ME: I see where you're coming from. Check out where I believe memento mori sits on the Hierarchy of Death-Creepiness.

Memento mori has less to do with the morbid and creepy parts of death and so much more to do with the profound opportunity to celebrate and focus on life. Reflecting on our mortality by using this reminder of death can prod us to thoughtfully tweak our lives, without having to encounter

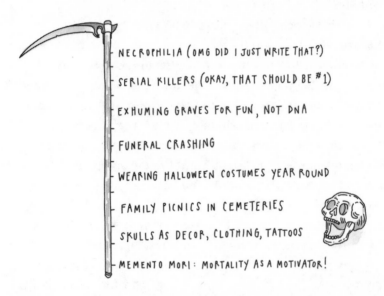

The HIERARCHY of DEATH CREEPINESS Scale

- NECROPHILIA (OMG DID I JUST WRITE THAT?)
- SERIAL KILLERS (OKAY, THAT SHOULD BE #1)
- EXHUMING GRAVES FOR FUN, NOT DNA
- FUNERAL CRASHING
- WEARING HALLOWEEN COSTUMES YEAR ROUND
- FAMILY PICNICS IN CEMETERIES
- SKULLS AS DECOR, CLOTHING, TATTOOS
- MEMENTO MORI: MORTALITY AS A MOTIVATOR!

a bracing near-death experience wake-up call—which is what it usually takes for us to snap to attention and start living on purpose. Remember when the phrase "Valar Morghulis" (All Men Must Die) set Arya off on the most epic adventure and arguably the best GoT plotline? Yeah.

The acknowledgment of death can arouse a sense of wonder[6] within us, which can percolate questions like "What is my destiny? What might be in store for me? How do I want to shape my remaining Mondays?"

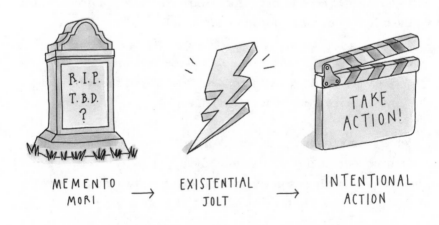

MEMENTO MORI → EXISTENTIAL JOLT → INTENTIONAL ACTION

Deliberately relating to death can provide an existential jolt that leads to a transcendence of our monotonous daily existence. It awakens us from the "drowsiness of the human condition."[7]

Memento mori is not only a mechanism to appreciate life but also clearly a means to become better versions of ourselves. Did counting your Mondays in your pre-mortem not make you feel an uncanny sense of urgency? How can we afford to not be practicing this regularly?

> YOU: So how do I practice memento mori and not be morbid enough to turn off all the people around me?
>
> ME: Screw them!
>
> ME, getting a do-over on my answer: Great question! Now that I have convinced you memento mori is a lifestyle, not an event, we should talk about how you can unweirdly weave it into your way of being on a day-to-day basis.

Most people I work with come up with little symbols or structures to stay in touch with their end:

- Memento mori on the go: You can get a coin, like mine, or maybe a small trinket to carry around that makes you think of your impermanence. You can buy the coolest little skulls carved in lots of different gemstones. Some of my clients carry a death-inspired quote on a card in their wallet around with them.
- Memento mori at home: I spray-paint decorative skulls in fabulous colors to put on display. . . . Hourglasses come in all shapes and sizes these days, too.
- Calendars galore! Any calendar is a countdown timer if you look at it through the memento mori lens, but what about a weekly life countdown calendar? (I gave these out to a bunch of clients as a holiday gift one year, and it went over like a lead balloon—fair warning that it'll need a bit of context.)
- I have jewelry made with memento mori engravings; every time I glance down at my skull necklaces, I think of my life with fondness. One of my clients has a bracelet with a tiny coffin charm that I'm quite envious of.

- Some people look at a photo of a lost loved one and use that as a reminder of their own limited time.

- Back in the Middle Ages, vanitas still-life paintings were big in the art world—allegorical depictions of death, death, and more death... images of skulls, watches, soap bubbles about to burst, hourglasses, burning candles, and dying flowers. Maybe flowers become a symbolic memento mori for you from now on, because they're beautiful and not around that long? Maybe you never look at your watch the same way again? Maybe your crazy-expensive candles take on all new meaning?

- Why not appreciate works of visual art that feature mortality? Vincent van Gogh's *Head of a Skeleton with a Burning Cigarette* is a classic (and can be purchased as a poster on Amazon for slightly less than Damien Hirst's £50 million platinum skull encrusted with more than 8,601 diamonds). Google "Art with Death Themes," and see what inspires you.

- Big reader? Volumes have been written about the big sleep. Dylan Thomas advised us to "not go gentle into that good night," and Hamlet famously shuffled off his mortal coil. Leo Tolstoy wrote *The Death of Ivan Ilyich*—a fictional focus on the liberation of death—in the aftermath of an existential crisis. Emily Dickinson had such a preoccupation with death that she wrote it into more than a quarter of her poems. If that's not enough to get you started, Google "Books with Literary Themes About Death" and put the tea kettle on.

- Many people meditate on death throughout the day, like Buddhists, who believe that death is the key to the mystery of life. More on that in a few pages.

- Many clients I work with journal on the topic or take a personal retreat day once a quarter to reflect on their temporariness. Taking a few hours to redo the Astonishingly Alive Assessment (page 32) can help you zero in on bright spots worth enhancing and the dark spots worth enlivening. I recommend cute notebooks with skeletons on the cover, but this is not required. How about asking yourself questions like ...
  - How many Mondays do I have left as of today?
  - How many Mondays have I lived so far in my life?
  - How many Mondays have passed since my last memento mori check-in?
  - Examples of how I have felt full of vitality in the last week ...
  - Examples of how I have felt meaning-full in the last week ...
  - I'm grateful to be alive because ...
  - Thinking of my mortality right now makes me feel and think ...
  - In light of all this death chatter, I'm motivated to ...
  - Which questions from my pre-mortem should I revisit and reflect upon?

- A company I lead retreats for has adopted a pre- and postmortem for every project and regularly practices gratitude for their existence in a competitive market.

- One particularly spiritual client prays with her family before dinner with a specific nod of appreciation for being alive. "It's not enough to be grateful for the food on the table," she says. "We also have to appreciate how lucky we are to be here."

- Let's not forget memento mori attire! There are plenty of cashmere sweaters out there with skulls and crossbones on them, and if that's not in your budget, you can buy a great pair of socks that encourage you to "Carpe the Fuck Out of This Diem." Indeed, indeed.

Memento mori ups our game. Life is a game after all, and while the Grim Reaper always wins in the end, he levels us up if we're willing to pay attention. Knowing he's out there, lurking in the shadows, can make us mindful of the time we have left until he sends the car around.

Apprentice yourself to the curve of your own disappearance.
—DAVID WHYTE

A Quick Story about Making Time for Bora Bora (i.e., Death as a Deadline)

In a recent Zoom conversation with the godfather of positive psychology, Dr. Marty Seligman, I asked him about the role of death in his life.

"I think about death very often," he said. "But I'm not afraid of death—it just reminds me how much time I have left. And why it's important to go to places like Bora Bora. [Marty and his wife had just returned from a snorkeling-filled sojourn to this French Polynesian island.] The fact of death is omnipresent for me.... It's like a calendar in some ways. It sort of tells me I've probably got, you know, at age eighty, I've probably got ten good years left, so I want to budget accordingly."

I then asked if death helped him focus on what mattered.

"It does help me prioritize in some ways. It's the same way as telling me that I have a deadline on January 1 to get a manuscript in. Yeah, I have a deadline at age ninety to try to get down on paper whatever useful thoughts I have. I want to make sure I get my work done."

What work (literal and figurative) do you want to complete before your own deadline?

Thing #4 Worth Knowing about Death

People who have had brushes with death know things we don't.

Think of someone you might know who has had a close call with death—maybe through an unsettling medical diagnosis, a close-call motorcycle accident, maybe a treacherous military experience—any kind of nearish death experience. Have you not noticed how on purpose these people live after the wake-up call of all wake-up calls? How much they treasure each day? Study after study shows how these people approach their lives with fresh eyes—clarified priorities and profound attitude adjustments about life.

In the stark face of abbreviated life spans, terminally ill patients often report feeling a poignant appreciation of the present moment and even blessed by the gift of being able to reprioritize their precious time left.

A Quick Deathbed Perspective Story

Victoria was diagnosed with stage 3 bowel cancer in August 2021, which progressed to stage 4 about six months later. She sent this email to her colleagues about a month before she passed away in September 2022, at the age of thirty-three—just a month after her wedding day.

> Its been a heck of a ride, and I'm afraid my diagnosis has gone from bad to worse. But I'm feeling incredibly lucky, all things considered. I couldn't have asked for more support from [the organization] . . . as well as my loved ones who have all been amazing. My goals in life have changed somewhat—from wanting a successful career and babies I now just want to get through each day and smile. And you know what? The days when I don't feel like total cr*p feel happier than ever. But it's tragic that it took a cancer diagnosis to teach me what living is really about. It's about cups of tea, enjoying the sunshine, having a laugh, and sharing love. So when you are worrying about stuff (and I of all people know how easy it is to worry!) just remember: you are healthy, and you are loved, and every day the sun rises you get a new opportunity to feel great. Its easier said than done, but please, for me, remember how blessed we are to have this thing called life. It's so beautiful, and I would do anything to have more of it left, so don't let it pass you by.
>
> All my love,
>
> V. x

To what extent did this email grip you as you read it? I'm never left unaffected, and I've read it countless times. Did you feel anguish, sorrow, panic, a can't-put-your-finger-on-it kind of existential despair? Maybe you experienced the fright/flight/freeze response that typically accompanies danger. Don't worry, it's a natural response. But shoving those feelings down deep and pretending you never read this email won't change a thing. Here, try this instead: How might you catapult those important and tender feelings into something productive—which is why we're here together? How can you extract the lessons from Victoria's story and apply it to your own life?

To what extent are you worrying about trivial things, instead of savoring the sweet, simple things in life—like cups of tea, sunshine, laughter, and love? To what extent are you taking for granted that "you are healthy, and you are loved, and every day the sun rises you get a new opportunity to feel great"?

I want us to see life through the same viewfinder as Victoria and those who have made it back from the brink of death, without first having to teeter on the edge of survival. More on this in chapter 5.

SO MUCH TO SAVOR

Thing #5 Worth Knowing about Death

Thinking about death is like a natural gratitude booster.

Every day the Grim Reaper doesn't pick your name out of the death jar is a good day. Would we prefer to get that gratitude glow by recording our little list of "Things to Be Grateful For" before bed every night rather than appreciating a bony figure holding a scythe? Of course. But we must zoom out and see the big picture. If you woke up today, and if you get to tuck yourself into bed tonight, you've got a lot more to be grateful for than the 151,200 souls who made Grim's short list for the day.

Coaching Chestnut: Gratitude Gravy. The authorities would revoke my coaching certifications if I didn't elaborate about gratitude for a second. In the first day of class in the Master of Applied Positive Psychology program at UPenn, Angela Duckworth (Yes! The author of *Grit!*[8]) said in her science-swathed-with-wit way that "gratitude is like ketchup—put it on anything and it tastes better."

Researchers[9] have found that long-term happiness can be enhanced by more than 10 percent by exercising gratitude through journaling.

Grateful people are more satisfied with their lives, are more agreeable and open-minded, and have deeper and more forgiving relationships, boosted self-esteem, greater self-control, less stress, better sleep, improved physical health, and shinier hair. So here is the chestnut: if you haven't completed a gratitude journal for thirty days in a row (listing five things to be thankful for that day—minuscule and/or monumental), you are missing out on an awful lot of love for life. Consciously appreciating what happens in your life inherently helps you appreciate that you have a life to enjoy. Your gratitude challenge has officially been issued.

Are you willing to give the gratitude journal challenge a go? What might you have to gain by doing so? Take this a step further: think of a special person in your life and five specific things you appreciate about them. Reflect for a moment on their impermanence. Does this heighten your gratitude for the relationship you share with them?

Thing #6 Worth Knowing about Death

Death denial is the default setting for humans.

It's normal to have an animalistic fear of death.... It's the number one fear out there, even more so than public speaking. Death terrifies and intrigues us in seemingly equal measure; we have a morbid fascination with death and destruction, and we flirt with it by watching gory movies or car accidents—but ask us to think of our own demise, and we head for the hills, don't we?

We're in such denial of our blatant endings that we consistently purchase insufficient life insurance; we postpone transfers of wealth between generations—even when significant tax savings are to be gained—and just 25 percent of us have living wills in place. Do you have insurance? A will? A living will? Your funeral plans mapped out with your loved ones? And if not, why not? Don't worry—I'm not here to badger you about getting ready for death...I'm here to badger you about getting ready to live. More on your denial in our very next chapter.

So...(*me looking at you, expectantly*)? After reading through these six points, are you starting to feel any special feelings for Grim? He has more to offer than you thought, doesn't he? We're going to come back to these "selling points" about death throughout our conversation together in this book. Let's summarize before we move on...

Here's a Quick Roundup of the Things We Know to Be True about Death:

1. The research seems fairly conclusive—100 percent of us will die.
2. Scarcity (for once in its life) can be a good thing.
3. A daily dose of death is good for us.
4. People who've had brushes with death know things we don't, but the rest of us can still live with urgency and intention without having to nudge the bucket first.
5. Memento mori can be a natural gratitude booster.
6. Denial is our default setting, but acceptance of death is a good first step on the path to a life with more width and depth.

THREE THINGS TO DO ON YOUR DATE(S) WITH DEATH

I know this has been riveting for you so far—all this mortality enlightenment—but you might be the type who likes a little more action on your dates (even if it is just you and you). I've got you covered with three different activities.... You can cram them into this special evening or spread them out over subsequent dates with death.

Death-Date Thing #1 to Do: The Death Meditation

The country of Bhutan, nestled deep into the Himalayas, has been measuring their Gross National Happiness levels since 2006. Things have been going well over there; over 90 percent of their residents report being happy, to one extent or another. Following the Buddhist tradition, many Bhutanese people practice their death meditation five times each day. Fatality is the farthest thing from a taboo topic in this culture.

Eastern religions and philosophies, traditionally more open about the topic of death, have connected death and contemplation for ages; the Vedic texts in India have woven in themes of death reflection, and Buddhists—believing that death is the key to the mystery of life—extol the virtues of mindfully meditating on the thought of *maranam bhavissati*, meaning "death will take place." *Maranasati* is the meditation we are talking about; *marana* translates to "death" in Pali (the language of the Buddha), and *sati* refers to "mindfulness." In the words of the Buddha: "Of all the footprints, that of the elephant is supreme. Similarly, of all mindfulness meditation, that on death is supreme."

The goal of death mindfulness is not merely to check the box on death awareness but to act as a catalyst for positive influence—like shifting our attitudes on the meaning of life, increasing our acceptance of death, and committing to a life of intention. All of this sounds lovely...but does it really work?

One study[10] dug into whether this "mindfulness of death" practice could lead to positive psychological impact. Korean students were asked to meditate for fifteen minutes on the question "If there was not much more time to live, what would I do?" After the intervention, their attitudes about life tilted in favor of intrinsic values, they felt likelier to partake in prosocial behaviors (e.g., helping, giving, being better citizens), and they were more accepting of death's inevitability.

The Five Remembrances

These central Buddhist facets of life's fragility are from the *Upajjhatthana Sutta* ("Subjects for Contemplation") and are intended to create personal awakening:

1. I am of the nature to grow old; I cannot escape old age.
2. I am of the nature to get sick; I cannot escape sickness.
3. I am of the nature to die; I cannot escape death.
4. All that is dear to me and everyone I love are of the nature to change; there is no way to escape being separated from them.

5. I inherit the results of my actions of body, speech, and mind; my actions are my continuation.

How might you feel about reciting these remembrances daily? How about *five times* each day? What would it be like to read these off a sticky note placed on your mirror, as you prepare for your day in the morning and get ready for bed at night?

Perhaps you'd prefer a softer touch.

Inspired by the Buddhist mortality meditation, the WeCroak app conveniently texts users "Don't forget, you're going to die" five times each day; over 150,000 people have paid to be reminded of their impending fates since the app's inception in 2017. Their texts arrive "at random times and at any moment, just like death." I can attest that each message arrives with a wee jolt (especially for the person next to you who might happen to get a glimpse of your phone when the message appears; I've had some explaining to do over the years).

Death-Date Thing #2 to Do: The Obituary Exploration

Yet another DIY-date activity, perfect when you're curled up with yourself in front of a fire (and a good Internet connection). Let's talk about obituaries (a.k.a. Grim's scrapbook) and how they can help us live in earnest.

Every January my dad and I play the morbidly amusing game of "Look Who Died This Year" over the phone. I read out the notable deaths from the *New York Times*, he reminisces about the sports players and glamorous movie stars on the list, and we have an all-round great conversation at the expense of a lot of dead people.

Famous people's deaths do a bang-up job of underscoring the "seize the day" message, and while I'm all about acknowledging the Deaths of the Rich and Famous if it helps us mediate our own relationship with mortality, I'm also curious about the unfamous people who've died.

News outlets don't highlight the obit for Reg the accountant from Boise; nor do they feature the write-ups for the countless girls and grandmas next door. While their lives aren't notable enough for headlines, they are no less remarkable. Dare I say that these everyday people's obituaries are even more compelling, because their lives resemble our lives more than those who've walked the red carpet? We can relate to Reg's life—the to-and-fro commute between the office, home, the pharmacy, and Applebee's—in ways we can't seem to do with the Queen of England.

Here is a random sampling of word-for-word ordinary human obituaries found online:

- Linda from Pennsylvania passed away at 82; she was an animal lover who fostered several seeing eye puppies and brought home a duck she named Waddles. She loved to garden and made the most delicious iced tea.
- Ron, 71, was an avid fisherman who loved the outdoors in Minnesota. He had a love for his grandchildren, great grandchildren, as well as his four-legged friend Daisy. He unapologetically hated Trump to the end.
- Dean, 45, loved to cook and showed beef cattle at the Delaware County Fair.
- Bubba from Tennessee loved playing Xbox, spending time with his dog, and riding his bike on sunny days. He died at 18.

When almost-centenarians die, we tend to accept and even dismiss their deaths. Death is on the to-do list when you're north of eighty-two, right? Yet when people our own age or younger die, we snap to attention with the gripping fear that "it could have been me." Our ephemerality comes into much clearer view in these moments, and that's what we're after—the vicarious wake-up call to live—because our next car ride might be our last, because that mole on our shoulder with the funny edges could be malignant melanoma, because Anything Could Happen. Life could happen, and we might be the next obituary that other people are startled to attention by.

I can't help but acquiesce to the inevitability of it all when I read every-day folks' obituaries. I look deep into the eyes of their photos and wonder about the lives they lived. Were they happy? I wonder about my own life and how it would be summarized in a small square on the Internet. Was I happy? It's profoundly impactful.

Your Obituary Draft

You know how there are things in life you don't want to do, but they end up being absolutely worth it in the end? Like getting a root canal, or maybe a colonoscopy? Here is a seemingly morbid—possibly gut-wrenching—assignment that has a payoff of memento mori proportions. You get to draft your obituary. This colonoscopy-of-the-soul-like task will help ground your mortality in reality, which is what we are here to do. Pull out a fresh page of paper, get comfortable, and take your time as you consider the following points:

- Aim for about two hundred words. You can be short and sweet* at around fifty words, and if you're a little long-winded, you can bloat up to five hundred words (surely referencing your loquaciousness?).[11]
- Skip the details and date of your death in this draft, unless you want to jinx your life forever. (I do give you permission to make the date of your death on your one hundredth birthday. Just not sooner.)
- Hit the highlights of your life story, which may or may not include your date and place of birth, your hometown or places you've lived, schooling details, employment details, and any special interests.
- Ask yourself if the obituary captures the essence of your youness, so that readers would say, "Yes, that sounds like Sophie—late for her own funeral!"
- Obituaries usually include shout-outs to key people in one's life: sur-viving and already-dead family members, friends, pets. Who might make the cut in this brief encapsulation of your life?

---

* Fun fact: you might have a hard time beating the brevity of Fargo, North Dakota, resident Doug Legler's obit, which by his witty request came in at just two words: "Doug died." I think we'd have liked Doug a lot.

☠ Do you want to include charity details for donations to a cause you care about . . . possibly in lieu of all those carnations?

☠ What photo would you select? (I recently read about a perfectly healthy eighty-seven-year-old man who had professional headshots taken for his inevitable funeral, so he'd have a good-looking shot published with his obituary in the paper. God, I love people who are planners, not to mention overly vain, like me.)

Now that you have a mock-up of your obituary, what was it like to draft this write-up? It likely stumped you at points. What might that indicate? What feelings emerged as you drafted this version?

Sure, it's convenient to have an item ticked off your Things to Do When I Die list, but I'm less interested in your tasky bits being nailed down here. I'm interested in the emotional experience of wrapping your life up in about two hundred words. I'm interested mostly in the part about your life story—how you'd like to be summed up. This might drive some of your decisions about how you'd like to live your life from now on, as we make our way through this book.

I encourage you to peek at the obituaries of everyday people from time to time, just to see what it stirs up in you. Getting a glimpse into what other people have lost—like their grandma Linda,* for example—can spark empathy for others, an appreciation for the people you care about, and, if nothing else, gratitude for the life you still get to live.

Death-Date Thing #3 to Do: The Cemetery Walk

Things have been going well on this little date with death, and the party's just getting started, so. . . . What do you say we keep these good vibes going! It's time to go on a little field trip.

The "get out there" intervention I'd like you to complete within the next thirty days of your life is a visit to a cemetery, graveyard, mausoleum, or other resting place. Immerse yourself in the utmost finality of it all.

---

* Gardening appears to be a super popular pastime noted in the obits, especially for seniors. At first I thought it was charming that "Myrtle loved tending to her begonias." But then I started wondering . . . do you think it's the gardening that's killing these people? Let's keep working on this hypothesis before alerting any authorities.

If you're in the middle of nowhere and can't make this special field trip work, go online and Google famous people's graves. I urge you to make this in-person effort as a part of your commitment to living like you mean it, if you can swing it.

- ☠ While walking through a cemetery, look at some of the gravestones and imagine the lives of the people who once walked the same earth as you.
- ☠ Zero in on a particular tombstone and notice the name, date of birth and death, and any other engravings.
- ☠ Imagine a day in their shoes—what their hopes, dreams, and longings might have been.
- ☠ Imagine what they felt like near the end, what they might have been proud of, and what they might have wished they'd done differently.
- ☠ Spend as much time as you realistically can on this: I encourage a minimum of fifteen minutes to really be present with the idea of death.
- ☠ What was it like being in the cemetery? What were you thinking of, trying not to think of, or noticing?
- ☠ What other observations occurred to you on this field trip?
- ☠ Might you be willing to visit cemeteries in new towns or cities you visit? What might you have to gain by witnessing our shared human experience of dying?

Of the three activities you just tried out / read about trying out on a future mortality-contemplation date with yourself, which ones resonated the most, and for what reasons? Perhaps they all felt hideous, and if so, for what reasons? All good fodder for contemplation.

RIP
ONE
DAY
HOPEFULLY
NOT SOON THO

SO NOW WHAT?

Your date with you, yourself, and death is over. The good news is that since you went on this date solo, you don't have to worry about being rejection-murdered in your sleep tonight by Grim. The goal of this self-reflection date was for you to get to know Grim just enough to respect the power he possesses...not just to eliminate you but to spur you to live. #respectthescythe

Clearly we wouldn't be meeting here in these pages if there weren't countless benefits of reflecting on death. When we're forced to look at our inevitable demise in a deliberate way, it tends to not only wake us up to our finitude, but it also forces us to count our blessings that we are still alive, that we can breathe fresh air, that we have time left to do something special with our existence. Halle-fucking-leujah.

If the ~~threat~~ reminder of death is what it takes for us to breathe some life back into our lives, then I'm all about starting the International Council for Grim Reaper Aficionados. Interested in starting a local chapter? Imagine the cool branded hoodies we could wear!

I encourage you to go on this solo date with death on a regular basis. You can treat yourself to an all-expenses-paid personal retreat to Bhutan or maybe just snag the corner table at Starbucks and reflect on some or all of the following:

- Count your Mondays. Every. Single. Monday.
- Adopt the memento mori lifestyle. Find ways to remind yourself of your temporality, and regularly switch things up. Maybe have this date with death in the coffee shop across from a funeral home? Maybe wear your new skull T-shirt?
- Meditate on death—even for two minutes—focusing on the Five Remembrances.
- Read a handful of obituaries of the Average Joes and Janes. Make sure to read a few of people in your age group for a more poignant experience.
- Revisit your obituary draft. Do the words still feel like they synopsize the always-improving life you're leading?
- Cap your date off with a walk through a cemetery or a scroll through the Père Lachaise Google images page. Might this shed light on the life you've been living, as the exercise is intended?

Was this date with death a tad overwhelming? I can see how you might be nodding. (You can't see me, but I'm nodding with you.) I'd like you to hold on a bit longer though, because our next chapter will sort through the gory details of this mortality conversation—pulling you back from the brink of a full-blown existential crisis.*

Memento mori, as you well know by now, is about remembering we will die. This practice is really in service of *memento vivere*, which translates from Latin to "remembering we must live." So we're going to get you doing that—living full out, spurred by the awareness of Grim's looming and inevitable presence. Don't be alarmed if you catch him stalking you; you did share a blooming onion appetizer with him, and he thought he stood a chance. You don't have to put him on your vision board (*I totally did that*), but do use him to your advantage as we continue on this astonish-your-life adventure together. As they say . . . keep your enemies close.

_____

* For the record: nose-diving into existential despair isn't on the agenda for our adventure here together. Tap-dancing near the edge of existential discomfort—that's okay. We just want you to wake up to the absurdity of your finite human condition and to live like you mean it in the midst of said absurdity.

CHAPTER 4

DEATHLY DENIAL: AVOIDING YOUR EXISTENTIAL CRISIS

 We pay expensively for the taboo we affix to the subject of death.
—HERMAN FEIFEL

Welcome back from your hot self-guided date with death! Although you didn't get lucky, it wasn't a total train wreck either. At least you learned how memento mori helps us live like we have something worth dying for.... Between that and drafting your obituary, it sounds like a real night on the town.

And here is where I'm going to get nosy about the date—in a "How are you feeling about death?" kind of way. Were the Things Worth Knowing about Death uncomfortable to hear? Did you feel yourself recoiling... questioning... flinching... nodding... *denying*?

As it should be abundantly clear by now, we're all going to die. Every second on our planet, 1.8 poor souls drop dead, and we're all just walking around hoping we're not one of them. We're not just trying not to die; we're trying not to think about dying. It's normal to be anxious about not being around in the future.

We tussle with an instinctive fear of death, buried at our deepest, primal levels. You may not think that you have existential angst, but if you're human, it's there. Some of us don't have to scratch the surface too far to find that animalistic fear, and for others, we bury our mortal dread deep down under cartons of pistachio gelato, refilled prosecco glasses, infinite social media scrolling, Amazon shopping marathons...

scads of ways we numb our anxieties of not being enough and/or doing enough.

Even you—someone as evolved as you to be reading a book about such a wildly ostracized topic—might tippy-toe around death, even though it holds such great potential to help us live like we mean it. The way we approach or avoid death profoundly impacts our well-being and the ways we live our lives.

So let's dive deep into how we deke and deal with death. We'll get into the studies, and we'll get you doing a few reflective exercises. See if you recognize yourself in our discussion—as a card-carrying death denier—because the acknowledgment of when and where you might swat the idea of death away can help you stop the swatting and start the living. Awareness, after all, is the precursor to change. (Can I suggest a "dead eye" to drink during this chapter, which I've just learned is a coffee with three shots of espresso? Your call.)

A SOCIETY EVOLVED TO DENY DEATH

We come by our disdain for death honestly, in light of the times we live in.

Death used to be a social experience that brought communities together through collective rituals; it was familiar and literally out in the open—wakes were held in home parlors up until the end of the nineteenth century, so the whole family could give Uncle Melvyn a last goodbye from the comforts of home.

It was around this time that death became professionalized, and corpses were swiftly whisked away to funeral homes or hospitals. (And consequently home parlors were given the ultimate home makeover, ingeniously rebranded as *living rooms*. No more dead bodies stinking up the house, please and thanks.) Death is now a medicalized event, cleaned up of its inherent messiness, and hidden from plain view.

Out of sight death became seen as a physical malfunction or a medical letdown. The medical, scientific, and technology fields have done wonders for extending our life spans, yet our discomfort with death appears to have grown in direct proportion with our ability to postpone it. We can't even utter the word; Thelma didn't die; she "passed away." This sanitization has left us floundering in the face of something so natural;

we're often woefully unprepared to handle the distasteful act of dying, let alone the finality of death.

Existential Exception Alert! Some cultures are more accepting of death than others. "To the people of New York, Paris, or London, 'death' is a word that is never pronounced because it burns the lips," wrote the Mexican poet and diplomat Octavio Paz. "The Mexican, however, frequents it, jokes about it, caresses it, sleeps with it, celebrates it; it is one of his favorite toys and most steadfast love. Of course, in his attitude perhaps there is as much fear as there is in one of the others; at least he does not hide it; he confronts it face to face with patience, disdain, or irony."

Many Mexicans and Latin Americans pay respects to their ancestors on Dia de Los Muertos, or Day of the Dead*—a joyful and exuberant celebration that spills into the streets and graveyards. We can connect the dots of this annual party back to ancient Aztecs, who viewed death as an integral, ever-present part of life.

Communities in Ghana, Africa, also celebrate death with the help of elaborately designed fantasy coffins that honor the life of the person who passed away. Why go with a pedestrian, run-o'-the-mill mahogany casket when you can be carried by dancing pallbearers in a chili pepper coffin? Or go away in style in a giant Nike shoe coffin? Or a pack of Marlboros? Ghanaians know how to put the "fun" in funerals.

Novelty caskets can also be found at daylong Ngaben cremation ceremonies in Bali. After a day of raucous partying and sacred dancing, the deceased person's soul enters into reincarnation, and their ashes are sent out to sea. It is a joyful occasion to watch a casket in the shape of a cow, for example, be a part of such a celebratory cremation.

These examples indicate how influential our cultures and religions can be in shaping our acceptance or denial of death. What do we have

---

* Please refer to the Disney movie *Coco* for a highly academic exploration of this ritual.

to learn from them? How was death viewed in the culture you grew up in—was it a never-to-be-uttered topic, or were you encouraged to talk about it openly at the dinner table? Were funerals purely mournful or partly celebratory experiences? How would you like to approach the topic of death? I realize you can't snap your fingers and become full-on equanimous about the Reaper. We have some work to do...and so the journey continues.

DEATH-DODGING DENIAL

No discussion about mortality evasion would be complete without hearing from the cultural anthropologist Ernest Becker; in *The Denial of Death*[1] he addressed the existential matters that contribute to our fear of the end. Fun fact: academics[2] credit Becker's bible—for which he posthumously received a Pulitzer Prize—as one of the five most important works published on meaning within twentieth-century social science history.

A Pulitzer is great and all, but you know you're a big deal when they create a foundation after you. I spoke with Deborah Jacobs, executive director of the thirty-year-old Ernest Becker Foundation, about all things death denial. "You want to know the simplest way I explain to someone in the elevator what the deal is with Ernest Becker? Well, you know how Freud thought everything was about sex? Well, for Becker, everything was about death. And the difference is that Becker's theories have scientifically borne out and Freud's have not." I liked her from the get-go. "Awareness of our mortality can make us live more—or less—fully. And if you know about it, and if you confront it, and if you embrace it, that's how you live more fully."

Rather than denying our denial, Becker recommended that we stoically accept the limitations of being human (fatal flaws and all), the limitations of our bodies (which are destined to perish), and that we give up the ghost on trying to stifle our natural impulsive responses to death. The paradox is clear: we must accept our denial.

Becker noted that a productive way in which we often handle the dilemma of death is by cooking up an "immortality project"—a set of beliefs that make us feel heroic and symbolically immortal. We're sober enough to realize we won't be here forever, but we find comfort in the notion that a sliver of our existence might just persist beyond us, don't we? An immortality project could look like having your name chiseled into a brick on the new wing of the library at your alma mater, devotedly adhering to a religious doctrine, getting a facelift to stave off the appearance of aging, or having kids who will have kids who will have kids, and so on. Fear—or denial—of death, to Becker, was the "mainspring of human activity"...a fundamental motivator behind why we do what we do.

OUR MISGUIDED SENSE OF SPECIALNESS

The existential psychologist Irv Yalom[3] writes about the concept of "personal specialness" as the most common way we deny the idea of death. This "conviction that we are exempt from biological necessity and that life will not deal with us in the same harsh way it deals with everyone else" is as illogical as it is predictable. Oh, how we love our self-deception strategies. See if you recognize yourself in this little human head game.

Bad things happen to other people, and we find ourselves startled when they happen to us. Other people have their cars broken into...not us. Other people get laid off in a recession...not us. Other people age into wrinkled raisins and ultimately breathe their last breaths, but we somehow think we'll dodge the bullet and come out...unscathed? With remarkably smooth skin and implausibly immortal? Intellectually we know it's foolish, yet we cling to the idea that we're special and immune to the negative experiences all the unfortunate *other people* have to endure. Sucks to be them!

I remember laughing with a client who shared the details of her recent optometry appointment. She was baffled that she needed reading glasses and pressed her doctor

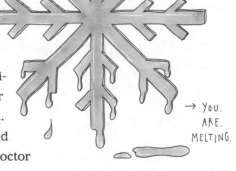

→ YOU.
ARE.
MELTING.

to run special tests to "get to the bottom of this." She imitated her doctor's response, replete with his southern accent: "Honey, this ain't no mystery. You're forty-two. What did you think was going to happen?" She thought she was exempt. She thought her eyes were special.

It's true that no one else out there is quite like you—you really are a special snowflake. But you know what happens to snowflakes? They melt. You are a special, melting snowflake. Beautiful (well, some of you are*), but fleeting. Melting.

 The writer William Saroyan once said, "Everybody has got to die, but I have always believed an exception would be made in my case." (An exception was not granted; he died in 1981.)

So how do we stop specialness† bamboozling ourselves? We face the truth about death; we remind ourselves that zero exceptions have been made and ever will be made. (Again, except for vampires. We must ask them their secret.) What realities might you need to face today? If your father and grandmother had arthritis, for example, might you want to anticipate it for yourself and get on with your active lifestyle now? Get on with traveling to Machu Picchu now—while your knees still bend—instead of "one day down the road"?

THE DANGER OF DEATH DODGING

Denying the idea of death comes at a cost. No, literally: Bryan Johnson is slated to spend $2 million per year as part of his project to turn back the clock from forty-five to eighteen years old.[4] While trying to put the lid on our thoughts about the big sleep, many of us experience anxiety, worry, depression, and negative emotions; trying to quell death anxiety through avoidance ironically brews a batch of even more anxiety. Conscious and unconscious worries about death, if unaddressed, put a dent in our

---

* ☺

† An important note about specialness: It's true that you are extraordinary, exquisite, and unique. You have talents and traits unlike anyone else out there. You are important and special! Just not special enough to not get old and die.

ability to show up fully for life. Denial exacts the price of a compromised inner life.

The troubling thing about avoiding death is that death always wins. In all of its annoying omnipresence, death isn't afraid to make itself known—through our own health scares ("there's an abnormality on your X-ray"), through the 24-hour "if it bleeds, it leads" news cycle, in the lyrics of a popular song, driving by a funeral procession, or through the unfortunate passing of someone we know. We can try to play dumb, we can try to avoid reality, and then we end up in another round of therapy and wonder why. Unaddressed death anxiety just morphs into anxieties about other things in life, creating what psychologists call the "revolving door" in their clinical practices.[5]

 Perhaps Otto Rank, the first existential therapist, said it best: "Some refuse the loan of life to avoid the debt of death."

The "What Does Your Death Mean to You?" Scale

The meanings we attach to death, as complicated as they may be, act as triggers for our emotions, motivations, and actions. But how do we gain this valuable self-awareness? We turn to scientific scales.

Psychologists[6] assembled a list of thirty "meanings statements" from a bevy of academic sources. What is the extent to which each statement represents the meaning that death has for you personally? (Imagine a 5-point scale where 1 means you vehemently disagree and 5 means you heartily agree.)

1. Death means pain and suffering.
2. Death means personal extinction.
3. Death means the end of one's dreams.
4. Death helps give meaning to life.
5. Death is a relief from the struggles of life.
6. Death challenges one to take high risks.
7. Death provides the opportunity for our accomplishments to be evaluated for posterity.
8. Death makes us all equal.

9. Death means separation from our loved ones.
10. Death means reunion with our loved ones.
11. Death means the opportunity to attain symbolic immortality (leave a legacy).
12. Death means the opportunity to die nobly, to die with honor and glory for a cause.
13. Death means the elimination of adversaries, outliving competitors.
14. Death means eternal punishment.
15. Death means loss.
16. Death means the beginning of something beyond.
17. Death is absurd.
18. Death is sexually exciting.
19. Death is the impetus for setting goals.
20. Death is the beginning of a new adventure.
21. Death makes us all humble.
22. Death motivates us to achieve.
23. Death motivates us to provide an inheritance for our children.
24. Death is an opportunity to be eulogized for our great accomplishments.
25. Death makes us concerned with others more than ourselves.
26. Death makes us live to prepare for it.
27. Death means that life is uncertain.
28. Death is remote from everyday life.
29. Death is a disease that medicine will cure.
30. Life gives death meaning.

(Should we agree to not comment on #18? It's settled, then—no comment.)

The scale above measures how we view death along four dimensions:

- Death as Afterlife (i.e., pearly gates): items 2 (reversed), 10, 16, 20.
- Death as Extinction (sheer and utter oblivion): items 1, 2 (reversed), 3, 9, 15.
- Death as Legacy (leaving something of significance behind for others to benefit from): items 7, 11, 12, 13, 24.
- Death as Motivator (the firecracker in the behind to set and reach goals in life): items 4, 7, 19, 22, 30.

What dimension resonates the most with you? What dimension do you identify with the least? Continue reading to make even more sense of your feelings about your mortality.

THINGS WORTH KNOWING ABOUT OUR ATTITUDES TOWARD DEATH

- **Feelings about death carry over to feelings about life.** If you're feeling consistently queasy about your inevitable expiry, studies show you're likelier to be depressed, anxious, have lower self-esteem, and pretty much everything that's the opposite of people who neutrally accept death . . . because they tend to experience more life satisfaction and meaning.[7]

- **Women are more willing to go there.** Academics[8] have found that females tend to be more open to the contemplation of death, whereas males are likelier to avoid the thorny subject.

- **Death awareness leads to . . . growth?** A genuine understanding of our own mortality is seen to have profound psychological benefits and can be a prompt for growth, whereas fearing death can meta- phorically kill us before we die.

- **Death acceptance can provide a wonder-filled wake-up to life.** Some academics[9] note the acceptance of death rouses a sense of wonder, which flips the script on life and turns it into a game of figuring out our destiny. Might you need a bit of wonder to wake up from your life nap?

- **Having a point of view on "what death means" is good for you.** Psychologists[10] study death attitudes by analyzing responses to light 'n' fluffy questions like "What is your personal philosophy of death?" and "What is death? What does it mean to you?" People who actually have a personal philosophy of death tend to feel a greater sense of purpose and have a great acceptance of their mortality. If you were pressed to write a few lines about your philosophy on death, what would you jot down?

- **Meaning + connection matters.** Research[11] shows that people with high perceptions of meaning in life and people who define them- selves as socially connected find themselves relieved from many death anxieties, without dips to their well-being when they talk about death. Key takeaway: boost meaning and meaningful relationships (see you in chapter 9, "Living Deeper with Meaning").

- **Positive illusionists.** Some researchers[12] believe that negative attitudes and avoidance behavior toward death are more of an illusion of self-control than a form of denial, especially in people with a high level of desire for personal structure and control (so...a lot of us?). You might just be a positive illusionist if you fail to take your mortality seriously, even if you've had a brush with death and lived to tell the tale. Are you avoiding the truth just to keep that feeling of control behind the wheel of life?

- **Humility tames death anxiety.** The personality trait of humility (fondly called the "quiet ego") has been shown in several studies[13] to cushion the anxiety of death. Being humble involves self-awareness— that keen understanding of our strengths and imperfections. Humility leads to an acceptance "that against a cosmic scale of time and space, every human being is minute." This awareness downgrades mortality from a DEFCON 1 situation into a more manageable tragedy and conceivably into a compass to direct us on how life could be lived.

 As I've gotten older, I've become enthused about viewing myself as radically inconsequential. After all, I am a respiring piece of carbon-based meat, born in a time and place not of my choosing, here for an infinitesimal amount of time before I will be summarily obliterated and my atoms redistributed. I find that self-image ironically uplifting at this point in my life. I can be proud of becoming a psychologist and writing some books, but I'm no less enthusiastic about getting a lungful of fresh air on a beautiful day or taking the dog for a lap around the block.

—DR. SHELDON SOLOMON, WHO STUDIES MORTALITY AS
PROFESSOR OF PSYCHOLOGY AT SKIDMORE COLLEGE

ATTITUDES ABOUT DEATH: WE MELLOW AS WE AGE

We tend to get all jacked up about death when we're young, and then we chill out as we age and accept that death really is the grand finale of life.

In one study,[14] younger adults aligned with death as a motivator more than older adults, who have theoretically achieved many of their hopes and dreams. Older adults don't just put their feet up, though; many are still motivated to reach meaningful goals—like wrapping up that family tree project, finishing memoirs, or mentoring a grandchild.

Research[15] on thanatophobia (fear of death or dying) shows that grown children experience more anxiety about death than their elderly parents tend to. We assume that those near death's door are the ones shaking in their boots, but no. Older folks are more afraid of the dying *process* than their grown kids, but they tend to have accepted the construct of death, while their adult kids have yet to soften to its inevitability. Apparently this gets in the way of crucial end-of-life discussions, as adult children prefer to avoid the topic of death with their parents and miss the window to help plan a "good death" for them.

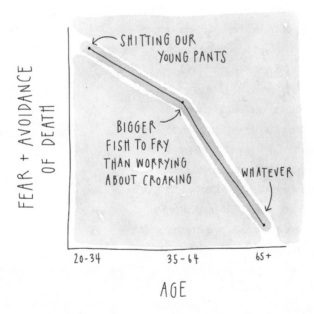

People with a positive attitude toward death feel like they have had a fulfilling life.

People with a gloomy attitude about death (at least when they're under sixty-five) feel like they haven't met or might not meet their life goals. While this question is unbearably obvious, I'd be a cruddy coach if I didn't ask it: What's even one small goal you might have for yourself?

A "fulfilling life" is really just a collection of life goals that have been reached or at least attempted with intention.

> **Coaching Chestnut: Goals vs. Dreams.** Speaking of goals... do they make you break out in hives? That's okay. Not everyone gets jacked up by scrawling out SMART (specific, measurable, attainable, realistic, and time-bound) goals on a whiteboard; some find them constricting and pressure filled. In your desire to "do something" with your life, all hope isn't lost if goal setting doesn't float your boat.
>
> Researchers[16] have validated the tension that bubbles up in some goal phobes. The goal-setting process activates our sympathetic nervous system (you know—the jacked-up go-go-go system inside us), whereas our parasympathetic nervous system (you know—the lean back, chill-out system) is activated when we fathom and talk about dreams, possibilities, aspirations, hopes, visions, and things we might be curious to explore. If specific and measurable goals with a deadline do it for you, go get 'em, tiger. If you're more of a free-range dreamer who appreciates fewer constraints around your ambitions, spend quality time drumming up your dream and imagining it in vivid color. Think for a moment.... Are you more of a goaler or a dreamer? This will have implications when we start planning your next steps near the end of our adventure in chapters 10 and 11.

DEATH AWARENESS = UNSHAKABLE JOY?

Dr. Sheldon Solomon—the respiring piece of carbon-based meat guy—might sit on the top of my list of academic idols, and not just because he's a giant in the world of mortality studies. He's a quick-witted, tie-dye wearing, very sweary, unconventional professor. He checks all the boxes.

Here's the first thing Sheldon said when I interviewed him: "Let me know when you get your first death threat because what you're saying is, 'fucking wake up,' and not everybody wants to be woken up." I nodded in earnest over Zoom, barely concealing my enthusiasm that (a) he had watched my TEDx talk and (b) he attributed swear words to me. I felt so seen.

Sheldon continued: "The point of memento mori, as you've stated it and to channel Lincoln, is, 'it's not the years in your life, it's the life in your years.' And if you want to avoid becoming essentially a culturally constructed meat puppet tranquilized by the trivial, oblivious to what's happening around you—yeah, then keep doing what you do. On the other hand, what you're proposing is like what [the philosopher] Camus said: 'Come to terms with death, thereafter anything is possible.'"

Coming to terms with death is less about the agreement that we're going to die later, at some vaguely unspecified future moment, and more about accepting it as a distinct possibility that informs the way we live our lives *now*. "We're just kicking the temporal can down the road," Sheldon said, "without a genuine confrontation with our mortality. And you said this in your talk. It's like, I'm not counting Mondays because I'm an accountant. I'm counting Mondays in order to make myself poignantly and profoundly aware that every moment counts, because whether I like it or not, I could be summarily obliterated at any time—a comet could come through my window and knock my head off."*

Following a candid acceptance of mortality, one might expect to look forward to a life that has meaning and purpose.† Sheldon continued: "And then this sounds like fucking Mary Poppins, but Heidegger says when things are like that, your life feels like it is an ongoing adventure perfused with unshakable joy." (Did you just gasp audibly at the *ongoing adventure perfused with unshakable joy* part? Good, me too.)

"We're in a pervasive state of chronic mortality salience,‡ you know— between the pandemic, the planet melting, fascism, the fact that the

---

* *You have an academic crush on this guy now too, and you can't deny it.*
† For you students of philosophy, this is the experience Heidegger referred to as "anticipatory resoluteness."
‡ Or, for those who like smaller words, these days we're constantly being punched in the face by the presence of death.

global economy is about to implode on itself. You know, all of those things mean that death is on our minds constantly, whether we're aware of it or not. I just say look, whether we like it or not, malignant manifestations of nonconscious death anxiety bring out the worst in us, you know; that's what makes us just hateful, warmongering, protofascists plundering the planet in an alcohol, Twitter, Facebook stupor—that's bad."*

(*Insert record scratch sound here*)

YOU: Wait, what? What is mortality salience?

ME: It's a fancy phrase for being made aware of death.

YOU: And it can bring out the worst in us? Isn't that what we're doing in these pages—making mortality salient? Am I going to become a drunk warmonger?

ME, making my most reassuring coach face: I assure you that you will (probably) not become a warmonger.[†]

Let's talk more about wielding the sword of mortality salience without falling on it and dying . . . because there's a good way to use death to your advantage, forgoing the whole hateful, warmongering, protofascist planet plundering in an alcohol, Twitter, Facebook stupor . . .

THE GOOD, THE BAD, AND THE DEAD: WHAT GOES ON IN OUR HEADS WHEN WE THINK OF DEATH?

Here's a quick recap of what we know to be true so far re: death denial:

We're dying, which is a shame, and we're denying that we're dying, which ironically deprives us of aliveness.

So the answer is to face the facts of life—er, death—correct? The answer is to memento mori all over ourselves, right? Right.[‡]

We humans are burdened with the cognitive capacity to be aware of our own mortality and to fear what may—or may not—follow after death.

---

* Dr. Solomon Decoder: The anxiety felt by individuals who haven't taken the time to examine their own mortality is the root cause of most of the bad things out there.

† The drunk part is up to you. What're you serving? I might join you.

‡ Yes-ish, if we do it right and proceed with caution. Here is where we must make an important distinction between subtle death reminders, which are around us all the time, and conscious death reflection, which we're getting you to do in these pages.

As we've been discussing, our tendency is to deny the idea of death... avoid the conversation... and then maybe eat a chocolate glazed donut or two. Although we evade the idea, let's not kid ourselves: there's a lot going on under the surface that ultimately influences our behavior.

Studies[17] show that our "psychological immune system"[18] kicks in when we're initially faced with the idea of death; we unconsciously seek out and glom onto happy thoughts as a way of protecting ourselves from the downer of death. This is a charming and well-intended coping mechanism, isn't it? Yet we are still waters that run deep. The happy-slappy thoughts don't sufficiently distract us.

Thousands of experimental studies show that death reminders have the potential to make us act like either angels or assholes as Sheldon made so eloquently clear above. It all depends how intentional we are in our exposure to those death reminders.

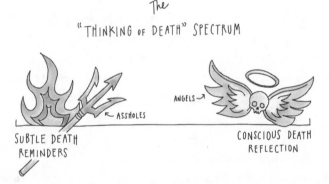

The "THINKING of DEATH" SPECTRUM

ANGELS

ASSHOLES

SUBTLE DEATH REMINDERS

CONSCIOUS DEATH REFLECTION

Researchers[19] distinguish between these two discrete psychological pathways we traipse down when we're made conscious of our mortality. I affectionately call them Dark Alley of Death and Light Alley of Death. Let's take a walk.

DARK ALLEY OF DEATH: WHERE THE ASSHOLES LIVE

Terror management theory (TMT*)[20] is what paves the road in this dark alley of death. This social psychology theory explains how certain

---

* This theory was conceived of in 1986 by psychologists... our friend Dr. Sheldon Solomon being one of the theoretical baby daddies.

individuals turn to fear, hatred, alienating beliefs, and discriminatory acts in response to death awareness. These actions stem from the discrepancy in the fact that we're wired with a drive to remain alive and add some sort of value as long as we get to be alive, but we simultaneously understand that we won't, in fact, exist forever: conditions are ripe for discomfort and dread to potentially fill the void.

It's a staggering existential dilemma, isn't it—our human desire to survive and flourish in spite of suffering and death? This existential terror runs deep, to be clear—it usually manifests as an unconscious angst that unfolds in unexpected and insidious ways, not so much a blow-in-a-paper-bag kind of stress.

According to TMT, when some of us are faced with mortality salience (i.e., the subtle awareness of our inevitable death), we manage this unsettling anxiety in two ways:

1. We become increasingly committed to a particular cultural worldview—a set of shared beliefs and values found within an in-group—because they are the very constructs that provide order and meaning to us. When we're reminded of death, we might align closer to our religious beliefs, national identity, political party, workplace culture, alma mater, and so on. Go Bears!

2. We seek to bolster our self-esteem, which is contingent on how well we believe we've been a good little follower of our cultural worldviews. If our worldview includes a capitalistic ideology, for example, when reminded of death, we might strive to spend money in such a way that people are acutely aware we have it . . . conspicuous consumption at its finest. When death is made salient, this self-esteem boost provides us with a sense of significance and meaning.

TMT allows us to suspend the disbelief of death and buy into the notion that some valued part of us will live on forever, even after we've bitten the dust:

- ☠ We might believe that we'll literally carry on in an afterlife-like heaven or a reincarnated existence.

- ☻ We might subscribe to the fantasy of immortality arising from some kind of cultural achievement, like winning an Academy Award—or maybe more reasonably, winning the Sales Performer of the Year award.

- ☻ We might symbolically seek to create a legacy through our children, or any other kind of aforementioned "immortality project" that affords us the chance to make a meaningful dent in the world. Research[21] around the planet illustrates that reminders of death heighten the desire to have children, because it helps us feel like we somehow transcend death.

Do these approaches solve the problem of death? No, and rationally we know they don't. But they do shift the problem of death to a symbolic realm: we feel a sense of symbolic immortality by living up to the standards of a meaningful worldview that will continue to endure.

All of this sounds fine, but where does the asshole part come in?

Psychologists[22] point out that the typical mortality salience scenario features death in a subtle, subliminal, and abstract fashion (like watching a character die onscreen, hearing the sirens of an ambulance, reading about a train crash, or losing the gray-hair battle); yet these sprinklings of death can spur us to react in subconscious ways.

AN ASSORTMENT OF FASCINATING TERROR MANAGEMENT THEORY EXAMPLES

When the idea of death is made salient, study participants double down on their existing beliefs that align with their worldviews and then circle the wagons, often disparaging others for presenting views that don't match what they believe to be true. Here's a wee sampling from over 1,500 experimental TMT studies:

- ☻ **Judges judge more harshly.** When municipal court judges were reminded they were going to die, they were nine times more punitive than judges who didn't happen to be reminded of their mortality. In this seminal TMT study,[23] the death-primed judges set an average bond of $455 in a hypothetical prostitution case, compared to an average bond of $50 for the judges in a control group who weren't reminded of death. By punishing the prostitutes who violated their worldview, these judges reinforced their own beliefs about life to alleviate the tension caused by the death prompt. Sheldon Solomon weighed in on his experience leading this study: "The fact that every judge in the debriefing room, when we said, 'We asked you to think about death, and then you made this harsh judgment on a case,' they said, 'There's no fucking way your idiot questionnaire could have influenced how we judged this case.' So that surprised us." TMT runs deep; we aren't cognizant of our worldview reflexes to death awareness. (And Sheldon Solomon continues to be the best.)

⊙ **Our choices are typically made in service of maintaining our self-esteem, even at the expense of our health.** Study[24] participants were split into two groups; one read an article about fears of death, and the other read about fears of public speaking. Both groups were then asked to read one of two fashion magazine articles: one with a "pale is pretty" theme (with images of fair-skinned Nicole Kidman and Gwyneth Paltrow) and another with a "bronze is beautiful" message (with images of tanned-skinned Jennifer Lopez and Jennifer Aniston). What happened when asked afterward about their inclination to suntan in the future? Those who read about public speaking fears reported average intentions to bake in the sun, regardless of which skin-tone article they read. The death-primed participants exposed to the "pale is pretty" article reported a marked decrease in tanning intentions, and the "bronze is beautiful" article readers reported a notable increase in plans to tan. Death reminders cause us to align more vigilantly to the social norms that make us feel better about ourselves.

⊙ **Speaking of self-esteem . . .** Male study[25] participants who wrote an essay about their death reported more of an interest in acquiring power than participants who were asked to write an essay about dental pain.* Being primed to think about death spurred men to behave more dominantly in the week following the study . . . indicating that

---

* Writing an essay about dental pain would surely make study participants want to die, no?

their self-esteem hinged on a worldview that valued power, and the thought of death spurred them to take action on that worldview.

⊙ **Death reminders make us uncomfortable with our decayable bodies.** Subtle reminders of death cause us to distance ourselves from our physicality. This means we avoid sex and other bodily activities when death is made evident, because on some deep level our bodies signal that we're creatures prone to perish. Women's bodies are veritable land mines in TMT studies, because as reproductive epicenters who menstruate and lactate, female bodies are as creaturely as it gets... And that doesn't sit well in our subconscious psyche because no creature gets to live forever, and we darned well know it. In one study,[26] students were either primed with a death reminder or a neutral topic. They were then asked to sit beside their supposed lab partner, a woman (an actor hired as part of the study) who then accidentally dropped a tampon out of her purse. The participants were asked to rate "how competent, intelligent, focused, friendly, and likable you perceive your partner." Those with the death reminder rated her negatively and chose to sit farther away from her upon returning from a break. Those without a death reminder rated her far more positively and plopped themselves in the chair right next to her. (In another version of the study, the actor dropped a hair clip, and no one batted an eyelash.)

⊙ **Subtle death reminders can spur us to react with hostility and aggression toward outsiders who don't happen to share our beliefs.** Flashing the word "death" on a computer screen to American research study participants, for just fractions of a second, turned them against an author who criticized the US. The participants reported feelings of contempt for the writers not because they wrote essays that included anti-US sentiments; it was only after being unconsciously primed to think about death that people donned their "you vs. us" hats. Death greased the skids of polarization.

⊙ **And then there's the hot salsa study.**[27] Politically conservative and liberal study participants were divided into two groups and asked to jot down answers to questions about either their own death or a neutral topic. They were then asked to read a paragraph that was derogatory toward either conservatives or liberals, including lovely statements like "The best place for a Liberal [or a Conservative] is out of my sight. They make me sick." At this point, thinking they were in a study about personality and food preferences, participants were asked to dole out the amount of painfully hot salsa that the supposed author of the political paragraph would need to consume for the taste test. Right on cue with TMT's hypothesis, participants who'd been prompted to think about death scooped twice as much hot salsa into a cup for those who didn't share their world-view as they did for those who happened to share their political beliefs. Participants in the control condition (who didn't write about their mortality) couldn't care less about the author's political beliefs either.

Terror management can turn us into assholes. And yet when we become aware of death in the right circumstances, we can turn into angels. Read on.

LIGHT ALLEY OF DEATH: WHERE THE ANGELS LIVE

Welcome to the land of death reflection . . . still a dim alley (because *death*) but so much warmer and so much fuzzier than the Dark Alley above.

Remember when we talked about intentionality? We've established that thoughts of death are unavoidable, but whereas Dark Death Alley is a path lined with denial and suppression and lots of little pebbles in your shoes, Light Death Alley is one where those who willingly and mindfully open themselves up to the Contemplation of Death walk. Death reflection is a more thoughtful, internalized, intentional process as compared to subtle death awareness. This experiential style of memento mori prompts us to put our lives in perspective, contemplate our meaning and purpose, and consider our legacy after we've shuffled off our mortal coils. This is why we are here reading together, to elicit all sorts of self-transcendence and generativity and reprioritization and waking-up-ness to the widest and deepest versions of your life. To be extra clear: we're here to collude with the angels, not the assholes.

This study[28] captures—rather dramatically—the essence of death reflection. Researchers split study participants into three groups:

1. A control group, where study participants were asked to imagine waking up to an average day in their life.
2. A "mortality salience" group, where participants were asked, "In as many words and in as much detail as possible, please describe the thoughts, feelings, and emotions you experience when thinking about your own death."
3. A "death reflection" group, where participants were asked to "imagine waking up in the middle of the night in a friend's apartment on the 20th floor of an old, downtown building to the sounds of screams and the choking smell of smoke." Study participants were asked to envision "making futile attempts to escape from the room and burning building before giving into the fire and eventually death." (Isn't science a riot?)

Important detail: study participants were asked to complete a "gratitude for life" assessment before and after being whisked off into their three groups.

Wondering how things went down in the study?

- Participants in the control group (the ones asked to think about a typical day in their mundane lives) bored themselves to death. (I jest. But they actually experienced a decline in gratitude through the duration of the study.)
- Participants in the mortality salience group (thinking about their death in a more abstract way) experienced a mild bump in gratitude.
- Participants in the death reflection group (i.e., the scorching fire scenario) "significantly enhanced state gratitude compared to subjects that did not think about their own mortality."

When we look at our inescapable demise in a way that feels more real to us (i.e., with vivid details that make our death-by-fire mortality more concrete), that deliberate, striking exercise tends to not only wake us up to our mortality, but it also forces us to count our blessings that we are still alive, that we can breathe fresh air, that we have time left to Do Something with our existence.

Consciously thinking about our mortality—and it doesn't always have to be in vivid, glaring, fiery detail—tends to get us thinking about death differently than the way we think about it after, say, visiting a funeral home or reading a murder mystery. The context in which we think about death is important; when we're exposed to our mortality as an abstract concept (like hearing about the war in Ukraine in the news), we look for support in abstract ways—like intensifying our worldviews and religious and social affiliations, which can cause us to go a bit overboard and disparage those who don't believe what we believe. When we intentionally expose ourselves to the concept of mortality in a specific and personal fashion (like through conscious death reflection), we seek out support from internal resources—like setting goals, finding creative ways to meet our own needs, and going after intrinsic growth.

Here are a few examples from research and studies that illustrate the positive and productive role that death reflection can play in our lives:

- **Goal clarity.** Consciously thinking about death can act like a clarion call to authentic living. Studies[29] highlight how a deeper contemplation of death makes extrinsic goals like notoriety, wealth, admiration, and power feel more trivial. We tend to lean into intrinsic goals when we're jostled awake by deeper death reflection—like focusing on personal development, contributing to our community, building healthy relationships, and pursuing well-being. "The bullshit flies out the window," said a client after completing a death reflection exercise at one of my retreats. "I put so much energy into my image, into caring what people think about me and my job title on LinkedIn and what kind of handbag I'm carrying. It feels so superficial. I'd rather be spending this emotional energy helping people." This woman went on to initiate a program at her company that matched disadvantaged youth in her community with mentors in her industry.
- **Death reflection puts a dent in greediness.** Thinking mindfully about our mortality can shift us from a "me" to a "we" mentality. Study[30] participants who were primed to reflect on their death and

their values were subsequently less likely to take raffle tickets for themselves and likelier to leave raffle tickets for other study participants to possibly win $100. Angels, not assholes.

- **Deep death thoughts make us generous into the future.** Being primed with reflective thoughts of death made study[31] participants more likely to donate money into the future for their heirs, evidently a lovely display of intergenerational beneficence and a powerful demonstration of how inclined we are to want to leave a legacy that lets us live beyond the pesky boundaries of our life spans. If I had a nickel for every workshop participant who has mapped out a more generous plan for their estate after participating in a visualization exercise about their mortality... well, I'd have a casket full of nickels.

- **Gratitude + death continue to have a symbiotic relationship.** Reflecting on one's own death enhanced the levels of gratitude in study[32] participants, as well as their appreciation of the simple pleasures in life. When people are asked to think about a time in their life when they've felt particularly grateful, it tends to shrivel unconscious thoughts of death. (Have you started that gratitude journal yet?)

- **Terror management theory's silver lining.** Rabid adherence to our worldviews doesn't have to lead to the dark side—à la TMT discussed above—especially if one's self-esteem is conditional on being a good person. Death reminders can also include prosocial values like equality, compassion, empathy, forgiveness, and helpfulness.[33] Conscious reminders of death increase our charitable[34] and altruistic[35] behaviors. Studies[36] show that people (predominantly women) act in more prosocial ways in the week following death prompts.

- **Death reflection can lead to better character.** In the wake of the 9/11 terrorist attacks—which brought awareness of death to the forefront for many—the character strengths of gratitude, kindness, hope, love, spirituality, leadership, and teamwork were elevated in surveyed individuals as far out as ten months after the event.[37]

- **You, but better.** Experiencing mortality salience in the right context can increase your desire to be your best self.[38] Conscious thoughts of death can also lead to healthier lifestyles,[39] including firmer intentions to exercise and eat well.

● **Buffers against worldview defenses.** If we do happen to experience vague, abstract death reminders—which usually trigger protective defense strategies—there are ways we can mitigate the reflexive asshole response. Actively reflecting on our mortality awareness with openness, mindfulness, and curiosity has been shown to have a mediating effect on the guard we put up.[40] Elevated self-esteem also tends to reduce our worldview defenses and has a protective quality against death anxiety.[41] Are you willing to pause when faced with subtle prompts about death, now that you know they could lead to less-than-amazing thoughts and behaviors without a little intervention? Let's say you learn about a colleague's cancer diagnosis. . . . Might you slow down and check if you are fiercely clinging to any of your beliefs or if you're trying in vain to boost your self-esteem, in the midst of this abstract death reminder? You are fully empowered to steer your thoughts and actions down the angel alley.

THE RESEARCH WRAP-UP

Whee! Do you also feel the need to put a bow on all this Dark Alley vs. Light Alley of Death research? Okay, let's bullet point it out:

● Thinking about our mortality needs to be done with a little TLC, lest we ignite the flames of TMT (terror management theory).

● Mortality salience "done wrong" has the potential to make us bigoted, self-centered assholes (camping out in the Dark Alley of Death). We'll pass on this kind of abstract thinking, thanks.

● Death reflection "done right" (down the Light Alley of Death) can spark the very productive, agentic, motivating thoughts we're here to make happen.

● Since I want you to be thinking of death as often as you bathe (so, daily?), we shall steer your thoughts through concrete, straightforward questions and answers. No dicking around here in the Dark Alley!

● Start to notice your behavior if and when you find yourself clinging fiercely to your beliefs or if you're feeling desperate to elevate your self-esteem. Maybe the topic of death surreptitiously entered the picture, which can signal the next step of truly contemplating what you're thinking and feeling.

☠ Speaking of next steps, let's talk about when you don't want to talk (or think) about death...

UNDENYING DEATH 101: FOR PEOPLE WHO AREN'T BUYING DEATH ACCEPTANCE

Look at you over there, digging your heels in! I respect your desire to feel safe and comfortable, glossing over this mortality stuff.... It's evidence that you are fabulously human. And yet you do know that death is going to slap us all in the face someday, right? I know you know. You're just apprehensive about diving into the deep end of the death pool. We need to de-deny-ify you one step at a time.

Acceptance of Change

If death reflection doesn't sound appetizing just yet, how about an amuse-bouche to whet your appetite? How about embracing the wee impermanences of life as a warm-up act? Let's consider **The Many Ways Things Inevitably Change and Die:**

☠ The prettily arranged hydrangeas on your kitchen counter will drop their leaves and die.

☠ Your sour mood, or deliriously happy mood, or any mood for that matter, will pass.

☠ Your ill-conceived bad haircut will grow out.

☠ Your golden retriever will die. (Ugh, this one might be the worst of all.)

☠ Your son will grow out of his terrible twos.

☠ Your favorite diner and/or boutique and/or bakery and/or dance studio will close.

☠ Your body will start to slow down.

☠ Some of your friendships will fade over time—and some of your friends will even have the nerve to die before you.

☠ Your neighbors will move.

- The org chart at work will get reshuffled; Tom will get promoted another level, and you'll report to someone else.
- The leadership of your country will turn over.
- The yogurt in the fridge will expire.
- Your attitudes will soften and change over time as you morph into better and better versions of yourself.

We are ruefully susceptible to wrinkles, weakness, accidents, illness, and extinction. Accepting that change is the only constant helps us see impermanence less as a threat and more as an opportunity to grow. Reflecting on the short-term-ness of just about everything prepares us for our own mortality meditation.

There is always something ending and beginning, all around us. What change is going on around you right now? What change are you instigating? What change feels like it's happening *to* you? How can you accept—and maybe even surrender to—the ebb and flow of growth, adjustment, and even death?

Positive Psychology Interlude: You Win Some, You Lose Some. Research is clear that progress toward a goal provides a motivational and well-being lift. While setbacks toward a goal are usually frowned upon, it's often because we have a socially constructed relationship with What It Means to Be Successful (i.e., a winner, and definitely not a loser). And yet! What if you reframed loss? What if it was noted and appreciated for its instructional value? What if we deliberately mined the change and loss in your life for its insights and meaning?

One of my clients used to overlook her wins and self-flagellate her losses. I encouraged her to keep track of both, so we could talk about them in upcoming sessions, and something interesting happened. She saw her ups and downs in a completely new light. By highlighting her wins—usually tiny triumphs like "Finished the client proposal today," "Figured out that move in karate class," or "Had that awkward-but-necessary conversation with Elaine"—she became aware of how many steps forward she was taking each day.

Counterintuitively, her setback list didn't turn into fodder for an imaginary list of Ways I Am an Unmitigated Disaster of a Human. No, this list put all the right things in perspective. "Got Madison to ceramics class 5 minutes late," for example, wasn't as big of a deal when she saw it in writing. Seeing "Didn't hear back from problem client again today" helped her size the problem, too. She started to stoically accept that she might not retain a big-but-annoying client at work, and she started moving toward acceptance rather than rumination.

Tracking your wins is a slam dunk win on the path toward living like you mean it, but don't underestimate the impact of tracking your losses, too. It helps us build equanimity—a sense of levelheadedness about our thoughts and experiences, that we win some and lose some and life will go on regardless. We need these practices of loss on our way to the big finish.

What About a Practice Run?

There is an art and science of "practicing death"—dipping our toes into the idea of our mortality. This often looks like:

- ☠ Interacting with people who are grieving;
- ☠ Pulling over for a funeral procession and imagining our own;
- ☠ Coming to terms with smaller losses in our lives—like lost jobs, friendships that fade, fizzled romances, great ideas that died on the vine at work; or
- ☠ Catastrophizing that our loved ones will surely be snuffed out by some horrible demise because we forgot to say goodbye that morning.

Research[42] shows we're better equipped to handle anxiety and appreciate life by trying death on for size in even these subtle ways.

Are there other ways you might practice death, even unwittingly? And if you're not practicing it in pocket-sized ways, how might you start?

JOIN ME IN THE CRUSADE TO DEFANG DEATH

Face the facts, my friend. You have an expiry date, I have an expiry date, Tigger your cat has an expiry date, and your carton of milk in the fridge has an expiry date. We're all just hoping that the milk goes first.

What a grave error we make, this propensity to ignore the facts of life—given death's role as an instigator. The Grim Reaper spurs us to behave differently and make more powerful choices while we're still here.

Can we just call it like it is here? **It's not so much the big idea of death that scares us as much as the dawning awareness that we might reach the end of our life and realize we never truly lived.** (*And a hush fell over the land. Now might be a good time for a moment of silence?*)

Aaaaand, we're back.

Let's stop pussyfooting around death. It's a fundamental motivator behind why we do what we do, and I don't know about you, but I need a healthy dose of motivation to do things that are even three degrees out of my comfort zone. *I am very comfortable over here in my fleece-lined comfort zone, thank you very much.* It's only when I focus on the preciousness of my petering-out time that I make life-affirming choices instead of zombie-zone, autopilot choices. When I face the real facts of life—which include the shitty truth that everyone I love and care about will die, including the person I see when I look in the mirror—that's when I come alive.

Join me in contemplating your "ultimate life event" (no, not the Ice Capades coming to your town). The more we expect, accept, and reflect upon death, the more we have to gain by putting our priorities and goals into focus.

In light of all we've covered about the bright side of mortality reflection, I think you're ready to bravely walk down that well-lit Light Alley of Death. No denial for you. You're ready to let death punctuate your life . . . on the way toward living as though you've been warned that you won't, in fact, live forever.* You've seen the light!

Speaking of seeing the light, let's talk next about lessons learned from brushes with death. There's no denying that premature encounters—near-death experience and the like—can wake us up to live in astonishing ways. Let's go take a safe field trip together.

---

* Consider yourself warned: *you definitely won't live forever.* (Sorry.)

CHAPTER 5

THE ULTIMATE WAKE-UP CALL: BRUSHES WITH DEATH

> YOUR DOCTOR, asking with a furrowed brow: How long have you had this lump?
>
> YOU: Lump?

Oh shit.

And yet.

Close calls with death are profoundly effective at waking us up to the kind of lives we really want to be living. Those who've had "precipice moments" with mortality waste no time solving the predicament of finding meaning, fulfillment, and joy in their Mondays-till-the-morgue. They get down to the business of living with a new lease on life, because they've seen with crystal clarity what they almost lost.

That's what we're after in this chapter together—the wake-up call that shines the spotlight on the value of life, without having to walk the near-death experience tightrope. So no, you won't be asked to pin yourself under a crumpled car in these pages, or some other kind of epiphany-inducing near-death experience field trip (because that would be risky and probably a lawsuit waiting to happen). But we are going to simulate the experience from the safety of our couches to (hopefully) spur the same sort of meaningful change as we see in those who have come back from the light. We'll learn vicariously from others who've had moments of truth with life and death, so you can in turn take your own life more seriously in some ways and less seriously in other ways.

Thank you for continuing to take such good notes and for being a sport when asked to participate in unconventional thought-inducing exercises. These aren't easy pontifications, so please keep trusting me that it will be worth it in the end.* Buckle up for some exceptionally safe, glimmers o' death enlightenment.

THE ROAR OF AWAKENING

The Grim Reaper does us a favor sometimes and introduces himself to us ahead of schedule: he invites himself over unannounced for the weekend ("I'm sorry, but the test results are positive"), makes a complete mess (i.e., chemo, radiation, decimated assumptions about life), and then leaves us to clean up after him (i.e., putting the pieces of our existence back together, hopefully infused with a newfound appreciation for life).

For many, these dabblings with death act as the ultimate wake-up call. Finding ourselves on the brink of whatever we believe to be in store for us when the undertaker calls is a rare event that most of us will never experience. But for the 5 percent[1] or so of the gen pop who have brushed up against death, they've seen the proverbial light and are basking in the glow of it.

Think of anyone you might know who has had a life-threatening episode—maybe someone who has wrestled with an ominous diagnosis. Maybe you're thinking of someone who survived a car crash where the doctor marveled, "Whoa . . . if the damage had just been half an inch to the right," and then mimed the keel-over-and-die move. Have you not noticed how purposeful these people are after emerging from what psychologists[2] have called "the roar of awakening"? Studies consistently show how these people wake up to their lives with fresh eyes—with clarified

---

* Worth it in the end of this book *and* in the end of your life.

priorities and profound attitude adjustments about the ways they want to live "from this day forward."

Some of the most vitally alive clients I've had the pleasure of working with are the ones who've been awakened by the alarm clock of death. (For the record, they pressed the snooze button; they're still alive and kicking after being yanked out of complacency.)

One client, for example, survived an overseas military convoy bombing with a renewed sense of aliveness. "I want to wring out all that I can from however many years I have left. I've been living with blinders on. I've passed the point of no return, and there's no going back to that way of living," she acknowledged. She put an end to the indifference and routine in her life and is now outrageously appreciative for every sunrise, every belly laugh that comes out of her toddler, every simple pleasure.

And then there's the gentleman I worked with who fell off a ladder while hanging holiday decorations on his roof. After waking from a coma, he felt like he had officially woken up to his life (despite endless ribbing from his brothers about the giant inflatable Santa who took him down). He looked back on the pre-Santa years as time he took for granted, stuck in autopilot mode. He systematically overhauled the way he spent his time both in and out of work, using his newfound awakening as a reset button he didn't know he needed.

These clients and others who've had intimate relationships with death seem to know things that the rest of us don't. Why can't we—the supposedly lucky ones who haven't had one foot in the grave—feel that same sense of urgency, motivation, and desire to *live*? Or can we? We can, by digging into the revelations people who've survived close calls with death typically experience. Take note of your observations.... Which insights could *you* benefit from, *without* having to fall off a roof?

10 INSIGHTS FROM THOSE WHO'VE SEEN THE (LITERAL AND PROVERBIAL) LIGHT

1. **Reshuffled priorities.** When a person looks death in the eye, their to-do list and day-to-day bullshit becomes less and less consequential, and they begin to hyperfocus on what really matters. Like what? Like the people in their lives actually worth hanging out with, the interests that

captivate their souls, the work that makes them feel fulfilled, or any of the opportunities that intoxicate them with possibility.

Just as valuable as prioritizing what matters is their deliberate choice to *deprioritize* the BS (goodbye, counting calories) and *devalue* the culturally conditioned happiness traps (Fame! Fortune! Who we know! What kind of car we drive!) to honor more personal and intrinsic values. A brush with death can provide a wake-up to the ways we're living out of sync with our values. It allows us a second chance to live a life that feels authentic rather than a life full of values imposed on us by others.

Shay's Circle

"I am so grateful I had cancer because it put a giant stop sign in my life," Shay Moraga* explained. "Cancer gave me a second chance at life."

Shay shared that she had a ton of time to journal and reflect on how she wanted her life to be while she was in chemotherapy appointments for twenty weeks straight. She told me the story of how she flipped to a fresh new sheet of paper during treatment one day and drew a circle in the middle of the page. She recorded all the things she wanted in her life inside the circle and all of the things she wanted out of her life outside of the circle.

I loved her idea so much I could hardly breathe.

Outside the circle was her "people pleasing" mentality, things she didn't have time or energy for, and toxic relationships. Inside the circle sat her own needs and interests and spending time with people she wanted to.

What if you got a "second chance" at life? What and who would sit inside your circle, and what would be unceremoniously turfed outside of

---

* Shay is the founder of Shay's Warriors, a nonprofit that supports cancer survivors.

it, for good reason? What priorities need to bubble up to the top for you? What trivial things do you need to deprioritize?

2. Elevated gratitude for life. Many people who've faced a brush with death report a heightened appreciation for the life they're still fortunate to have. Mortality is the splash of cold water in our face to help assign greater value to life. A stark reminder of how ephemeral we are—that is, teetering on the edge of life—can act as the provocation to live more consciously. The opposite of being grateful for life is taking it for granted.

When was the last time you felt thankful to have a heartbeat, to have legs strong enough to walk up and down the grocery store aisles, to have the gift of Being Here?

Having an Avocado Removed from Your Brain

Chris Baccash found out he had an avocado-sized brain tumor in 2019, when he was twenty-seven years old. I spoke with him a few years after that—after three surgeries that "took out as much of the avocado as they could," he joked. It struck me how appreciative he was for things he'd previously have overlooked.

"I was flooded with the most profound gratitude of my life. I'm very frequently in awe of my mother's love that I couldn't appreciate when I was young. She'd do these things like leave Post-it notes on the seat of my bike that said, 'Welcome back, I missed you.' She'd put a Post-it beside my chemo drugs that said, 'Loving, healing drugs.' I would hardly have noticed before the avocado."

Chris recalled his experience on a June day after receiving great news from a clear MRI, as he sat outside the hospital and observed what was going on around him. "There were all these crazy helicopters dropping people off for care. I felt so grateful that as people we've been able to harness these machines and so delicately balance them to land in place on hospital rooftops. I was so grateful for the capacity humans have to care, both physically and emotionally." Chris now calls these waves of gratitude "helicopter moments."

"I want people to know that it's possible to be destroyed by life's circumstances, and yet it's possible that it could be the best thing for you. This experience of having my brain chopped open has made it clear what matters and what to savor. Brain cancer is the best thing I never want to do again."

Imagine you were sitting on a hospital bench after a favorable post-avocado MRI, like Chris. What seemingly simple things would you feel grateful for? What if you felt that sense of appreciation without having to go through brain surgery—what would your life look like? What helicopter moments might become wildly apparent to you all of a sudden?

3. Dismissing expectations. After flirting with death, people often turf the expectations they believe society has placed on them and grant themselves permission to live in more authentic, "this is the real me" ways. The pernicious question of "What will people think about me?" seems to fall by the wayside because *it just doesn't matter.* Seeking and gaining approval from parents, bosses, board chairs, and the Joneses down the street no longer seem like valid concerns. Boundaries are built and respected.

A participant in a corporate workshop I delivered shared with his team how he felt about responding to emails and messages at all hours. "You've probably noticed that I don't tune in at night anymore or on weekends, and I know that's different than how I used to be before my accident." After his near-fatal motorcycle crash, he stopped caring about what his colleagues would think if he worked a paltry ten hours a day and

 You've heard Steve Jobs's famous Stanford commencement speech, right? Remember when he said, "Almost everything—all external expectations, all pride, all fear of embarrassment or failure—these things just fall away in the face of death, leaving only what is truly important.... Your time is limited, so don't waste it living someone else's life. Everything else is secondary."

not a minute more. "You guys know I've got your backs, right? But life's too short to worry about playing the game of 'who responds first' or 'look who's working on Sunday.' I want for you guys what I've found: freedom to work hard and be okay to live hard outside of work, too."

Imagine what your life might look like if you were the real you, in every setting? If you cared less about what (you believed) people thought of you? If you felt like you had to impress yourself on your deathbed instead of other people while you were alive? If you put your head down on your pillow each night, proud for living *your* life, not someone else's?

4. Deeper immersion in life. Nothing boosts one's participation in life like almost losing it. Being made hyperaware of one's ephemerality tends to motivate us to get on the field and play. Death-brushed clients I've had the chance to work with have started online dating profiles once and for all, traveled to Morocco, learned to snowboard at fifty-two, started nonprofits, moved somewhere warm, started spending Fridays with their grandkids, gotten tattoos, arranged three-day workweeks, gone back to school to become a personal trainer, and you know this list goes on. All sorts of stuff is waiting for us in the life of our dreams.

A Quick Story about Vicarious Wake-Up Calls

Scott DeLuzio blew my mind while I was a guest on his *Drive On* podcast—a show with a primary audience of military veterans interested in resilience. While discussing the concept of memento mori, he said, "If you're going to just sit there on your ass at home doing nothing with your life, like how much of a slap in the face is it to that person who sacrificed themselves to give you that next however many more Mondays? In your life, you know? I lost my brother in Afghanistan, and I feel like if I'm just gonna sit around wasting away, then his sacrifice, as far as I'm concerned, was for nothing. And that's not okay with me. And so I feel like I owe it to him to live a life that's worth living."

Mind. Still. Blown.

Where do you need to show up ready to play in your life . . . because you have a life you get to live? What activities and goals and dreams would you *get on with* if you had a heightened awareness that your time was truly limited?

5. Embracing the mundane. People who've walked under the shadow of death appreciate the day-to-day moments that pass the rest of us by, despite their seeming ordinariness. In a world where we acknowledge and celebrate the Big Moments like birthdays, holidays, anniversaries, proposals, babies birthed, marathon finish lines, making partner at the firm . . . what about the juice we can squeeze out of our everyday existence?

Life gets incrementally better when we revel in the tiny joys eked out of our mundane moments—like the feeling of warm bathwater, the sound of your favorite song turned up loud loud loud, the smell of your favorite bakery as you walk by, the first sip of your beverage (Hello, Mr. Moscow Mule!). Might you add a few magical mundane moments to your What Makes Me Happy List from your pre-mortem, just so you're careful to pay attention when they almost pass you by, to not gloss over them?

Shopping for Light Bulbs and Other Mundane Treasures

Chris-Tia was a dear client who passed away from her third bout of breast cancer in 2021 when she was just forty-two. In our last session—just a few months before she died—she shared that she was choosing to slow down and embrace boredom:

- She was enjoying walking up and down the Home Depot aisles looking for light bulbs.
- She was actually enjoying watching the exposed pipes get dusted in her high-ceilinged loft.
- She was enjoying sifting and sorting through her junk mail.

☠ She was enjoying her time spent sitting on the big red lawn chairs scattered around the University of Illinois Chicago campus, around the corner from her place—just sitting there, *being.*

☠ She was enjoying walking to Mariano's grocery store and eating chocolate ice cream bars on her way home.

If life is what happens as we're busy making plans to "really live," then what simple moments might you benefit from really tuning into? What absolutely average thing are you overlooking right now? What simple pleasures are you taking for granted? What if you imagined you almost died this morning—might you celebrate the crap out of the simple pleasures you just might be overlooking around you?

6. Rekindled connections. People who are here one moment and almost gone the next tend to look around and cherish the characters in their lives a heck of a lot more. Approaching death highlights all that we have to lose—*who* we have to lose. We know this is true when we attend a funeral; we do that mental inventory of the people we dread the idea of losing next: "Deb, Alan, Esmerelda—Alan killed my jade plant that time I asked him to house-sit so he can go, but holy shit, what would I do if Deb died?" Imagined loss helps us value the time we spend with people who matter in our lives.

One of my clients was carjacked at gunpoint and experienced clarity in a way she didn't expect. She "learned the hard way," as she framed it, that her relationships had fallen off the map. After returning home from the police station the evening of her ordeal, she felt scared and alone, without anyone close enough to reach out to. Her life was full of surface-level acquaintances and colleagues galore—all sorts of laughs and happy hours and birthday cakes shared at the lab—but no one to call in a real moment of need. She had friendships that she let fade in favor of her career. She was motivated to resurrect her relationships one by one, even if it meant producing less in a "publish or perish" profession. *She* didn't want to perish without meaningful human connections to lift her life.

Who in your life might you want to reach out to before they bite the dust? Who might you want to reach out to before *you* bite the dust? Who would you call late at night for support if you had a brush with death?

7. Maximized mindfulness. Folks who've had brushes with death are more mindful of the present moment—whether it's fantastical or crap-tastical—because they've almost lost the luxury of living in the here and now. They don't need to spend inordinate time ruminating about the past and worrying about the future, because they understand that now is all they have in ways the rest of us mere mortals take for granted.

We're mindful when we intentionally make new distinctions about all the nouns in our field of awareness: we see people, places, and things bathed in new light. When we're mindful, we stay attuned to the present moment and widen our apertures to receive new information that would've passed us by if we were busy staring at other people's lives on our phones.

A former MAPP student and now-friend Duncan had a heart attack a few years ago, and while it didn't strike him until a couple of months afterward that he could have died, he awakened to what I like to think of as extreme mindfulness: "I saw my life through a completely new lens; I was seeing the buildings, the trees, the clouds in a completely different way. It was jaw-dropping. They were *so* beautiful."

So much of this comes down to the deceptively simple concepts of *noticing* and *attuning*. What are you choosing to notice in any given moment? What are you attuned to? What are you observing, ideally without judgment? Being mindful takes effort, because our monkey minds are wont to hop backward into what happened and forward into what might happen. That's okay. We just need to pause, breathe, take a sip, notice, and attune.

8. Creating meaning and growth. Sidling up to death and experiencing traumatic events don't necessarily make us happier or smarter, but survivors do consistently report increased self-awareness, more wisdom in life, more of a sense of purpose, and greater self-actualization. Coming within reach of death inspires many to open themselves up to new educational, career, and relationship experiences as they grow and metamorphosize into new versions of themselves.

A client's son almost lost his life through an accidental overdose. Home from the hospital, he reported feeling like he knew himself on a whole new level: "It's like a classic before-and-after picture. Before, I knew myself like an acquaintance, like a neighbor I'd wave at over the fence. I think I was avoiding myself? After, I'm confident about the things I stand for and the things I don't. I want to go back to school and study psychology."

Mortality awareness undeniably acts as a jump start for growth. Where can you reframe or catapult the challenges you've endured, to make more meaning in your days? You might be overlooking ways to grow and evolve. Where are there even the smallest green shoots of growth possible for you?

Positive Psychology Interlude: Introducing the Opposite of PTSD. Have you heard of post-traumatic growth? The lemonade made from the lemons of life? Psychologists[3] refer to post-traumatic growth as the positive psychological change that can emerge from adversity. We actually have the capacity to rise to a higher level of functioning as a result of brushes with death, major life crises, and any of the other shit sandwiches served on the Platter of Life. This growth usually stems from a casting aside of the values, expectations, and goals that no longer serve those individuals.

An exquisite relief can be found from letting overripe goals go. Are there any projects you've got a death grip on—stubbornly trudging forward to finish—when maybe they're past their prime and your life would be better if you just changed course? I've worked with people who became 950 times happier overnight when they just let their drag-me-down goals go—like complicated work projects that were deenergizing them (How about just abandoning that New York office idea?), renovation projects that were killing them one light fixture at a time (Why not just move?), or training for a marathon that didn't feel fun anymore (How about just running short distances for the joy of it again?).

RELINQUISHED GOALS → BYEEE

I was working on an art piece last year that zapped the life out of me every time I looked at it. I painted over my gaffes so many times that the canvas was heavy with acrylic and defeat. At no point was I energized or excited when working on this creativity and happiness sponge.

"I'm going to give it one more go," I'd wanly proclaim to The Husband, with feigned fervor.

"It looks like a lot of zucchinis," he hesitantly (but astutely) observed after one of my attempts.

I had no intention of painting zucchinis. The Husband doesn't even like zucchini, so why would I paint a three-by-four-foot painting of them for our foyer?

I made the tough decision that the zucchinis can- vas had to be put to rest. And oh, the sweet relief! Had I imagined myself returning home from the hospital after a brush with death, would I have been so insistent to work on the calamity-on-a-canvas? No. Had I tuned into my Monday countdown, would I have picked that paintbrush up again? No. I'd have started a canvas bonfire and danced around it, toasting marshmallows in its fiery flames.

Sometimes we think it's a sign of good moral character if we "stick with it," or perhaps we succumb to the sunk-cost fallacy (you know—when we're stubbornly reluctant to move on from something we've invested lots of time and energy into, even when abandoning it would be the supremely smart choice). But you could die next week; wouldn't it be a bummer if you spent the last days of your life with books/shows/movies/podcasts/people/jobs/hairstylists that just aren't doing it for you? Do you need to give yourself permission to walk away from them? Poof. Permission granted.*

THESE ARE NOT ZUCCHINIS

---

* Well, let's not be rash. You really must finish *this* book.

9. Spiritual awakening. Many near-death folks experience a connection to something seemingly beyond themselves—a kind of transcendence that provides immeasurable comfort. Some rekindle a dormant relationship with organized religion or seek out a spiritual relationship for solace.

Psychologists[4] talk about this idea of "spiritual surrender," a phenomenon that puts people less at the center of their universe and more a part of an enlarged existence, a part of something sacred. In our ever-present desire to gain control of the goings-on of life, this surrender paradoxically creates even greater feelings of control. Placing trust in a benevolent higher power or being can lead to feelings of wholeness, gratitude, serenity, calmness, and compassion.

Is there a spiritual element you might want to enhance in your life? Might you benefit from being a little less at the center of your world? Are there things you might want to relinquish control over, with the help of some spiritual surrendering?

10. Rebirthing aliveness. Studies[5] of people who have faced death—specifically through serious illnesses, car accidents, near drownings, and falls—show that they seem to experience "rebirths" into newly enriched lives, notably described as brimming with aliveness.

Interestingly, research[6] shows that the positive side effects associated with near-death experiences don't tend to diminish over time; transformed values and views on life were maintained over two decades for study participants. I want a life described as brimming with aliveness, don't you?

Close Calls and Phone Calls

Trish Kendall rebirthed her life when she was twenty, right after she tried to end it.

Let's begin this tale with its happy ending: Today Trish lives in a quiet suburb with her husband, two kids, and dog named Wes. She is living a self-described dream life, which stands in stark contrast to her life twenty-five years prior as a full-on drug addict.

"I was on the bathroom floor, a cold and moldy and grimy and dirty bathroom floor," Trish said. "I made the choice that I was going to overdose on crystal meth by plunging a needle in my vein—because I didn't believe there was anything else. I didn't believe there was any hope or love for this twenty-year-old girl who was sexually abused by her dad every day. I had nothing to look forward to. In that moment, on the bathroom floor, before I plunged the final needle in my track-marked, bruised, skeletal arms, my sister called. And it was back in the day of those old caller ID boxes, you know, where you look down and you could see the area code really big. And I saw area code 254, which was my sister in Texas. And I picked up. I thought I wanted to die, but deep down I didn't want to because I chose to pick up the phone."

After this fateful phone call, Trish's stepbrother picked her up and put her on a plane to Texas, where her sister was waiting at the gate to look after her.

"My biggest fear was, who am I without this, and what is life without this? And I tell you that because there's not dying, and then there's not knowing how to live. I didn't know how to find joy in the ordinary. I didn't know how to *be* ordinary. I had no belief in myself, that I could live an ordinary life."

I asked Trish if she had a point where she looked back and thought, *Whoa, I almost ended it.* She blurted out a resounding yes. "It was in the moments that I felt joy and love with my sister's children, like when they would wake me up at seven in the morning with their dry Cheerios, crawling into bed with their auntie Tishee to watch *Rugrats*. Those moments of ordinariness punched me in the face with such pure, healing joy. I was so grateful to be alive to experience that ordinary joy—that's what taught me to live again. I'm profoundly grateful to this day."

 Coaching Chestnut: Addition through Subtraction. Psychologists[7] tell us that the exercise known as "mental subtraction" can boost our subjective life satisfaction. Imagining the loss of positive things in our lives (like that you never met your spouse) evokes what researchers refer to as "gratitude induction"—but we're just going to call it *waking the fuck up to what we've been taking for granted.* Research confirms that mental subtraction opens us up to what we've been overlooking, keeps us curious, and helps switch us out of the all-too-natural autopilot state we find ourselves in.

Other examples include imagining that you lost your mobility or health, that you no longer possessed your greatest talent, that you lost Pickles the family ferret. You see where this is going, right? Imagine you are not, in fact, going to live forever. Imagine you weren't here at all. No loved ones (of the two- or four-legged variety), no delightful and touching memories, no more autonomy, no reaching your potential, no plans for your future, no more Twizzlers. Now look around you. What do you want to do in life that you've been putting off, thinking you have all the time in the world to get to it down the road? What kind of person do you want to be, with this amplified realization that you can rebirth yourself within this finite period?

INITIATING A PINT-SIZED EXISTENTIAL CRISIS

The jury is in: people who've looked death in the eye (while squinting; apparently it's a pretty bright light down that tunnel) live their days with a matter-of-fact approach to living like they mean it. Their eyes work differently when they've seen the edges of death. They gain the ultimate consciousness.

So how do we wake up to the absurdity of our finite human condition and live like we mean it in the midst of it all . . . if we haven't been granted the gift of a brush with death?

The best way I've found to live astonishingly albeit temporarily is to peer over the edge of an existential crisis. It's not as dramatic as a near-death experience, but it earns a silver medal in the Existential Wake-up Call event.

Karl Jaspers, the nineteenth-century existential psychiatrist and philosopher, believed that being alive is about finding ourselves in situations. Some situations are trifling in the grand scheme of our lives (e.g., submitting TPS report #395 and picking up the dry cleaning), whereas some situations have the capacity to wobble our world (e.g., having a baby or turning fifty).

Our highest degree of self-awareness—when we become the most authentic versions of ourselves—comes from "boundary situations." These are the consequential moments that expose us to the boundaries of our existence. World-rocking boundary situations emerge from change, suffering, struggle, guilt, and, last but not least in this lighthearted line-up...death.

Psychologists[8] explain that an existential crisis (or its cousin, the midlife crisis) can occur because of a confrontation with mortality that's spurred by a boundary situation—a more urgent event that either hints at our impermanence or boldly thrusts death to front and center stage. Examples include:

- Birthdays that end with zeros (these are significant because the decade to come feels subjectively different than the one we just crushed, even if we're the same person when we turn forty on Wednesday as we were on Tuesday when we were only thirty-nine)
- Significant anniversaries
- Retirement
- Job loss
- Serious disability or illness
- Relationship commitments
- Relationship separations or endings
- Relocations
- Major financial change
- Deaths of loved ones
- Evidence of aging (e.g., gray hair, wrinkles, sagging body parts, menopause, erectile dysfunction, and the list goes on)

Many of my clients find themselves in a quandary as they approach and enter retirement—the classic life-jolting scenario. In a "So Now What?" event I lead for groups of soon-to-retire leaders, they often articulate the tension between having freedom and choice ("Woo hoo! Every day is like Saturday!") with a loss of their professional identities ("Who am I if I'm not Dr. Ali anymore?") and uncertainty of purpose ("So now what do I do?"). The liminal space between Then and There can feel daunting and paralyzing. The fear-based belief that "my options are limited" can creep in. The stage is set for existential despair. And yet this boundary situation offers a tremendous opportunity to redefine and redesign life: for some of us, boundary situations can create mammoth shifts in the way we live our lives.

SUPERPIVOTAL SOUL-SEARCHING MOMENT ALERT!

Fair warning: these questions are intended to poke, prod, and then light a firecracker under your tushy.

If you don't have a turning point on your near-term horizon (damn—no bankruptcy or divorce planned this year?), that doesn't mean you have to sit around and wait for a boundary situation to pound at your door. Go AWOL on a personal retreat and visualize your next big birthday, life event, or retirement. Get comfy and reflect on the following:

- How are you *really* feeling right now? What feelings are you afraid to admit?
- What's the difference between *reacting* and *responding* to what you're feeling in this transition?
- What feelings of loss and gain will you likely experience?
- How do you want to look back on this time of change, and what will you do to feel proud of how you handled it?
- How would you like to describe this transition (e.g., graceful, exciting, curious, calm, adventurous, life-altering, open, inconsequential, inspiring)?
- What would the most alive version of you do next?
- What version of yourself might you need to become to best handle this transition?
- How does this period of change make you reflect on your impermanence?
- Knowing your time is limited (as it always has been and always will be), what sorts of things are you motivated to do with your remaining Mondays?

Write, read what you wrote, write about what you thought about what you just wrote, and then repeat that all over again. A good bottle of wine helps.

The encouragement here is to celebrate the boundaries of your being (every big milestone, every big birthday, every big beginning and ending, every change you put up a pointless fight against)—even if these situations feel discombobulating at first. Let's embrace these wake-up calls for the gift they usually are (albeit in disguise): opportunities to live wider and deeper.

FOR WHEN WE'RE NOT ON THE VERGE OF DEATH: ENGINEERING EPIPHANIES

Thankfully most of us haven't had a brush with death. And don't worry! I'm still not going to encourage you to rock climb with a sketchy rope just to heighten your appreciation for being here. So much of what we're talking about here are epiphanies, right? Head-jerking moments that forever change our paths forward, our thinking, our being, our usness. Can we engineer our own epiphanies? Can we jerk our own heads without almost dying?

Brushes with death bear a family resemblance to the concept of "quantum change"—the sudden light-bulb moment epiphanies that lead to deep and lasting transformations of values, priorities, and perspectives... think of Ebenezer Scrooge from *A Christmas Carol*[9] as an example. Psychologists[10] describe this big-deal subjective experience as a developmental metamorphosis, like a "fast-forward in what Maslow described as self-actualization." I know we both want the fast track to the top of the pyramid.

When our preconceived notions and roles and identities and expectations are stripped away, what's left is an urge to reshape that moldable clay, to create a new way of living that feels legit to ourselves, not just a version that earns a seal of approval from someone whose opinion we care a little too much about. And here is where the quantum change magic happens: this tectonic-plate shifting is what causes us to build new constructs of how we see ourselves and plan for the future. It appears as though this dismantling of Reality 1.0 can lead us to a more thoughtfully lived 2.0. We can rebuild what needs rebuilding. We can let go of what needs letting go. We can do both. We just need to start the earthquake ourselves.

So what if we played the "what if" game to get the earth moving?

If you were pulled back from the brink of death today...

- What would you do tomorrow?
- Who would you be?
- What would you savor, with the wisdom of knowing what it felt like to be without it?
- What would you dispense with in your life? What would you say "fuck thank you very much, but no" to?
- What would you do with your remaining Mondays?

And with your answers to each of those questions, what is stopping you from being that person and living that life today, to shine the light on all you're taking for granted? Keep these notes safe for the grand finale action-planning chapters.

What we know to be true about ontological confrontation (one of the fancy names for when we're faced with the inevitability of death) is that it sparks that sense of temporal scarcity and that our priorities are more finely tuned in the face of a perceived expiry date on life. We don't need to survive a plane crash or go into remission from cancer to experience this wake-up, thankfully. Deliberate death reflection can induce epiphanies.

Now do you see where I've been going with all of this death talk?

The only way to experience a manual "roar of awakening"—the wake-up call only death can trigger—is by going full-tilt memento mori:

- Memento mori reinvigorates us with that sense of "let's get on with it-ness."
- Memento mori reminds us of the fragility of our existence and dials up our appreciation for having an existence at all.
- Memento mori reprioritizes how we want to spend our time—choosing activities that can simultaneously bring us pleasure (like the hobby of

learning how to paint) and also deepening meaning (by connecting with others at art class, gifting a Van Gogh-sunflower-inspired canvas to a friend on her birthday, and feeling that undeniable sense of accomplishment).

Actively wrangling with your mortality provides the kick in the behind your cute little ass needs and wants in order to snap out of autopilot and live an astonishing life.

In this chapter, we've pictured your almost-death and channeled the lessons learned from those who've been given the gift of a second chance. Now imagine you had the opportunity to direct the course of your life—oh wait! You do! So let's step forward into a lifetime of regret-free Mondays. Speaking of regrets...

CHAPTER 6

REGRETS: THOSE (HELPFUL) LITTLE ASSHOLES

 Of all sad words of mouth or pen, the saddest are these: it might have been.
—John Greenleaf Whittier

Regrets: they *are* assholes, aren't they?

So far we've been talking all about the Grim Reaper, who is a grade A asshole for sure, but *regrets*. . . . (You can't see me right now, but I'm shaking my head in that slow, squinty-eyed, part-disappointed-part-menacing way.) The Reaper happens *to* us, but we're responsible for the regrets we let pile up. True, it's much more fun to blame our problems on someone else, but when it comes to these little buggers having the run of the place, we have only ourselves to blame (*sigh*).

But I didn't invite you to a pity party about all the ways we let our lives fall apart before we decay and die. So as much as we're starting a chapter together *about assholes*, I do solemnly swear that we'll make this worth your while. We're going to delve into the inner workings of regrets and how they can be the exact lifesavers you need to live the life you're longing to experience. By the end of this chapter, you'll

A. Have become a card-carrying member of the Regrets Prevention Department (don't worry, membership is free) and
B. Have a list of eurekas and notes to hold onto until further notice.

There will be zero pressure to Do Anything until the end of our adventure, of course, but since action is at the heart of a squander-free

OFFICIAL
MEMBERSHIP
CARD

the
R E G R E T S
PREVENTION
ASSOCIATION

NAME: *Your Name Here*
MEMBER Nº: 36910432-7

"I SOLEMNLY SWEAR TO LIVE A REGRET-FREE
LIFE UNTIL THE DAY I BITE THE BIG BISCUIT."

existence, if in the course of this chapter you feel called to Take Astonishing Action on Something Big or Small, no one here is going to stop you. We can't have you regretting not taking action on something that matters to you during a discussion about regrets.

And now—lessons learned about Coulda Shoulda Wouldas...

WHY I'M REPELLED BY REGRETS

Of all the things I fear (spiders, rejection, needles, ambiguous lineups... and we're just getting warmed up here), regrets take the cake. I have a deep-rooted fear of getting to the end and feeling woefully disappointed— not so much by the life I lived but by the life I *didn't* live.

For this I have my mom to thank.

I've already mentioned that she died with a full Compendium of Lost and Unfulfilled Dreams. I've also already mentioned the vestiges of half-baked plans I sifted and sorted through as I cleaned up her place after she died: writings, drawings, business cards made at home on her inkjet printer (you know the ones you buy at Staples—with the perforated lines to tear the cards apart?). She was a wondiferous dreamer... but not so much a doer. Some of us are content to dream all day and not execute on the idea du jour, but my mom did indeed feel the sting of stagnation.

As a manic-depressive, creative soul who churned out chapters and ideas and homemade dog treats and hand-carved hiking sticks through her manic highs, she'd pull the pin on her plans when she was down in the dumps. The cycle was predictable and heartrending to watch unfold, again and again. I'd cheer her on for every newfangled notion ("Wow, Mom! *Take a Hike* is an amazing name for your hiking stick business!") and then watch her bury the idea alive. I have a photo of her at some kind of outdoor flea market in British Columbia, sitting behind a makeshift table with her sticks on display. She had tied cute little handmade logoed price tags on the tops of them, which somehow makes the story sadder. She didn't sell any hiking sticks that day, and so the Take a Hike empire folded before it really even began.

My mom wrote a children's book in the early '80s called *Dreamdust*, and it included everything a bookworm daughter wanted in its pages: a beautifully illustrated protagonist mouse named Arlo, a cast of cute and clever animal sidekicks, and the fantasy of all the dreams that would come true after Arlo sprinkled his dreamdust willy-nilly over his buddies in the forest. (My mom would sprinkle imaginary dreamdust on me every night at tuck-in time, à la Arlo; it didn't stop me from peeing the bed, but it did curb my bad dreams.) She sent the manuscript out to a few publishers and lost the nerve to press on after the first wave of rejections. Where was her own sprinkling of dreamdust?

This irony-laden tale is what I grew up with: I learned to value the glimmers of creativity, to hope for dreamdust to do its thing (I no longer pee the bed, FYI), and then to throw in the towel before a project even stood a chance. I come by my own fears of rejection and failure honestly. Witnessing my mom's dormant dreams splayed out bare as I cleaned out her apartment woke me up to my own chickenheartedness. I did not want to live a life with dead-on-arrival dreams.

So I took a Take a Hike perforated business card out of her desk drawer (for posterity's sake), stuffed her *Dreamdust* manuscript in my backpack (right beside her box of ashes), and packed her orange cat named Teddy into his carrier, and as I locked up her empty place, I committed to live a regret-free life. At least I'd die trying.

REGRETS: THE BEST OF THE WORST

Despite my harsh stage setting, regrets aren't *always* assholes.

Regrets can motivate us to change our behavior and improve our lives, after we simmer in the uncomfortable awareness of "what could have been" if we'd only made a way better decision. Oh, the benefit of 20/20 hindsight.

Regret actually wins the Best of the Worst award; studies[1] show we value regret more than any of the negative emotions* out there, because we accept its functional value to help shepherd our decisions. Regrets play an important role in an astonishing life, so we're not just here for a bitchfest in this chapter.

There are two main categories of regrets[2] you'll want to pay attention to in today's lesson:

Regrets of commission include things we did and wish we didn't. Here's a true-crime sampler from my clients and workshop attendees:

- "Being mean to Kandy on the schoolyard in sixth grade"
- "Having an affair"
- "Telling that client what I really thought of them"
- "Getting a DUI"
- "Leaving my vintage baseball card collection at home for my mother to later *throw out*"
- "Giving Tom the finger after quitting in a huff"
- "Eating three-day-old sushi"

These are known as hot regrets[3]—stupid things we do that burn hot in the short run with shame, guilt, embarrassment, or remorse—and cool off over time.

And then we have **regrets of omission**, which include the paths we didn't take. These are known as wistful regrets[4]—supernovas that pretty much burn bright and torment us until the end of time. Real-life client examples include:

- "Not backpacking across Europe after college"
- "Not running that marathon"

---

* We value jealousy the least of the negative emotions.

- 💀 "Not finishing law school"
- 💀 "Not fixing my relationship with my brother"
- 💀 "Not writing that children's book"
- 💀 "Not ordering desserts just for myself; I wish I'd had more pieces of cake all to myself"
- 💀 "Not telling my first crush I loved him"

→ AN ASSORTMENT OF PATHS NOT TAKEN

 Mark Twain nailed it when he said we're more likely to regret the things we skipped than the things we went through with (and just wish had gone so much better): "Twenty years from now you will be more disappointed by the things that you didn't do than by the ones you did do. So throw off the bowlines. Sail away from the safe harbor. Catch the trade winds in your sails. Explore. Dream. Discover." I love this quote so much it makes me briefly consider becoming a sailor, but for the unflattering horizontal stripes.

We can rationalize our regrets of commission through the softening of time, but regrets of omission tend to haunt us, mostly because these paths not taken shine a glaring spotlight on the chasm between our actual selves and the person we've imagined as our ideal selves—the versions of us that make dreams and goals come true and have their shit together in general.

"THE 12 FLAVORS OF REGRETS" ASSESSMENT

Just as we diagnosed the dead zones in the Astonishingly Alive Assessment, we want to identify your regrets-in-the-making hotspots.

Anticipating our regrets—"pre-grets"—before they come to fruition gives us a chance to live a life that feels right to us rather than one that's riddled with the crestfallen "It could've been so much better if" or the "If only" grimace that trails off into a somber silence. Ew and ew. We don't have to continue down the paths not taken; we can traipse down entirely different paths if we so choose.

The list below, adapted from regret psychology research,[5] offers twelve areas where your regrets might be brewing. Read through the examples and select your best number according to the "Coulda Shoulda Woulda" Scale:

1 = Zilcho regrets-in-the-making!
2 = A sprinkling of regrets
3 = Hand-to-the-forehead... regrets brewing
4 = Riddled with regrets

FLAVOR	DETAILS	EXAMPLES	COULDA SHOULDA WOULDA SCALE			
Family	Interactions with parents and siblings	• "I wish I'd called my dad more often" • "I wish I had gone home for more of the holidays"	1	2	3	4
Parenting	Interactions with offspring	• "If only I'd spent more time playing with my kids" • "I could have been less overbearing toward my daughter"	1	2	3	4

FLAVOR	DETAILS	EXAMPLES	COULDA SHOULDA WOULDA SCALE			
Romance	Love, sex, dating, marriage	• "I wish I'd married Ralphie instead of Howie" • "I could have canoodled more"	1	2	3	4
Friends	Interactions with close others	• "If only I went out for more Girls' Nights" • "I could have kept in touch with my work friends"	1	2	3	4
Career	Jobs, employment, earning a living	• "If only I were a set designer" • "I wish I had applied for bigger jobs along the way"	1	2	3	4
Education	School, getting good grades, earning advanced degrees	• "If only I had taken my time in college more seriously" • "I wish I'd gotten an MBA"	1	2	3	4
Finance	Decisions about money	• "I wish I'd gotten into the stock market earlier" • "I wish I had saved more when I was younger"	1	2	3	4
Health	Exercise, diet, avoiding or treating illness	• "If only I could stick to my diet" • "If only I went for that colonoscopy when my doctor encouraged it"	1	2	3	4
Leisure	Recreation, fun, hobbies, sports	• "I should've gone on that safari" • "I wish I had picked up the guitar again after all those years"	1	2	3	4
Community	Volunteer work, community engagement, political activism	• "I should have volunteered more at the library" • "I could've gone campaigning door-to-door"	1	2	3	4
Spirituality	The meaning of life, religion, philosophy	• "I wish I'd found this purpose sooner" • "I wish I had explored other world religions"	1	2	3	4
Self	Improving oneself in terms of abilities, attitudes, behaviors	• "If only I had more self-confidence" • "I wish I didn't care so much about what people thought of me"	1	2	3	4

What observations jump out at you from the chart? I suspect you have an inkling of your possible regrets, but in my experience, we need a little help to underscore them. We need more examples...

AN ASSORTMENT OF POIGNANT REGRET-INSPIRATION

If I've learned one thing from presenting to large and small groups on this topic of "please don't die jam-packed full of regrets" (other than the importance of having enough portable potties available at outdoor retreats), it's that people love to hear where other people are selling themselves short. I believe it's less about schadenfreude—that sick pleasure we derive from other people's misfortunes—and more about feeling less alone in our "oh fuckness" about living this life right. It's helpful to know we're not alone, that we're not the only ones giving our goals a raincheck year after year.

When Donna shares how she'd regret not learning how to flamenco dance if her plug was pulled tonight, for example, Fatima remembers her long-lost burning desire to breakdance. We learn vicariously through others, so this little list, gathered from presentations where I've gotten nosy and asked participants to share their deathbed regrets, might inspire you to stop procrastinating your aliveness and start living the better version of your life, now.

I present to you an assortment of paths not taken . . . gripping tales of the "coulda, shoulda, woulda" ilk:

- ☠ "I'd regret not standing up for myself against my tough boss"
- ☠ "I could have spent less time worrying about what might happen and just trust I'd be able to handle whatever came my way without planning for every contingency"
- ☠ "I'd wish I had gone to med school"
- ☠ "I should have visited my mom more before I moved out east"
- ☠ "I'd regret not getting healthy and feeling lighter of body and soul again"
- ☠ "I wish I had listened to my intuition more"

- ☠ "I'd regret not dressing up for Halloween and having more fun"
- ☠ "I'd have regrets about not leaving my dead-end job"
- ☠ "I could have become a vet"
- ☠ "I'd regret not ending my friendships with the people who drag me down"
- ☠ "I'd wish I went to the doctor sooner"
- ☠ "I spend time worrying about what people think of me, when it's really none of my business, right?"
- ☠ "I'd regret not being a more involved uncle to my nephews"
- ☠ "I regret not entering a fitness physique competition"
- ☠ "I could have checked out Buddhism, or at least meditation"
- ☠ "I'd wish I had applied for the bigger stretch jobs at work, like the secondments to Asia"
- ☠ "Why didn't I take the kids to Disneyland?"
- ☠ "I'd regret not patenting my hosiery invention"
- ☠ "I wish I had the courage to take a creative class, like painting or woodworking"
- ☠ "I would regret not living off the grid"
- ☠ "I'd regret not learning how to teach yoga"
- ☠ "I could've gone on an overseas mission"
- ☠ "I wish I had learned how to speak another language"
- ☠ "I wish I'd have asked more for forgiveness instead of permission"
- ☠ "I'd regret not eating more cheese"

Even with all that morphine coursing through their veins at the end, people on their deathbeds kick themselves for the following:

- ☠ "I regret not getting to know my dad better before he died"
- ☠ "I really wanted to publish a memoir"
- ☠ "I wish I had come out sooner and stood up for other LGBTQ+ people"
- ☠ "I wish I put myself out there at work more, offering up my ideas and taking more initiative"
- ☠ "I regret worrying so much about how my body looked"
- ☠ "I wish I had gotten sober sooner"
- ☠ "I hardly traveled when I was healthier; I wish I had explored more"

- ☻ "I regret working so many weekends when I could've been hanging out with my kids"
- ☻ "I regret not treating myself and my husband more to the special things, like using the good dishes, getting dressed up, lighting more candles, making more fancy meals"
- ☻ "I should have told my wife I loved her more"
- ☻ "I wish I had made more of an effort to keep my friends close"
- ☻ "I regret not having more fun; I worked so much and did all the responsible things at the expense of good times"

I'm inspired by the memento-mori-slash-regret story of Alfred Nobel, of Nobel Prize fame. Apparently when his brother Ludvig died in 1888, he was horrified to read his obituary in the paper, because (oops!) the paper published their draft for the wrong brother. Alfred sat reading his own obituary, and it wasn't flattering.

Newspapers apparently have drafts of famous people's obituaries ready to go at a moment's notice, and the headline for his published version read, "The Merchant of Death Is Dead!" (At the time, Alfred was a big player in the world of dynamite and ballistics manufacturing, which made him a bit of a social pariah.)

The story goes that Alfred, seeing his death and bad reputation basically stare back at him in print, was motivated to leave his fortunes and estate to the improvement of humanity (i.e., the Nobel Prizes). Alfred Nobel dodged a bullet of regret by a wake-up call published in error. You might not be making weapons, but is there a version of a regret wake-up call that would snap you to attention?

You'll notice that almost all of the examples listed above—including the story of our friend Alfred—are regrets where the regretee had an option to prevent the regret from manifesting. Some are easier than others to intercept, but possible nevertheless. It's never too late. People get educated, get published, get clean and sober, get confident, get reconnected, get healthy, get bold, get fun, and get gussied up at any age. The only limitation is the story we tell ourselves—that the ship has sailed or, if it's just at a new dock, is waiting to "sail away from the safe harbor."

THE DEATHBED REGRET EXERCISE

This one's an oldie but a goodie. Get comfy in bed. Yes, for real—recline your body and take a deep breath. Imagine you are lying on your death-bed, with all but a few hours to go. You're not in pain, you feel lucid and at peace, and you look fabulous. You're near the end and reflecting back on your life. Start to zero in on your regrets—not the things you *did* do but rather the things you *didn't* do.

These missed decisions, or chances, could be ancient history—like wishing that you took that dance theater program in college—and maybe some of your regrets are more recent, like not applying for that cool job in San Francisco or never getting around to renovating the basement. Some of your regrets might be hefty, and some might be trivial. They are all valid.

Jot down your list of deathbed regrets. Look at them looking back at you. What does it feel like to think about these missed opportunities? Do they feel heavy, like a full-body cringe?

We'll spend time later figuring out what—if anything—you want to do about these little life robbers, but for now, let's talk about how to counter-intuitively leverage these pre-grets.

SEVEN RESEARCH-BACKED WAYS TO USE REGRETS TO YOUR ADVANTAGE

#1: Improved decision hygiene.

- Regrets can spiff up our future decisions because of the "once bitten, twice shy" effect; being burned from a previous regret slows us down and broadens our perspectives, so we don't make the same mistake twice.
- What regrets from your past can you learn from today, to help steer your decisions in a healthier and happier direction?

#2: Common regret danger zone: social relationships.

- Regrets surrounding personal relationships cut deeper than other types of regrets because they rankle our perception of belonging—something our species has been wired for centuries to value quite heartily, lest we be cast aside as dinner for the hyenas. We tend to have a tough time when our connections to others feel at risk in some way, even if we've contributed to the disconnection.

⊙ A vast majority of the people I work with are in the messy middle of a burgeoning regret known as Not Making Time for People Who Matter. This might sound familiar to you? "People Who Matter" could include daughters, sons, partners, friends, moms, dads, mentors, and the list goes on. Do we always have to hurt the ones we love, as the saying goes? Do we always have to take them for granted?

Positive Psychology Interlude: Supra-social = supra-happy. Researchers[6] compared very happy people to happy people, wondering what made them different. Of the very happy (or "supranormal") people in their sample, the striking thing was that they all had close relationships with others. I want supranormal happiness, don't you? Good relationships with others may be the single most important source of life satisfaction and emotional well-being, across different ages and cultures. What a shame it would be, then, if we let these relationships flounder because we were swept up answering three more emails.

Are there any troubled relationships you might want to mend—even with a simple "thinking of you" text? Are there any long-lost friendships you'd like to search and rescue again? Reconnections are rarely as awkward as we fear they'll be. Are there any relationships you'd like to devote even more time and love to, because they're so mutually rewarding?

#3: Performance booster.

⊙ "If only" thinking often leads to the wistful feeling of regret, which typically leads to reflection, then some kind of revised strategy, and then—voila—improved performance and results. The path isn't always direct, but it's fairly clear when we're willing to tune into regret's possibilities in disguise.

- One of my CEO clients missed the boat on hiring a fabulous team member. "She's the one that got away," he'd moan (until I encouraged him to stop talking about her in thwarted romance and/or fishing derby terms). After wallowing in his mistake, he worked with his HR team to come up with a more efficient hiring process and credits his lost ~~fish~~ VP of Operations for upping their game.

- Are there lessons you've learned in the past that have improved the way you live your life now? If you've been beating yourself up for a transgression or mistake from days gone by, it might be time to reframe it as a helpful tutorial in what not to do / what to do moving forward. You're doing the best you can.

#4. Closed vs. open doors.

- I regret not reaching out more regularly to a dear mentor who recently passed away. That's a "closed door" regret because there's not a darned thing I can do about it (short of arranging some kind of seance... "Barry, are you out there?").

- An "open door" regret, in contrast, still offers the chance to take action—like tracking down your old college roommate after years of zero communication. Open-door regrets sound lovely, but we need to be honest that they can feel bothersome because they require effort. We're not always up to the task.

- Is it worth the effort for you to take action on one of your open-door regrets? For some regrets, it might not be—we only have so many Mondays left, and you might be just fine not going back for your black belt or visiting that cool ice hotel or taking a stab at turducken. We must be judicious with our time, and we can't do it all. And yet... only you know, deep down, which open-door regrets doors are worth walking through to live like you mean it.

DON'T BE AN IDIOT WALK THROUGH THE DAMNED OPEN DOOR LIKE RIGHT NOW

No Regrets

> It's never too late to be what you might have been.
> —GEORGE ELIOT*

#5. Mustering up bravery.

- It takes the strength of courage to live like we mean it with zest, it can take courage to come to terms with regret-soaked dreams that died on the vine, and it can take courage to back up from the pre-gret path we're on to forge a new regret-free path forward.

- "I wish I had the courage to be bold, to be more spontaneous with my schedule," whispered a lovely woman on a break at one of my workshops. This woman didn't know it, but she echoed the voice of scads of other highly successful, organized, "in control" types. Spontaneity can be scary for those of us who like the trains to run on time, for those of us who like things "just so." Boldly busting a schedule can feel reckless and out of bounds . . . yet also a little alluring and alive, no? If this sounds like you, make sure you're alert in our next chapter when we talk about the art and science of shaking your life up (in a gentle, mostly in-control fashion).

- Summoning up the conviction to color outside the lines of life might be the best regret you never had.

Coaching Chestnut: Lost Possible Selves. Just as courage is required to thwart future regrets—like starting over in new careers or relationships, for example—we need courage to face up to dreams that went down the toilet. Many of us have idealized versions of our "best possible selves," and we want to keep trying to become that person, with gusto! Add to that the practice of letting go of what psychology researchers[7] call "lost possible selves."

Like any goal we shoot for, we often attach ourselves to their outcomes and find it hard to be with ourselves when we miss the mark. Wanting to become the Chief Marketing Officer, dreaming of being a parent, setting a

---

* George Eliot was the pen name for Mary Ann Evans, a woman who lived what sounds like a regret-free life in the 1800s with an open marriage.

goal to climb Kilimanjaro...these dreams and desires aren't always in the cards for us. Tom might get the CMO appointment. You might not be able to have kids of your own. Altitude sickness at basecamp is a thing. Pulling the plug on who we wanted to be isn't always easy, especially when it's a closed-door regret that's locked tight—yet acknowledging the selves we've left behind paradoxically leads to a richer, mature, developed life. (Note I did not say *rumination* over goals gone awry; this is about acceptance.)

How courageous are you willing to be, to reinvent parts and pieces of your life, in service of living a life that feels true to you? How courageous are you willing to be, to face up to your lost possible selves and see that *different* best possible selves might fit even better into the landscape of your life? Remember that courage is like confidence: if you wait for it to find you before taking action, you will wait until you are full of formaldehyde at the morgue. You must drum up that courage yourself, while you are very much alive and formaldehyde-free.

#6. Regrets run out of time.

Research[8] highlights how hospice patients are often preoccupied by missed chances, with little or no time left to course-correct their missteps. It's tough to make that oft-thought-about trip to New Zealand, learn how to play the pan flute, or make amends with your cousin when you've got one foot in the grave and the other foot on a banana peel. Are there things you long to do yet keep deferring for "later"? Are there goals you've been telling people about, maybe for years and years, that you haven't taken action on? If so, what is stopping you from taking a step in the direction of that dream? Would anyone shake their head at your funeral, grieving not just for you but also for your dreams that were buried right along with you?

The graveyard is the richest place on earth, because it is here that you will find all the hopes and dreams that were never fulfilled, the books that were never written, the songs that were never sung, the inventions that were never shared, the cures that were never discovered, all because someone was too afraid to take that first step, keep with the problem, or determine to carry out their dream.

—LES BROWN

#7. Avoiding despair—and regret—at the end.

☉ Our eighth and final stage of being alive, according to Erik Erikson's[9] stages of development, is known as the *Ego Integrity vs. Despair* stage.

☉ Ego integrity is full of fabulous feelings of fulfillment, the pursuit of wisdom, and rocking-chair contentment. Check, check, and check. This special flavor of maturity is the reward for those who believe they've lived their lives well, minus a list of "coulda shoulda wouldas." Erikson believed that despair is inevitable for those who feel disappointed about their past, for those who look back with the melancholic belief that they didn't reach the goals they had fathomed for themselves. Anyone smell a bunch of pre-grets turned into deathbed regrets?

☉ My friend Dana told me how struck she was by something her dad said after he was diagnosed with a terminal illness: "I've lived the life I wanted to live." He had spent time golfing and with his girls during his life wind down and possessed a calm clarity that he had lived a full-blown life. It might not have been full-length, but it was *full.* If you breathed your last breath during your sleep tonight, would you say with conviction that you'd lived your life well? That you'd reached ego integrity, instead of despair?

WELCOME TO THE REGRETS PREVENTION DEPARTMENT

Welcome to the Regrets Prevention Department (*rolls out red carpet*)! Can I offer you a drink?

Now that you're sufficiently educated on the upsides of regrets, let's talk about how to drive a stake into the heart of your pre-grets...all in service of living an astonishing life.

Most of us get the drift that we're not going to reach all of our goals—we know we're going to lose a few of our possible selves along the way—but how can we ensure we don't miss out on the things that matter? How can we tell when looking at our deathbed regrets list which pangs are worth pursuing? How can we tell which regrets-in-the-making are worth taking to the grave with us, because they're "nice but not necessary" to accomplish?

I encourage my clients and program attendees to pay attention to their lists, to treat them like precious instructions on How to Live the Good Life: Me Edition.

Some regrets-in-the-works will jump off the page, demanding to be acted upon pronto...like one woman at a workshop who got up from her seat, left the room for fifteen minutes, and came back bursting at the seams to announce she had just booked her Outward Bound mountaineering expedition.

Some pre-gret bullet points take root over time—maybe starting out as seedlings of goals that grow like bamboo over the months to come. One client kept checking in on her regret list and noticed that she was increasingly interested in point 3: "Becoming a volunteer Big Sister." It was a goal she could no longer *not* act upon.

Some regrets-in-the-making would be lovely to put into action but don't make the cut in the grand scheme of life...like the client I worked with who peered at his list of twenty-seven items and scratched two off in the moment. "I *want* to learn how to use sign language, but I don't *have* to." It's all about prioritizing what we'd like to fit into our Mondays.

Your mission right now—should you choose to accept it and all that— is to:

- ☻ Make a deathbed pre-grets list and keep it a living, breathing document. Mark it up. Highlight it.
- ☻ Circle the entries that make your heart beat fast, that make your heart ache, that make your heart skip a beat—anything heart-related is a good indication *it matters*.
- ☻ Make note of the pre-grets that aren't shy to make their presence known.

☻ Pay close attention to the gossamery pre-grets that want to hide on the page because they're fragile and afraid to be exposed out of fear of failure or rejection or ridicule.* Protect those dreams.

☻ Start pontificating ways to take even one step forward. Better yet, write one down here: _____

_____

We are going to culminate the shit out of all your dreams and ideas and plots and plans and ploys at the end of this book, so if you'd prefer to let your regrets-in-the-making percolate until then, I'll catch you on the flip side. If you prefer to book your first fencing lesson or request a transfer to the London office or try to have a baby before you get to the last chapter, I will not reach through these pages to stop you.

IRREGRETFULLY YOURS . . .

"Live Squander-Free™" is kind of my motto (that and "The More Swedish Fish, the Better™"), so I'm downright fanatical about the ways we might "if only" ourselves to death.

Identifying our regrets-in-the-making and course-correcting along the way to prevent them from materializing—that's a recipe for a life well lived, full of agency and intention. You know what else is? Reflecting on our no-way-out-alive, no-ifs-and-or-buts, *death*—because it forces us to be intentional. Since our lives aren't long enough for a collection of do-overs, it behooves us to pin down our most pressing wants and create a sense of urgency to *do something* about them.

We risk getting to our deathbeds with the unfortunate realization that we spent our time pursuing the wrong things, instead of the dreams that might've made us feel even more alive. I started Four Thousand Mondays because the idea of dying with that dream stuck inside made me feel like I was nailing my own coffin shut while gasping for air. Speaking of, have you recalculated your Mondays since you read your pre-mortem in

---

* One of my clients in his late forties said he would be deeply regretful if he didn't learn how to ride a unicycle. Zero judgment about the things that dreams are made of.

chapter 1 (page 25)? How many fewer do you have now? Are we on the same page about urgency yet?

An unflinching awareness of your almost-regrets can change the trajectory of your life. Consider, deeply, the pangs of regret you already feel in your life. Look at your list again. Contemplate the paths you have yet to take, the paths you know will lead to regret if you don't reorient yourself. Reflect on the paths you *are* on but might regret not hitchhiking your way out of.

Cue the Turkish proverb: "No matter how far you have gone on a wrong road, turn back." Turn. Back. Now.

Make the time before time gets the best of you. Don't die with all that life left inside you. Go all Grim Reaper on a regret today. Let's tell our regrets to Take a Hike, shall we?

CHAPTER 7

HABITS: THE BLUNTING OF OUR ALIVENESS

 How we spend our days is, of course, how we spend our lives.
—ANNIE DILLARD

Habits? They suck. (The life out of us.*)

You might've seen my beef with regrets coming from a mile away in our last chapter—because they've been universally anointed as assholes, after all—but I bet you weren't expecting hostility toward The Habit.

We design our lives around habits and routines that are predictable, regimented, and nestled in comfort zones that feel satisfying for a while . . . until they initially dim and then eventually douse the fires inside of us.

(Quick refresher on why we're spending all this time together: we want to *stoke* the fires inside of us—set our lives ablaze with passion and fervency and interest and aliveness—not *extinguish* the flames with the soaking wet blanket of boredom.)

Am I aware that you might have feelings about habits, of the defensive "don't mess with the very things that keep my life on the rails, bitch" sort? Yes, I am in tune with that. We've come this far together, and after all these reflections and Kleenexes, I'd be out to lunch if I didn't sense that natural resistance.

I feel that resistance in my own life, too. I cling to my own litany of habits, and I too am wary of agitating the routines that make me feel

---

* I feel like I need to apologize to James Clear every time I rain on his habit parade. Sorry, James!

like life is less...flimsy. Less higgledy-piggledy. I appreciate an efficient, well-organized life; I am not interested in higgledy-piggledy-ness! But I'm even *more* wary of how habits can dull the edges of our lives. I've done the research, and I've worked with enough clients to twig how fastidiously adhering to routines invariably turn us into robots.[*]

"IT IS 6:33. MUST BRUSH TEETH."

In light of this insight, I'm probably going to overindex on the whole "Habits Are Heinous" theme throughout this chapter, in an effort to illustrate my point—because we want to upgrade our experiences of being alive while we have the honor of still being above ground. So yes, we'll talk about how habits and routines eviscerate our vitality and lead to the total yawnfest called *boredom*. We'll then transition into the antidote to autopilotitis, which is our jaunty little friend called *novelty*. Along the way I'll reluctantly acknowledge that routines have a time and a place in a well-lived life, and then I'll likely recalibrate by the end of our discussion about what a healthy amount of habit might look like within your astonishing life.

Just as you're now poised to use regrets-in-the-making to your advantage (Oh, and death!—let's not forget our good friend Grim), my goal is for you to learn to use routines to enhance your life, not diminish it.

Before we go any further, I'm going to insist that we do something a little different for this chapter. I'm going to encourage a routine rumpler, right here, right now. If you've read the first five chapters in your usual spot on the right side of the sofa (Look! There's your little dent!), can I suggest you move somewhere different? (I suppose the left side counts.) If you normally read and take notes in the lobby of your favorite hotel because it's just so beautiful (and hotel lobbies make great places to

---

[*] Robots are not living like they mean it. All robots care about is getting more oil, so they can become even oilier well-oiled machines. We must be wary of both robots and routines.

loiter), how about pulling a switcharoo for this chapter—maybe trying a different seat for a new vantage point or a completely different hotel all together? You get the idea: try reading this chapter outside, or in bed with a flashlight, or on a train, or in a meadow...just to shake things up. More on why this matters in a few pages.

AN INTRODUCTION TO THE HAZARDS OF HABITS + RISKS OF ROUTINES

YOU: Can you please draw me a doodle that explains why you're so hostile toward habits?

ME: I love nothing more than hostility-related doodles-on-demand! Here you go.

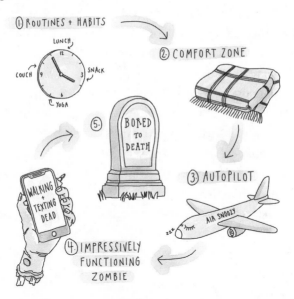

See that cozy-looking plaid blanket in my little drawing? See how it beckons you? We aren't idiots—we need and want the ease of well-ordered comfort in the midst of busy, hectic days. Habits can provide feelings of control in lives that, as liberally discussed so far, are uncontrollably terminal.

Succumbing to the same routines day after day and week after week numbs us all into pseudosatisfying trances that we sometimes confuse as helpful things called habits.... Well, we can see how this turns us into impressively functioning zombies, right? We can see how this switches us into autopilot mode?

When we find ourselves asking questions in the mirror like "Am I just going through the motions?" and "When did things get so fucking boring?," we know we're asleep at the switch of life—yet we typically lack the oomph to flick the switch back on. Is it not true that our fear of death is rivaled only by our fear of living (*insert a flinching grimace here*)?

We all too often move through our Mondays like automatons who wonder "Where did the month of February go?" because we've slipped into the warm embrace of routines that felt soothing at first—routines that let us control the chaos with schedules that got us up each morning at the same time, eating the same bowl of oatmeal, taking the same train to work, ordering the same macchiato, attending the same Wednesday status update meeting, rotating between the same six dinner options, and spending the last few hours of the day with the same variation of a theme involving kid's homework, TikTok, and folding the whites.

The routines that initially felt like a bear hug started to smother us, and then at some point, they snuffed the life right out of us—dulling our senses and robbing us of the joys of newness, of any semblance of surprise. Suddenly we realize we're in the middle of the slowest-motion-ever boredom-bear-attack that we didn't see coming.

Living our lives on autopilot can be comforting and efficient but also flatteningly dull. Lifeless. Hollow. Unfulfilled. Uninspired. Deflated. Godforsaken. *All sorts of words we don't want to use to describe our lives.* While we're at it, check out a few more "no thank you" words synonymous with habit- and routine-laden lives on the calendar.

Proust, the old-school French novelist, believed we deflate our lives by the "shroud of familiarity" that habits bestow upon us. Last I heard, familiarity breeds contempt. It's the insidiously familiar, mundane routines that muffle

NO ONE KNOWS WHAT THIS IS BUT IT DOESN'T SOUND LIKE SOMETHING WE WANT IN OUR LIVES.

our senses and make us feel stuck in stale, monochromatic versions of our lives—even when we're actively yearning for fresh, vivid versions.

So how do we break free? How do we "stop the squandering"...stop taking life for granted by living in autopilot like androids? We study our habits; we learn about how our routines are breeding grounds for boredom. And then we get to make choices about where we want to adjust the dials to live with more vitality and meaning.

THE HABIT PROS-AND-CONS LIST: FROM HELPFUL TO HOMICIDAL

We Bubble Wrap our lives with an arsenal of routines and habits that help make our lives feel manageable. So who am I to ask you to de-habit-ify your life and make life feel... *unmanageable*? What kind of animal am I?

Habits exist along a continuum,[1] from *Habit Impoverishment* on one end (where life is a clusterfuck of disorganized chaos with zero habits in place—likely involving sketchy personal hygiene), all the way over to *Habit Domination* (where habits rule the roost, lobotomize the habitee, and whittle away at life satisfaction; i.e., you skip a fun concert on Tuesday because On Tuesdays We Do Laundry). *Habit Utility* sits in the middle of the continuum and is characterized by habits that support the production of being alive, and successfully so. Knowing where your keys are, because you habitually place them in the same drawer, day after day, just makes life flow better. Using your seatbelt, because that's what you mindlessly do when you get in the car, keeps you alive. We like Habit Utility.

How do habits go from being blessings that bring order to our lives to "the fossilized residue of a spiritual activity"[2]... a.k.a. the curses that bore us stiff? The familiarity that breeds contempt? Now might be your opportunity

Habit Utility

Habit Impoverishment

Habit Domination

ALWAYS ON THE VERGE OF SUCKING

SUCKS A LOT

SUCKS THE MOST

to freshen up the routines that were born out of goodness but just got stale along the way?

Here is where I'd light a cigarette if I smoked (speaking of bad habits), lean back in my chair, and concede that habits and routines aren't *entirely* bad. Let's dig into the pros and cons.

PRO #1: Habits can act as training wheels when we're establishing healthy lifestyles. If we're trying to get fit, for example, it helps to have a Tuesday + Thursday + Saturday hell-or-high-water ironclad workout routine. But at some point, when the habit has formed and we can trust ourselves to not go to Cinnabon instead of the gym, the training wheels need to come off. We need to spice things up before our workouts become uninspired and lifeless.

What habits once served you, before the tables turned and you started serving them? Are there habits you're ready to take the training wheels off of?

PRO #2: Habits allow us to keep pace with the rhythms of daily life. Sometimes our life pace is a little too fast and frenetic, and habits let us coast in ways that let us go with the flow and recharge. Falling into a mindless habit rhythm—like how you make your coffee in the morning or how you drive to work—might be exactly what's needed to get our heads on straight. Being meticulously mindful of the coffee-making moment or fully present for the commute might be a big, stupid ask when systems are already overloaded. Think about your own life rhythms. Where do routines help you—like paying your bills on the first of each month? Are there habits that make sense to glaze over while doing, because too darned much is going on, or are there opportunities to be more thoughtful and tune into your routinized moments?

PRO #3: Habits help us leave room for important things like cognition, emotional responsiveness, and skilled task performance. Sometimes we just need a less preoccupied inner life, and having a routine allows for more efficient outcomes and less nervous breakdowns.

Maybe you've honed your craft of delivering client presentations at work, for example. You're killing it! Clients are loving you! Why fix what isn't broken, right? Of course you're going to keep your supersuccessful presentation process, *for a while*. And yet you see where this is going. We need to be vigilant about habits and routines that start to reach their expiry date. We need to sniff out the rot and proactively freshen up the process before gangrene sets in—because after X number of presentations, you will start to feel mind-numbingly bored. This is why I work with a lot of people, because they didn't get ahead of the gangrene curve. We're allowed to coast, for a while—but as they say, if you're coasting, it means you're going downhill.

What habits and routines allow you to be successful in your life right now? Which one of those might need refreshing *before* they start to perish (i.e., before you get bored)?

That's pretty much it for the good stuff about habits. Now over to the dark side . . .

CON #1: Routine-filled lives can erode our sense of happiness and agency. Routines and habits can put a dent in our satisfaction with life over time, even if they feel good in the moment. There's a natural tension that exists between structure and agency, between habit and choice. We like the safety of guardrails when we're driving, but we also like to be the boss of where we're going when we get in the car. Habits act as helpful guardrails in our lives but can unwittingly make us feel restricted and narrowed with our choices. And here is where our sense of agency finds itself potentially on the chopping block.

When we're at the mercy of the patterns of our lives—absorbed in routinized behaviors without awareness that we're absorbed in the first place—we run the risk of "choice capitulation." At its most banal, this looks like mindlessly reordering our exact same pizza as last time because the delivery app allows us to do so. At its more consequential, this choice capitulation looks like socializing with the same group of friends week after week, even though they might not actually be your ideal crew, spending precious hours of time with people that maybe aren't so additive or uplifting in our lives. Routines can stealthily rob us of agency. Psychology research confirms that the disruption of our habits can helpfully force us to make more intentional choices.

This might seem oxymoronic—because routines are designed to be mindless—but can you become mindful of your routines? What habits are you engaged in that might not be serving you as much as you think they are? What routines are on replay that you might want to throw a wrench into, to make more empowered choices?

CON #2: The irony of comfort zones. We engage in routines that make our lives feel comfortable. The definition of *comfort* is something that elicits a feeling of ease or relaxation. For the record, I love comfort, ease, and relaxation! I am not Lucifer. Oh, how we love our comforting cocoons. But we love comfort zones even when they stop loving us back. In the midst of lives that feel helter-skelter, it's comforting to abide by routines that keep the wheels on the bus.

As snuggly comfy as these habits and routines are, they don't make us feel really *alive* after a while, do they? These lukewarm, monotonous experiences of life might not make us feel like we're deceased either ... but we know we can do better than sleepwalking through our days.

ROUTINES TO ~~LIVE~~ DIE BY:
- ☐ SAME BREAKFAST SMOOTHIE
- ☐ SAME ROUTE TO DAYCARE
- ☐ SAME REPORT UPDATE AT WORK
- ☐ SAME VARIATION OF DATE NITE
- ☐ SAME YOGA-FIT CLASS WEEK AFTER WEEK
- ☐ SAME SATURDAY CLEANING RITUAL
- ☐ SAME SUNDAY SUPPER OPTIONS
- ☐ SAME SAME SAME SAME SAME SAME SAME
- ☐ SLOWLY BUT SURELY GOING INSAME

Our comfort zones become ironic the day they start stifling us. Some of us have a gnawing sense that our comfort zones really aren't all that comfortable anymore anyway, and the difference between Living Like We Mean It and Living Like We're a Wee Bit Dead Inside (remember back from your pre-mortem in chapter 1 (page 18)?) comes down to how much time we loaf in our *dis*comfort zones. "I really should try something different for date night" is what dawns on us, and then seven more date nights pass us by, and we've failed to pizzazz anything up. But habits are tricky because habits are sticky. They're designed to wrap themselves around our lives as they routinize our busy, stressful worlds—so it's hard to unwrap ourselves from the straitjackets that were once such warm embraces. It's up to us to prevent comfort zones from getting a little too handsy and a lot too smothering.

Where might some of your habits be getting a tad clingy? Any routines starting to feel claustrophobic? It might be time to question how comfortable your comfort zones really are as of late.

CON #3: Habits spread like spontaneity-sucking wildfires. Sometimes the spaces in between the routines are meant to be the enriching ones where we suck the marrow out of the bones of our lives, but those moments often get squeezed out in favor of *even more* insidious routines. We can make a habit of having habits.

A busy client used to include healthy and meaningful routines on her weekend mornings (like barre class on Saturdays and church on Sundays), leaving way for what she affectionately referred to as "TBD afternoons" full of the freedom to do whatever urges struck her. I'll never forget one of her texts sent on a Sunday night: SOS: WTF TBD!?!?!? She let Habit Creep happen. How? Gradually, then suddenly.* At first she stopped off at Target after her workout class, just to pick a few things up. Then all of a sudden she was toting laundry detergent and paper towels home every Saturday and (*shriek!*) opening her laptop while she dropped the stuff off, just to check on a few work emails.

What routines and habits are preventing you from living with a little more openness, adventure, and "TBD-ness"? Are you getting to improvise enough in your life, or are you feeling a bit too buttoned-down by routines? Could Habit Creep be infiltrating any parts of your life?

 Coaching Chestnut: Errands Are Errors and Chores Are Bores. It can be so tempting to look at the wide-open expanse of weekend hours and mentally shove all your housekeeping, cleaning, organizing, and so on onto those meeting-free planner pages. But devoting your precious weekend time to the things that drag you down might need a rethink. How can you hoard your most treasured time for well-being boosters? I do not live on Mars; I get that errands need running and that we can't run away from them (for long). What I'm suggesting is that we get creative about completing them

---

* Love that Ernest Hemingway line from *The Sun Also Rises*.

during times that aren't in our designated Prime Living Time. If you crave free Monday nights to ease into the work week, leave Monday alone, Ms. Get 'er Done. If Sundays feel essential to your mental health and you have 950 things that would make you feel alive *other than* tasks and chores, forbid yourself to fill the day with to-dos. It might serve your life better to stuff Tuesday and Wednesday nights with errand-y bullshit if you get a day of saving grace. Food for thought?

CON #4: Routines make time fly. And in our finite number of Mondays, we do not want time to fly, do we? We want the feeling of *more* time to fit more living into our days and weeks and years. Researchers[3] have studied our perceptions of time, and time and time again (bahaha), they find that when we're engaged in routines, time feels like it flies. Speaking of flying... frequent flyers on planes, for example, report "swifter passage of time during flights than did people who fly less often."[*]

In a study[4] conducted at a Club Med resort, guests were asked about their perception of time in the beginning, middle, and end of their beachy vacations. Most people found the *last* part of their vacation zipped by, as they likely settled into "this is the table we sit at each morning for the breakfast buffet" routines of familiarity. Time was perceived to pass slowly at the early stages of a vacation when everything was new and unfamiliar.

Can you think of routines in your life that have you going through the mechanical motions? How do these routines relate to your perception of time? Think of a recent week that felt fairly standard; how did that feeling of time compare to a week or weekend when you tried something new, like meeting a friend at a restaurant in a different part of town?

CON #5: As Aristotle said, we are what we repeatedly do. So let's shine the interrogation spotlight at ourselves (*squint up into the harsh, hot light*). Are we automatons traipsing between the office, the drugstore,

---

[*] Infrequent flyers have the pleasure of a four-hour flight feeling like five.

soccer practice, and a scintillating evening of Apple+ TV...because that's what we do, day in day out, year in, year out? Or are we vitality-filled versions of ourselves, because we've zestified our days and years with routine switch-ups, pattern-breaking excursions, and varied routes?

Our zestiest selves will still have mundane things to do—like completing spreadsheets, picking up the cough syrup, and toting offspring around—but it's an *and* situation, not an *or*. Our vitally alive selves *also* pick up popsicles to eat in the park on a whim after T-ball practice. That version of us is willing to watch a documentary about psychedelics because we'd normally watch a sitcom. That person takes the long way home from work every once in a while, just to see the old neighborhood.

If you are what you repeatedly do, what *are* you? How does that sit with you?

 Coaching Chestnut: How Murderable Are You? We've all seen the *Dateline*-type shows where the guy on death row shares his tricks of the homicidal trade: he'd stalk his victim(s) for a while, get a sense of what time they'd leave their SoulCycle class on Tuesday nights, what Sweetgreen they'd stop in at to pick up their Spinach Florentine Bowl, what route they'd walk home after hopping off the #457 bus, what PJs they'd change into before plopping down to watch HGTV, what time they'd put their mouthguard in to hit the hay with Chuckles the cat.

I haven't seen the studies on this, but a positive correlation surely exists between having a predictable routine and *getting murdered*. Stalked, at the very least. I'm a dick for talking like this, I know, but I ruffle your feathers because I care. Does your daily routine make you easy to stalk? Is your schedule of the rinse-and-repeat type? Would you be a slam-dunk victim?

Diversify your life—not so much because of the unlikely event of being stalked or offed by Jack the Ripper 2.0 but because you very much deserve to live before you die. You deserve to try different workouts, varied routines, new shows, and every now and then the Sweetgreen Shroomami Bowl.

BEDRAGGLED BY BOREDOM

 The average man does not know what to do with his life, yet wants another one which will last forever.

—ANATOLE FRANCE

Habits and routines have smoothed out our lives, sure, yet in all that smoothness things can feel void of texture, feeling, and interest. Airbrushed.

> YOU: Can one lead an astonishing life if it's also airbrushed?
> ME (with body language that involves pursed lips, side-eye, and an unrestrained look of skepticism): Living an airbrushed life is like trying to fit a tombstone-shaped peg into a round hole. I'm sorry, but no.

One way to pursue an astonishing life is to understand what it *doesn't* look like: habitually boring. Boredom is the all-too-common emotion where we feel restless and unchallenged in the midst of purposeless situations. Boredom isn't just dullness with indifference, though; the lack of interest is annoying and nagging, like a three-year-old at the mall.

We can be busy little bees with full schedules that keep us moving but still feel mired in monotony. Said differently, just because you're busy doesn't mean you're not bored. If you looked back on the last week of your life, how many times would you say you felt bored? Was this troubling for you, or did it feel like a nice break in the action?

Sometimes our lives do us the favor of broadcasting SOS calls to break out of our ruts, and the gnaw of boredom is one of those calls. That discomfort we feel is life kicking at us from the inside, insisting that we start living it as it was meant to be lived—even if we're not sure of what that looks like just yet. We just know it's lacking, and we want more. This is one of the most common issues clients come to me for, to help figure out why they feel bored on the inside when they're so freaking busy on the outside.

So what do we need to know about being bored, and how do we unbore ourselves when our lives murmur quietly or declare loudly that they're lackluster and uninspired? Jot down which points below feel particularly resonant or dissonant and why that might be the case for you.

SIX WAYS WE'RE BORING OURSELVES TO ~~TEARS~~ DEATH

1. Gaping self-awareness.

Boredom is a crisis of desire. We need an understanding of what we want, what makes us happy, and what energizes us in order to actually schedule those things into our lives every now and then and burst boredom's bubble. And the first step to having an idea of what we want is to develop self-awareness.

Psychologists[5] highlight that people with greater self-awareness are able to figure out how to satisfy their needs and remedy their boredom, specifically because they can pinpoint what an intrinsic reward might look like or feel like for them.

Some problems are easier to solve than others. Celiac disease? Not supersolvable (*insert a heavy, gluten-free sigh*). Boredom? We can work with that. One of my clients created a Breaking Up with Boredom list with a host of options to fill her "empty evenings." She tried racquetball and hated it. Great! Eliminating options can be instructive. She tried a book club and thought it was "okay-ish." Getting warmer! What clicked for her was starting her own podcast about the love of books. She more than broke up with boredom . . . She divorced it and fell in love with her evenings again.

What was your answer to the Alivealicious Question of "I feel most alive when _____" in the pre-mortem (page 47)? Might you be able to tune into that the next time boredom rears its ugly head? Can you keep a running list of activities to turn to before you start yawning?

2. Social media—enough already, I know.

(*Slow nodding*) It's still true: social media is boring us, and more insidiously, it's making *us* feel boring. Pictures and reels and stories of other people's sand-flea-free vacations and impossibly cool flash mob dances and all-you-can-eat nacho bars make our lives seem drab, unfun, and ruefully short on guacamole.

The members of a women's roundtable group I worked with committed to cutting back on their social media time by 50 percent, and not a single person came back to the next month's meeting in withdrawal. Every single person felt lighter and admitted to using the extra minutes (ranging from fifteen to seventy-five!) in their day for a good cause—like interacting with a friend, walking, reading, stretching, napping, or journaling.

What if you pared your social media time back by 33 percent and replaced it with something that breathed more excitement and life into you? Brainstorm a couple of activities you can turn to instead of scrolling when you feel the inevitable pull to that little icon on your screen.

3. Low...or no flow?

Flow happens when the relationship between skill and challenge in our lives matches up and complements our unique talents. If we're working on things that are too easy, we create the conditions for boredom and disengagement to prosper. If we're working on things that are too challenging for our current skill level, anxiety muscles in.

We know we're in a state of flow when we feel swept up in the thing we're doing...when we lose track of time...when we're anything but bored or tired when we're doing it...when we participate in the activity out of sheer and utter enjoyment (and not just because our boss or parent made us do it). It's up to us to find our flow zones by seeking out work, hobbies, and activities that offer a balance of our abilities with the demands of the task at hand...yet we're curiously lazy about seeking out these opportunities.

Only 16 percent of Americans in one survey reported being swept up in intense flow-like experiences daily, while 42 percent admitted they rarely or never lost track of time while being engaged in an intensely involved activity.[6] Said differently, we are inviting boredom over for a booty call and asking it to stay the weekend.

When was the last time you felt flowy? What activities get you into the revered state of flow? What undertakings challenge you to the brink of your ability?

4. The pesky problem of meaninglessness.

Some characterize boredom as the emotional manifestation of a lack of meaning.* Psychologists[7] call it an "existential vacuum," and it starts

---

* Oh, jeez—that hits hard, right?

with the tiny buds of boredom that grow like weeds into nihilistic despair... distress that can come from a sense of meaninglessness in our lives. We try to fill this existential vacuum with not-so-excellent defense mechanisms or substitutes for purpose—like pathologic shopping, overeating, manufactured drama, excessive TV, doomscrolling... and the list goes on.

One of my clients experienced what's known in existential psychology circles as "Sunday neurosis"—something even scarier than the dread we feel about going back to a less-than-fabulous job on a Monday morning. Sunday neurosis is characterized by that feeling of malaise when the whirlwind of the week is over and we realize we don't have a meaningful way to spend all that free time. "I was doing work on the weekends just to avoid the void," this client admitted. She needed to plug back into purpose. For her this meant looking after herself by hiking new routes in the woods each weekend and preparing nutritious foods to package up and freeze for meals later in the week.

When whatever we're doing in and out of work feels bereft of meaning, boredom's tentacles wrap themselves around our jugulars. Are you feeling connected to your purpose in life... or your purpose for now? Are you willing to take responsibility for your choices, to create a good life? See you in chapter 9 for a meaty discussion about meaning.

5. Giving the Grim Reaper the cold shoulder.

Taking for granted the number of Mondays we have left makes us lose perspective on how precious our time really is. If we knew you were going to buy the farm* twenty-six days from today, for example, would we be bored between now and then? Or would we be sure to stuff in as much meaning and vitality as possible? I'm fairly sure we'd overdose on life in those twenty-six days. It would be a preposterous hoopla—a whirlwind I'm not recommending for everyday living, of course—but it does illustrate the point, yet again, of temporal scarcity from chapter 3, right?

Boredom is the luxury of those who have lost perspective on their impermanence. If we begin with the Big End in mind, we usually snap

---

* Die. Possibly on a farm.

to attention and start participating in the ticking time bomb of our lives, less formulaically and more astonishingly.

Quick check: How many Mondays do you have left as of this moment? Great! Lots of time left to unhabit and unbore.

6. We slipped into autopilot, and now the plane is crashing.

The "last but not least" way we're boring ourselves to death relates to our entire autopilot discussion, since it's the wellspring of boredom. Given our crudely human impulse to Control Absolutely Everything, we reflexively create a matrix of habits—including but not limited to our time, our caloric intake, our finances, our emotions, other people, our pets, and the weather. But are we lost in that matrix, with our eyes all glazed over, swallowing the blue pill?* We all got a hall pass during The Plague of the 2020s . . . but we have to ask ourselves if we're *still* in walking corona-comas?†

 Coaching Chestnut: Quantifying Autopilotitis. In my research I have asked thousands of people, "To what extent is your life on autopilot?"

- 11.4% of survey respondents say, "Ugh—I am basically a highly functioning zombie."
- 42.8% of people say, "Quite a bit of autopilot in my life."
- 37.6% say, "A little autopilot but nothing worrisome."
- 8.3% respond with, "Autopilot? Me? Never."

First question: How would you answer?

Second question: 54.2% of people admit to being in quite a bit or constant autopilot. Should we be more afraid on the roads?

---

* Cue the scene in *The Matrix* where Morpheus says, "You take the blue pill—the story ends, you wake up in your bed and believe whatever you want to believe. You take the red pill—you stay in Wonderland and I show you how deep the rabbit-hole goes."
† And if we're being honest, most of us were in comas before The Plague.

Habits and routines are like makeshift rafts we believe keep us afloat but actually tend to fall apart at the first strong wave. Living in autopilot puts our lives on hold while we wait for the seas to calm down...which we will wait for an eternity to happen. We need to take control of the cockpit before the plane crashes—we need to identify where we're on autopilot and whether it's serving us or sapping the life out of us.

What habit traps are you stuck in? Where might you be in autopilot to your detriment?

AN IMPORTANT DISCLAIMER ABOUT BOREDOM

YOU: Are there times where boredom isn't so bad? I like zoning out sometimes.

ME: I'm right there with you, Zombie Buddy.

While life-infused lives aren't typically riddled with boredom, there is a time and place for the exquisite, just-what-the-doctor-ordered unplug sessions...best done on a beach with a slushy drink in hand. Sometimes boredom provides a restorative break after we've been living at a feverish pitch, verging on crispy-fried burnout. Vegging out on the couch can restore our sense of balance.

Psychologists[8] concede that boredom has been known to motivate us to pursue new goals. I'm imagining every disenchanted-with-work client I've worked with—sick and tired of Doing Nothing Interesting All Day, the repeated doing of nothingness was what led them to reach out for help in the first place. The right speckling of boredom in an otherwise lively life can lift the dam on the flow of our creative juices, too.

"The dose makes the poison,"* right? Everything in moderation, including boredom (and Botox, for some).

So we know that habits and routines are the double-edged swords that can be good for us until they aren't. The flip side of boredom—novelty—is what keeps boredom at bay and is at the core of what makes vitally alive people so decidedly alive. Are you ready? It's time to spice things up.

---

* Paracelsus actually said, "Sola dosis facit venenum," about five hundred years ago.

SHAKING UP THE SNOW GLOBES OF OUR LIVES

 The only difference between a rut and a grave are the dimensions.

—ELLEN GLASGOW

What's a human trying hard to hang on in this world to do? We all need coping mechanisms, and habits are among the most benign in a world where there are a lot of strong drugs out there that'll help "take the edge off." But habits grow weary on us.... They lead to the mind-numbing boredom you now know to be suspicious of. The answer is to mitigate the life-squelching effects of routines with variety and novelty.

We must shake up the snow globes of our lives.

Novelty is the saving grace of a dullingly narrow life. It responds to the basic psychological need[9] we have to experience "newness" and stray from the well-worn paths of our routines.

Research[10] highlights the connection between the amount of new experiences and novelty in our lives and our positive emotional state; the greater the variety in our day-to-day goings-on, the greater the happiness. Cha-ching!

Novelty seeking acts like a booster shot to motivation; the exploration of unfamiliar things jacks up our well-being and helps us function at our best. Variety is more than just the spice of life, though—it slows down the speed on the hedonic treadmill. Say what?

 Positive Psychology Interlude: Running on the Hedonic Treadmill. No, it's not an orgy on the piece of equipment gathering dust in the basement—it's a theory[11] that explains how we reliably adapt to the resplendent things that happen to us. We get accustomed to the things we thought would bring us everlasting happiness ... the high of a mega promotion at work, the glorious sunset over the water, the whirlwind of a new romance, the house with a big! wine! cellar!, the boob job, you name it.

We adapt to what life throws at us predictably and without fail, both the bad and, sadly, the good. Events that were once sources of great enjoyment—or pain—gradually lose their emotional power through repeated exposure and the passing of time. This is a soothing adaptation when things are shit (nice to know that if we're maimed in a shark attack, we'll end up just about as happy as we are today), and it's an off-putting adaptation when we want to hold onto the highs (like if we won the lottery—we'd be floating on air for a few months, buy a gaudy house, and then return to our pre-money-to-burn baselines of happiness). The treadmill of adaptation doesn't slow down, so we need to outsmart it. We need to shake things up. Variety reduces the risk of hedonic adaptation.

SIX "SHAKE SHIT UP" SCOOPS WORTH KNOWING

Now that you've busted yourself for being a routine fiend who may or may not be boring yourself to death, you need an antidote—an ennui elixir of sorts—and I can't make you wait until the chapters to come for solutions. I'm serving you six specially selected scoops (ideas) to help mitigate the impact of habits in your life. See which ideas click for you . . .

Shake Shit Up Scoop #1: Become a Neophiliac

Even if we self-identify as homeostasis lovers who prefer predictable structure, as humans we're driven from the depths of our genetic coding to go after new experiences, challenge ourselves in fresh ways, and explore new ideas, people, and places.

Whether we are *neophilic* (wanting shiny new everythings) or *neophobic* (very much disinterested in trying that newfangled cheese because "cheddar is just fine"), novelty is essential if we want to live the good life. Some of us need and want newness more than others, but research[12] is clear that we all need it; the introduction of novelty in our daily lives adds to our motivation and well-being, regardless of the importance we attach to it.

One of my clients scored low on the "openness to experience" personality trait,* which was made evident every time the business group we were a part of suggested a new location to hold our monthly meetings. "Why can't we just keep the meeting at the same place, with the same sandwiches for lunch?" he'd innocently ask. The group (wisely) insisted on changing the meeting venue for every meeting, which ended up being a good thing for Mr. Closed to New Experiences. After every meeting, he'd come around and admit that he appreciated the different perspectives gained from sitting at a different seat at a different table and that he did, in fact, like the falafel for a change. He would not have initiated the novelty and variety, but when exposed to it, he thrived.

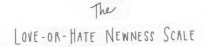

The
LOVE-OR-HATE NEWNESS SCALE

→ "I'M GOOD WITH MY MILD CHEDDAR, THANKS."

"OOOH! BRING ON THAT AGED MIMOLETTE!"

NEOPHOBIC   NEO-NEUTRAL   NEOPHILIC

Where might you plot yourself on this spectrum? Where would you like to be? Even a small nudge over to the neophilic side might infuse more vitality and satisfaction into your life.

Shake Shit Up Scoop #2: Beware the Responsibility Trap

Many of us are reluctant to stir up our routines and lifestyles because "that's not what Responsible Adults do." We succumbed to the belief that novelty is somehow synonymous with irresponsibility, and so we stick to the well-worn paths we've established for ourselves. The only problem is those paths are exactly that: *worn.* As in, worn out.

---

* The classic "Big Five" personality traits in psychology are Conscientiousness, Agreeableness, Neuroticism, Openness to Experience, and Extroversion.

I know of countless clients who've longed to go back to school, try a new job or (*gasp!*) industry, pick up a new hobby, move to a new city or side of the country or (*double gasp!*) new country, get a makeover, you name it . . . and yet they worried incessantly about looking like a bull in the China shop of life. "I went to school to become a nurse; I can't just switch careers and become a graphic designer!" Oh, um, yes, you can. "If we move to San Antonio, what will happen to the kids?" You'll take them with you, and they'll adjust. "I've had my hair like this since college!" *Exactly.*

Novelty and responsibility are not mutually exclusive. Spicing things up doesn't have to mean quitting your job every two years or moving the kids with you across time zones every time the urge strikes (unless you want that for some reason?). You can be Fully Responsible and switch careers. Picking up and moving to Boston doesn't make you reckless. Taking on new projects outside of your "area of expertise" doesn't mean you lack focus. Calling into work to extend your vacation by an unexpected day because you just *had* to stay in Joshua Tree for the full moon—that doesn't (necessarily) make you impetuous. Taking an Intro to Screenwriting class—if you're an accountant—doesn't mean you've lost it. . . . It likely means you've found it. These things reveal that you're interested in living before you die.

We are allowed to change course. We just need to give ourselves permission to do so. Sometimes this means tuning out the voices of people whose opinions might matter a wee bit too much to you. Usually this means thinking about memento mori and imagining getting to the end of it all, wondering how we'd feel about *not* becoming the DJ we've always wanted to be or *not* trying the scary-but-fun-looking dive bar at the edge of town.

What's an example of an idea or goal or dream that's simmering on your insides that you're afraid might look or feel irresponsible to take action on? What permission do you need to give yourself to pursue vitality, meaning, and aliveness? How would you fill out this permission slip to your advantage?

PERMISSION SLIP

I, ———, GIVE MYSELF PERMISSION TO SPICE UP MY LIFE BY: ———

PERMISSION APPROVED TO LIVE IT UP

BY THIS DATE: ———

Shake Shit Up Scoop #3: Novelty Might "Cost" Us Time but Be Worth It in the End

Routines and habits can absolutely save us time—and sometimes we need to adhere to our Tried-and-True Operating Systems to get to work on time and pick the kids up before the late fees accrue. Staying employed and keeping custody of our kids are good things. But this cracks the "saving time vs. enjoying time" debate wide open, and I suggest we pour our favorite drinks while we bandy this topic about.

Are there times when we might be adhering to our time-saving practices, when there might be wiggle room to live a little...with more variety? Sometimes we take the usual route home because it's a mindless choice, a shortcut in the brain that guides us to "do what we always do: turn left at the stop sign." But what if—on a day when we weren't late for dinner—we spiced things up and took a different route? What if we (*brace for impact*) pulled over, parked the car, and walked around the block in a different part of town, imagining what your life might be like if you lived there? What if we went into the impossibly cute health food store and had a green something at the juice bar? Or what if we stopped into a completely random restaurant and ordered takeout for the family, texting them an unrestrained message to be hungry bcos I M bringing home GYROS!!!!!*

Where might it be worth it for you to spend a bit of time to appreciate your time? Are there routines you abide by that would feel initially inconvenient to bust up but worth it in the end?

Shake Shit Up Scoop #4: Traveling, the Fabulous Routine-Wrencher

Oh, what a delightful discombobulation travel provides to our otherwise in-order lives! Vacationing or visiting a new environment upsets the applecart of habits that tend to meld our days together. The jambalaya of new stimuli is what wakes us up from our little vitality slumber sessions in new and unexpected ways.

---

* I really wish there was a gyro emoji.

Of course the bus tour around Montreal and all that poutine and the French language are the more obvious novelty infusers, but let's not overlook the subtler details. It's hard to form a routine after five nights in a hotel room.... It takes three of those mornings just to figure out how to get the shower knobs working just right, let alone how to use the fancy-pants coffee machine. Mild hassles? Sure. Major routine relievers? Absolutely. We need the autopilot reprieve from our back-home-on-the-ranch ways of doing things to feel alive again in both big and underestimated ways. Our brains benefit from novel situations, too; neuroplasticity—our noggin's ability to adapt, change, and grow—can be improved when we enrich our environments.*

The Husband was on a sabbatical for two months in 2021, and I joined him for five of those weeks. Not only did this time off teach me that big blocks of time away from work are Mandatory Living Experiences from Now On†—but that traveling has a profoundly positive snow-globe-shaking impact.

Even if you can't swing five weeks in a row jetsetting across the world, visiting new locations is deliciously disruptive to time. Jarring life with novelty in hotels and Airbnb's and new grocery stores and airports and rental cars can feel like a helpful redirection off whichever path we're wearing thin. And when you return home and resume many of your old habits, there's no reason you can't continue to put a wrench in some of your usual modus operandi ways of living. Why not go out for an early breakfast—*on a workday*? Why not eat dinner in bed, like one does in a hotel with room service? Why not read a novel at lunch? Why not channel the vacation lifestyle a little more into our nonvacation days? Traveling provides infusions of oxygen we often don't know we need and can inspire us to bring some of that oxygen home.

---

* Hot tip: fresh brain cells are what we're after, if we want to stay sharp and remember all the fabulous memories we're making. Let's not let our brain cells get stale.
† I've committed to (somehow) swinging a month off (Yes! Four Mondays in a row!) every couple of years until I retire and/or die, and I'd love for you to (somehow) do that too.

Are there ways you can let your traveling way of being help you shake up your at-home routine so as to inject necessary newness into your life and prolong the passing of time? Are there travel plans on your horizon? Might this make your giant to-do list?

Shake Shit Up Scoop #5: Slow and Steady Wins the Race

Since we know the hedonic treadmill is going to have us work for the rest of our lives to keep things fresh and alive, we do need to exert a modicum of effort to outpace the treadmill and ward off boredom. But that doesn't mean we have to sprint the whole way. We can run our hearts out when we're so inspired, but we can also jog for a bit, walk for a mile, and skip like a kid around one of the blocks if we want to.

Even a small dose of novelty can unbore our lives, and I feel the need for us to share a mutual sigh of relief right here about that. We don't have to fly to far-flung places for Every Single Vacation to earn an "apathy prevention" badge.* We don't have to eat new and exotic cuisines every night for the rest of our freaking lives. We don't have to dizzy ourselves with newness, because too much novelty and variety would be vertigo inducing and therefore counterproductive toward living like we mean it anyway. A consistent, slow drip of novelty can help bring us back to life when we've slipped into catatonic autopilot. We can handle slow drips, right?

 Coaching Chestnut: Determining Your Novelty FITTness Level. My first job out of college was as a personal trainer (yes, that was approximately 126 years ago, and yes, I wore those swishy track suits that were all the rage)—which means I know a thing or two about prescribing ~~burpees~~ life-changing programs to people looking to live even better.

I'd consider the FITT model when designing a workout plan for a client, and we shall do the same now when it comes to thinking of your novelty

---

* Apathy, that indifferent feeling of sluggishness, is the literal opposite of the *flow* concept we've been talking about.

plan. You don't need to *plan the plan* right now (chapter 11 awaits), but consider what strikes you with these reflection questions:

- Frequency: How often do you need/want to shake things up in your life? Does the idea of regular routine busters make you feel nauseated, excite you, or land somewhere in between? Make note.
- Intensity: How vigorously do you need/want to shake up that snow globe of yours? Are you thinking of a mild vibration or more of a tectonic-plate-shifting earthquake? You might find the idea of frequent, mild doses of novelty to be inspiring (like trying a different appetizer before every few dinners out), or maybe infrequent spurts of epic proportions might be more your style (like taking a three-week traipse-across-a-country trip once a year).
- Time: How long do you prefer your novelty interventions to last? You might feel more comfortable with quick bursts of variety (like a one-hour How to Make Tapas class), or maybe elongated durations of novelty floats your boat (like a seven-week course in the art and science of Spanish cooking)? Maybe a mix of short and long engagements?
- Type: What kinds of shake-ups might you want to infuse into your life? Might you need a little "adjusting" in your career, or maybe you want to get creative with your love life instead? You might feel called to spice up your R&R time, or maybe your meals, or even the podcasts you listen to.

Quick note before we move on, in case you feel the need to breathe into a paper bag with the panic of all the ways you think you need to transmute your life: many people need less frequent and intense interjections of novelty than they think to liven up their lives. There is no pressure to Change. Every. Thing. And there are no rights or wrongs when it comes to shaking up the snow globes, as long as a bit of shaking is going on, on the regular. Simply highlight a few areas that spark your curiosity and keep that page handy. You can decide if they make the cut when we get down to the official action-planning time together. Ooh! Speaking of curiosity...

Shake Shit Up Scoop #5: Join the Curiosity Crusade

Novelty is curiosity's fertilizer. Psychological scientists[13] are clear that the more willing we are to adopt a curious, variety-seeking outlook, the likelier we are to flourish.

Researchers[14] have caught onto the notion of "exploration and absorption" as paths toward living like we mean it. *Exploration* is when we follow the breadcrumb trails of things that spark our interest—which can be anything novel (like visiting the recently opened Punk Rock Museum in Las Vegas), challenging (like learning how to play the trombone), or fascinating (like getting lost in an enriching online rabbit hole researching the number of islands that make up the archipelago known as the Philippines*).

Absorption results from full engagement with an activity—like if you get swept off your feet at that Punk Rock Museum, or from those trombone lessons, or learning about new places on earth.

This exploration-absorption tango of curiosity is what adds to our subjective sense of life satisfaction. Are you dancing this dance often enough in your life to ward off boredom and make the most of the novel situations you might find yourself near? Are you curious to find out how curious you are? I think it's quiz time.

Select a number ranging from 1 to 5 for each question in this research-backed Curiosity and Exploration Inventory.[15]

1 = Very Slightly or Not at All; 2 = A Little; 3 = Moderately; 4 = Quite a Bit; 5 = Extremely

1. I actively seek as much information as I can in new situations.
2. I am the type of person who really enjoys the uncertainty of everyday life.
3. I am at my best when doing something that is complex or challenging.
4. Everywhere I go, I am out looking for new things or experiences.
5. I view challenging situations as an opportunity to grow and learn.
6. I like to do things that are a little frightening.

---

* 7,641. Wow, right?

7. I am always looking for experiences that challenge how I think about myself and the world.
8. I prefer jobs that are excitingly unpredictable.
9. I frequently seek out opportunities to challenge myself and grow as a person.
10. I am the kind of person who embraces unfamiliar people, events, and places.

The notion of *Stretching* (covered in items 1, 3, 5, 7, and 9) indicates how motivated you are to pursue new experiences and information. You might have a prolific Google search history, or it might be quite thin.

The notion of *Embracing* (covered in items 2, 4, 6, 8, and 10) reveals your openness to the novel, uncertain, and murky aspects of life. Oh, ambiguity—you're either willing to see it as an adventure or a nemesis.

Where might you need to work on stretching? Or embracing? Did one of the questions nudge you or straight up slap you in the face? That might be worth paying the most attention to.

 Positive Psychology Interlude: "Psychological Richness." Pseudo Spoiler Alert! In the next chapter we'll be talking about widening your life with vitality . . . something known as the *happy life*. Right after that in chapter 9, we'll dig into the deepening of your life with meaning . . . something known as the *meaningful life*. Researchers[16] have recently landed upon another dimension to live "the good life"—something known as the *psychologically rich life*. This rich life is characterized by novelty, curiosity, eventfulness, unexpectedness, complexity, and perspective change (so, everything we have been talking about in this chapter so far). The best part, other than the boredom busting? The psychologically rich life leads to wisdom. Who doesn't want to become wiser?

Large-scale examples of psychological richness include studying abroad, and small-scale examples include participating in a tough escape room with your work team.

Embracing novel and interesting opportunities in life, even if they are challenging, can lead to new ways of seeing the world and ultimately more wisdom. Combining these three dimensions of life together is what well-being scientists believe makes life worth living.

To what extent do you feel your life could be described as full of variety and interest? Are you wrapping your arms around curiosity and spontaneity? Are you entertaining your inquisitive desires to know or learn new things? Might these be areas to explore, in pursuit of a fully rich life... not just a happy and/or meaningful one?

Shake Shit Up Scoop #6: Let's Go on an Adventure!

Like, other than the one we're already on in these pages together? Because maybe the only adventuring we've been doing lately is via other people's escapades on reality TV?

Curiosity urges us to discover, get adventurous, and grow. So let's assume for a moment that we're doing a bang-up job of humoring our curiousness—we've been shifting our attention to the unfamiliar, to things we don't have the answers to already, to surprising delights. Sounds enchanting, right? Now we must ask ourselves if we're willing to take our curiosity to the next level... if we're willing to Do Something with our piqued interest. Are we willing to go on an adventure? Adventures, plural? Adventures as a regular occurrence in life?

I find myself yearning for something I can't quite put my finger on, usually in the evenings after boredom has joined my TV-watching party on the couch. Sometimes it feels like a desire to go out—and not in a do-my-makeup kind of way. More of a get-outside-and-see-the-stars kind of way, more of a walk-through-the-woods-at-night kind of way, maybe hear a wolf howl in the distance—that kind of thing. But the barriers are too great: we don't live near the woods, and I don't know where they even are; our 9:05 p.m. bedtime might be in jeopardy if we did drive out to a forest and then all the way back home; and I'm 650 percent certain I'd be murdered in the woods anyway. (I watch enough true crime shows to know how things go down in heavily wooded areas past sundown.) So I stay inside on the couch and go to bed, on time.

What I'm longing for is an adventure, and I'm thinking you have an inkling of what I'm talking about.

Life can be a series of glorious adventures or a monotonous bore.* I shall serve you a host of adventure-inducing options in our "paint-by-numbers" chapter 10, but for now, your job is to get self-aware and start to brew up some ideas. To what extent are you shunning vs. flirting with risk? What is your appetite like for adventure as of today? Is there room for more exciting or remarkable experiences? Write down a few ideas of what adventures might fit into your life.

 Avoiding danger is no safer in the long run than outright exposure. Life is either a daring adventure or nothing.
—HELEN KELLER

ENOUGH SHAKING SHIT UP. SHOULD WE HARK BACK TO YOUR REGRETS?

Oh, that's absolutely what we should do.

Can I ask you to flip back in your notebook to the page(s) where you identified your regrets-in-the-making—after imagining yourself reclined on your hypothetical deathbed? Yes, that list.

Are you able to connect the dots of novelty to any of your regrets a-brewing? For example, if you noted that you'd regret "not getting to Cinque Terre in Italy" (OMG I'd regret that too—should we go together?), might that indicate either a need for novelty or a solution that novelty could provide? If your deathbed regret list included "not going back to school," could that be an indication that you're in need of a snow globe shake-up to feel like you're learning and growing again, or that a shake up could be just what you need to solve the "bored with what I already know" dilemma?

I ask you these questions to hopefully highlight the crucial role that novelty can play in your astonishing life. Maybe an idea has bubbled up about an action you'd like to take? Note it! Highlight it! Circle it! We'll come back to it soon.

---

* I suppose there is a middle ground here, but hyperbole has a nice way of making a point.

AN IMPORTANT "ROUTINES VS. RITUALS" DISCLAIMER

YOU: Is there room for special stuff, like family traditions, or do I need to abolish all of our holiday celebrations from now on?

ME: Oh jeez—Christmas is definitely not canceled. I might've come on a bit strong with this Assassinate Your Habits message. There is a special place in a special life for special rituals.

Jan Stanley, a professional celebrant who specializes in the use of ceremony and secular ritual to help people find meaning and joy in their lives, is what I refer to as a Crackerjack Ritual Wizard. (She was also my thesis adviser in grad school, so she "gets" the memento mori ethos, and I knew her input would be on point.) Here's what she had to say about the difference between automated routines vs. rituals:

- The goal of ritual is to amplify what matters most to us. Wedding rituals are a "life milestone" example. Daily examples might be more like a gratitude practice or setting aside time every day to call a friend.
- We perform habits without intention (at least once they take hold) or thought, while rituals work best when we bring full presence to the experience.
- Habits are more transactional. Rituals can be more transformational as they connect us to what's important in our lives and help us to pause and experience them more deeply.

The difference between routines and rituals comes down to intention and awareness. How deliberate are we when we go through the motions of our tried-and-true routines? We're not so intentional, aware, or attuned into the moment when we're scarfing back a bowl of Honey Nut Cheerios while scrolling through the morning news, for example.

Rituals flip the routine script. They reflect conscious thought processes before, during, and after the experience, and they're rife with values, meaning, and symbols—not necessarily of the religious or spiritual sort. Thanksgiving dinner, for example, is an important yearly ritual for many families. It might involve special table settings, a prayer or sharing of gratitude before dinner, a hushed turkey-carving ceremony, Aunt Ginny's famous candied yams, and ~~passive aggressive bickering~~ a fun-loving flag football game in the park.

One of my client's most treasured times of day is her afternoon teatime. For most of us our caffeine fix is a mindless, vacant-eyed experience, but she couldn't be more plugged into this ritual-not-to-be-confused-with-a-routine. She puts thought into what cup and saucer to use (she's British, so she absolutely uses a saucer), deliberates what kind of tea to make each day, sets her table

RITUALS:
INTENTIONAL PRACTICES, ABOVE GROUND
CUSTOMS, CEREMONIES,
MEANINGFUL, BONDING,
MINDFUL, SPECIAL, SACRED

RIP ROUTINES

ROUTINES + HABITS:
MINDLESS, ZOMBIE GESTATION,
LOOKING DOWN THE BARREL
OF DEATH   6 FEET UNDER

with care as the water boils, and takes deep, cleansing breaths as the tea steeps. Pouring the tea is ceremonious for her: "It has become meditative. I watch for the right color, I anticipate the flavor, I notice the smell—is the tea floral today? Woody, maybe? I appreciate the entire experience. It gives me a chance to pause in my busy day and focus on this tradition that goes back for centuries across different cultures."

Beware the habitual ritual! When the rituals that were once special and meaningful start to feel washed-up and boring, that might be a good time to stir things up a bit. We don't have to forgo the sacred things—like if I didn't get my mom's Betty Crocker lemon bundt cake for my birthday when I was a kid, shit would have gone down—but we can spice things up for good well-being measure. Maybe we plan a plot twist for the holidays one year, like going to a Chinese buffet with the whole darned family and then coming home to a tradition-filled evening. Maybe we fly away for New Year's and do the midnight kiss in the middle of a street in San Francisco. Same rituals, different environments.

Are there rituals in your life you want to tune into even more so and savor? Are there rituals with a fine layer of dust on them that you might want to freshen up?

A SMORGASBORD OF INSPIRING LIFE REFRESHERS

Your habits might be hanging on for dear life, and in a way we should respect them for their death grip, yes? But fuck them. They are leeching your aliveness, and you haven't made it to chapter 7 just to go through the motions.

Variety, as they say, is the spice of life. So here are ideas, from real live people in my workshops, on ways to refresh your days and weeks:

- "I am doing the crossword for a change, and when I get bored of that, I'll move to another brain game"
- "Breakfast for dinner!"
- "I'm following different people on Instagram, and it's fascinating to learn about others' lives (and pets)"
- "I am listening to podcasts instead of music on my walks and switching up the genres"
- "I used to eat so many interesting, healthy foods and strangely forgot about them, so I'm having stuff like rainbow chard again"
- "I switch the kinds of books I read, so I try a biography, then an essay collection, then a spy story"
- "I'm using my mother's old cookbook and am making some of her old classics—it's fun to eat memories and reminisce about her and my childhood"
- "I insist that we change seats around the dining room table every night"
- "I sometimes mix up my get-ready routine, like by brushing my teeth before showering or eating first and then getting ready"
- "When we go out to dinner, we'll make sure to try a new place in a new part of town every other time or so"
- "I've been wearing brighter colors than I normally would, and people are complimenting me for it"
- "I'm letting my husband plan this spring break vacation; I told him to keep it a secret, so I don't know what to expect"
- "I am talking to different people around the office, which has been cool because I usually just mingle with my team or people on my floor"

- ☠ "I hired a trainer at the gym to try the things I'd never do on my own, like boxing"
- ☠ "I told my family I was going to a silent retreat over Thanksgiving and that they could order takeout turkey from Whole Foods"
- ☠ "We are trying to save money, so my husband and I issued a challenge to one another to use all the food in our cupboards and freezer for our meals, without spending a dime on groceries for two weeks"
- ☠ "I am having lunch outside every day"
- ☠ "Two words: open marriage"
- ☠ "I asked my friends with different backgrounds if they could take me to their religious services"
- ☠ "We started listening to eclectic music in the mornings as we get ready for the day"
- ☠ "I am swimming at night before bed a few nights a week, instead of first thing in the morning, and the experience feels so different"
- ☠ "We usually order Chinese food on Saturdays, and we've committed to switching it up a couple times a month"
- ☠ "My weekend routine is so boring, so I am turning it upside down—laundry can wait until the workweek, and Sundays are all about visiting museums and galleries and antique stores"
- ☠ "We have so many spices in our kitchen, and I'm using them in new recipes every couple of weeks"
- ☠ "I booked a trip to a national park when normally I'd choose a more luxurious urban vacation"
- ☠ "I'm a huge pessimist, so I'm imagining what situations would look like if I was a glass-half-full kind of person"
- ☠ I could keep going, but we all have things to do.

THE ANTI-AUTOPILOT ASSESSMENT

It's time to complete the Anti-Autopilot Assessment! This exercise will help you zero in on the ways you might be dulling your senses and see where that "shroud of familiarity" might be robbing you of vitality. There are quite a few questions (okay, there are fifty-two of them, but you are a champion and I believe in you), so cozy up to it, complete the reflection assignment at the end of it, and see where you want to add more novelty to your days.

#	Mark the box that most closely matches the statement that sounds like you as of today.	Yes!	Sort of	Sort of	Yes!	
1	I love my routines and habits; they give me comfort and control in a world that is so often careening out of control.					Routines and habits stifle my soul. Following a set pattern is an assault to my sensibilities.
2	My morning routine is set in stone; it would be weird for me to mix up exactly when I brush my teeth, for example.					I shake things up every morning. Sometimes I brush my teeth in bed just because.
3	Breakfast is exactly the same each day, and at the same time—naturally.					Breakfast? Cheerios one day, western omelets the next, sometimes even No Breakfast, or breakfast for dinner.
4	I take the same route to work / whatever activity I embark upon each day.					No two routes to work are ever the same; I'd be a hard person to stalk.
5	My morning coffee/drink ritual is something I could do blindfolded because it never changes.					My morning coffee/tea/smoothie/ juice-of-the-moment routine isn't a routine because I'm always trying new bevvies and locations.
6	My conversations with the "regulars" in my life are similar from day to day (the weather, what you did last night, when the report is due, etc.).					My conversations with the "regulars" in my life wildly vary, because I bring different kinds of topics up (global warming, the best burritos in town, etc.).
7	I tend to talk with the same people each day, without a lot of new characters entering the scene.					I interact with a lot of different people each day and have a lot of varied conversations with different people about different things.
8	My work is down to a science; it's a system I've mastered and then replicate daily.					My work is like an Etch-a-Sketch . . . Shake it up, and it's different each day.
9	I don't really get to innovate at work.					Creating, innovating, and trying new things out are what my job is all about.

		Yes!	Sort of	Sort of	Yes!	
10	The way I show up at work—like my interaction style and team approach—is predictable and consistent, like in meetings and in projects.					At work, I play different roles to gain and offer different perspectives; in some meetings I'll play the devil's advocate role, and sometimes I stay quiet to observe.
11	Lunch is predictable for me; I might rotate between a few options, and it's always at the time I like.					Lunch? Roll the dice. Different daily, although it usually does happen between 11:00 and 3:30, so is that a habit?
12	Going out with friends means we meet at the same place and order the same appetizer and the same drink. That's what friends are for.					Going out with friends means that every event is different, including the restaurant. Friends don't let friends get boring.
13	I haven't met a new person (that I could call on and have them remember me) within the last month.					I regularly add new people to my life, as friends or professional acquaintances.
14	When in a cab or rideshare, I ride in peaceful quiet.					When in a cab or rideshare, I chat it up with the driver and learn about them, their background, favorite restaurants, etc. Or I pool with others to meet new people!
15	I have a signature drink and stick to it.					I'm the one who tries the new cocktail or crazy craft beer with the trendy name.
16	I know what I like at restaurants and seek it out again and again. They sometimes know my order when I walk in the door.					I rarely order the same thing twice when I go out to eat.
17	Date night is highly ritualized with specific variables—like whether to order in or out and watch the movie or the new thing on Netflix.					Date night is mysterious.... We never know what we're going to do until 6:59 p.m.
18	Under the proverbial covers, things are predictable. Pleasing, yet predictable.					Under the proverbial covers, the covers get thrown off the bed with zest.

		Yes!	Sort of	Sort of	Yes!	
19	Dinner rotates between the same trusty options: the chicken dish, that red sauce thing, the two order-in options, and a couple others.					Dinner can be an adventure with so many cuisines and spices and recipes available to me.
20	My workouts are totally structured; I do the same stretches, for example, because they work just fine.					My workouts—and my stretches—are like snowflakes. . . . No two are the same.
21	Raising kids goes better with routine, structure, and habit formation.					Raising kids would be best done in the wild, with the sunrise and sunset as the basis of our routines.
22	The person who cuts my hair doesn't have to ask what I want when I sit in the chair; I've had the same 'do for decades.					My hairstyle changes with the seasons.
23	My style has stood the test of time; I buy the same wardrobe staples, styles, and colors.					My personal style is best described as "metamorphosizing."
24	My couch and chair and side table are just fine where they are, as are the pictures on the wall.					I'm always rearranging the furniture—at least the knickknacks.
25	I keep a happy homeostasis in my environment, like keeping the air and water temperature and the lighting just-so.					I thrive in a changing environment; I sometimes take cold showers just to feel something different.
26	I keep my smartphone with me, and on, at all times.					I often leave the phone behind, so I'm off the grid, even when I'm technically still *in* the grid.
27	I haven't had an outdoor excursion in the last six months.					I've had a notable outdoor experience in the last six months (like camping, taking a long hike, going on a ski trip, etc.).
28	I like to stick to the walking route in my area that gets me from point A to B.					I explore new routes in my area— walking down alleys, checking out new construction sites, going out of my way to see something new.

		Yes!	Sort of	Sort of	Yes!	
29	My leisure time tends to be repetitive; I do the same things in the same ways (like walk the same path in the art gallery).					My leisure time is like a cloud—always changing, morphing, and creative.
30	I pretty much have the same hobbies as I did this time last year.					I've introduced a new hobby within the last year—and have more on the docket to try.
31	I stick to the books, movies, and TV shows that I know I'll like; why read mysteries when I know I like biographies?					I try new genres of movies, books, TV, etc. all the time; I'm always listening to a new podcast.
32	I watch more than an hour of TV a day.					I watch less than an hour of TV a day.
33	The Internet allows me to shop, waste time, and get answers quickly; it's not an "experience" for me to use it.					The Internet is an exploration tool for me where I benefit from learning and growing after each session I'm sucked into.
34	I like my usual rotation of radio stations / music choices, thank you very much.					I listen to new music regularly, even in languages I don't understand.
35	I can't think of anything zany or childlike that I've done within the last year—although there was that one time I was caught in the rain without an umbrella for a block.					I've done something childlike in the last year, like jump on a trampoline, skip, or start a food fight.
36	I am happy with what I know and what I do right now; I don't need to discover new things.					I make it a priority to discover new things regularly; I wish there was a new continent out there for me to discover.
37	My bedtime ritual rivals my morning one in that it's militantly set in stone.					Getting ready for bed looks different every night; some nights I even sleep on the *other side of the bed*.
38	I have a patterned weekend routine that ensures everything gets done: groceries, laundry, workout, dry cleaning, kids' parties . . . *check!*					My weekends are quite flexible; I mix things up and sometimes kick errands into the next week.

		Yes!	Sort of	Sort of	Yes!	
39	My calendar for the next few months looks fairly repetitive with the last few months.					My calendar for the next quarter bears no resemblance to the last three months.
40	My daily schedule is set in stone.					I switch my schedule regularly, like going to work at 7:00 a.m. instead of 9:00 a.m. It's like a different world at that time.
41	My beliefs have all stayed intact within the last year; nothing has caused me to reevaluate and edit what I believe to be true.					I changed a belief within the last year because of new information or a new perspective I adopted.
42	Traveling can be stressful because it's a real routine buster, but I develop a routine while away to make it more comfortable.					Traveling means drinking from the firehose of a new culture; I take it all in and make sure every experience is unique.
43	When I like a place I travel to, I tend to go back there to experience even more of it.					The world is too big to go back to the same city in Italy or Iowa twice, even if it was spectacular the first time.
44	The festive holidays happen like clockwork; I know what's happening and when and what the side dishes are.					The festive holidays *are* festive because they unfold so serendipitously.
45	I don't really do the New Year's resolution thing or make goals for the year ahead.					I set ambitious goals and intentions each year.
46	I have ideas of what I want to do before I die, but there's still time, so I don't need to take action just yet.					I have a bucket list, and I'm steadily chipping away at it. Life's getting lived around here.
47	Time is flying by at an exponential rate.					Time isn't exactly standing still, but I feel like I'm able to harness it.
48	Spontaneity gives me hives.					Structure gives me a rash.
49	Curiosity did, in fact, kill the cat.					Knowing what I already know—and leaving it at that—feels suffocating, but curiosity adds oxygen to my life.

		Yes!	Sort of	Sort of	Yes!	
50	I sometimes feel like my life is like the movie *Groundhog Day*...the same day played out, day after day (but without Bill Murray).					I feel like I'm living a different life every day, since they're all so different.
51	I might be missing out on some parts of life, even if I'm not sure what those parts are.					"Carpe the f out of this diem" is my life motto, and I *am* making the most of each day.
52	I sometimes yearn for a new way of doing things, in some parts of life, just to spice things up.					I sometimes yearn to adhere to a routine, in some parts of life, just to automate things a bit.

Making Sense of This Anti-Autopilot Assessment

1. What was it like to complete this questionnaire?
2. What observations are most prominent about your answers?
3. Are there any areas where you feel inspired to build more novelty into your life? Make note of these areas below and what you might feel inspired to do to add more spice into your life.

#	AREA OF LIFE I'D LIKE TO BUILD MORE NOVELTY IN...	IDEAS (BIG, SMALL, IN-BETWEEN)

4. Are there areas where you want to add more routine and structure into your life? Make note of these areas below and what you might feel inspired to do to add more order into your life.

#	AREA OF LIFE I'D LIKE TO BUILD MORE ROUTINE AND STRUCTURE IN...	IDEAS (BIG, SMALL, IN-BETWEEN)

5. Where are you the most defensive about your routines? If you're feeling particularly rigid about an area, I encourage you to consider that might be just the spot you want to unpack first. Again—this isn't about abandoning all the habits that keep your life or family engine running. It's about the subtle tweaks that have the potential to add even just the smallest amount of life back into you.

6. Pick one thing to do between now and next week, and revel in your aliveness.

7. Go eat a brownie.

AN EXPOSÉ ON YOUR HABITS AND ROUTINES

It's the last notebook moment of the chapter, and I think you're ready for an exposé. You've been simmering in your habits for this entire chapter, and you're likely feeling itchy with ideas.

- ☠ Make a list of the habits and routines that exist in your life. Use the Anti-Autopilot Assessment as a prompt for ideas to make the list rich and robust.

- ☠ Identify whether each habit is a good thing in your life, a combo, or maybe worth revising. For example, weekly Friday date night might be a good habit to stay connected to your partner, but having the same Margherita pizza and 7:00 p.m. movie week after week might need a pick-me-up.

- ☠ Your next challenge is to identify a routine rumpler for each habit. How can you take an existing routine and infuse novelty into it? How might you mix things up for each one of those habits?

- ☠ On the topics of curiosity and adventure, how might you explore uncharted terrain? What can you do that's unpredictable? Is there some way to differentiate this week from the one before it and the one that looms ahead?

💀 While there isn't a scintilla of pressure to Get Going on any of these ideas right now, is there *one* notion that has emerged from your notes worth taking action on this week, in advance of our official action-planning-to-come? Do it if the spirit moves you.

Look at us—we made it through the Total Fucking Downer chapters together! We had to drag our limp bodies through all that death talk, all those regrets, and these life-draining habits to really hit rock bottom. We had to suss out where we've been unwittingly murdering ourselves, selling our lives short, living small, sliding down the slippery regrets-in-the-making slope, and habitually boring ourselves. It wasn't easy, but nowhere did I ever say—even in the fine print in the copyright page that no one reads—that it would be a walk in the park. But look how proud we can feel with how hard we've worked! We had to learn not just where things have fallen flat but how to better position ourselves to live like we mean it, minus all those mind-numbing habits. The good news is that the tide is turning with our remaining chapters (with the unwavering help of memento mori), to focus on the living. Because what we're after is aliveness, right?

In a reality where most of us are aching to feel acutely alive—in anti-autopilot mode—can we really afford to let a precious day go by without paying attention to it? Without throwing a wrench in our mechanical motions every now and then? Without getting curious? Without doing something simple and silly (like having breakfast fondue instead of the same-old, same-old), just to make the day stand out amid a calendar of 365 glommed-together days?

Our lives are an assemblage of minutes and hours and Mondays, and what we do or don't do with them is up to us. We can choose the unconventional option.... We can take the road less traveled.... We can do things that make us feel alive, using novelty to our advantage.

Habits, left unchecked, will govern and mummify our lives. We must de-mummify ourselves! If we don't pay attention to our slumbering existence, then the lives we lead won't be too far off from the deaths we'll die. We only die once.... Let's not die bored.

CHAPTER 8

LIVING WIDER WITH VITALITY: FUN + PLEASURE + JOIE DE VIVRE

 People say that what we're all seeking is a meaning for life. I don't think that's what we're really seeking. I think that what we're seeking is an experience of being alive, so that our life experiences on the purely physical plane will have resonances with our own innermost being and reality, so that we actually feel the rapture of being alive.

—JOSEPH CAMPBELL

Now that we've scrutinized all the ways you've been killing your vitality (who knew regrets and habits and routines were so mortally insidious?), it's time to fix that shit up!

This chapter has your name written all over it if you find yourself in one of these camps:

A. You're feeling a little bedraggled in the life department. You've lost that lively feeling* and now find yourself bored, humdrum, and spiritless, just going through the motions in your life. No one has accused you of being "fun" lately.

B. You're the "suck all the marrow out of life" kind of person, and while you're ~~annoying~~ inspiring everyone in the wake of your new recipes and travels and articles and hard-to-pronounce new workouts, you're always clamoring for more ways to feel alive.

---

* One might say your life is on life support?

C. You're somewhere in between flatlining and all-hopped-up-toddler-in-a-candy-store. Some days are more vivacious than others, and you're curious about this "rapture of being alive" idea from Joseph Campbell's most excellent quote above; you think you want a piece of that.

I'm pretty sure I've captured all of us? That was my intention because everyone's invited to the Vitality Bonfire Party!

Yes, we are gathered around the brightly burning flame called *vitality* in this chapter. We're here to metaphorically widen your life at this campfire full of sparks, starting with an awareness boost about what it really means to feel vitally alive and why it matters. We'll then talk about ways the flames of vitality within you get doused (so, what to definitely *not* do) and practical ways to fan the flames of your fieriness for life (so, what to definitely *do*). Our goal is to get you more than a little hopped-up on life, sure, but mostly walking away with an Inspiration Inventory—a range of possibilities that might make the cut in your One Hell of a Life Action Plan at the end of this book.

I encourage you to get on theme with vitality while reading this chapter...whatever makes you feel festive. Maybe skip the party hat (especially if you're sneak-reading this from your desk at work), but put on your favorite life-affirming soundtrack, wear something colorful,* put out the Skittles, sniff around the bar cart, and let's get this bonfire going.

LIVING WIDER WITH VITALITY

You make your life wider when you stuff it with vitality and zest—expanding the breadth of the fun, the pleasure, all the experiences that life has to offer.

Think of this on a horizontal scale that ranges from being in a Netflix coma on one end (blasé, listless, and eerily zombie-like), all the way over to winning the "A+ Participant in Life" ribbon on the other end (exuberant, playing all out, sampling the full smorgasbord of life's pleasures, every-day-is-a-freaking-carnival!). Flashback to the Astonishingly Alive Zones from chapter 2:

---

* I might get unruly and wear gray instead of black.

VITALITY/WIDTH

Vitality is officially defined as a positive sense of aliveness and energy. Some call it our "health of spirit," which has an undeniably nice ring to it. Who doesn't want a healthy spirit? Vitality has also been described as:

- Zest (a resounding interest in and experience of vitality),
- Psychological energy (a resource we can harness for valuable action),
- Vigor (the interconnected feelings of cognitive liveliness, emotional energy, and physical strength),
- Engagement (the potent cocktail of vigor, dedication, and absorption),
- Exuberance (joy's more energetic cousin),
- Thriving (the marriage made in heaven of vitality and learning), and
- Passion (which some say is a survival mechanism that keeps us interested in life).

East Asians refer to vital force or spirit as "chi," and the Japanese describe ki as a "fervor of vitality" . . . also known as the energy it takes to boil the lid off the top of a pot of cooking rice. Do you have enough ki to boil the lid off your proverbial pot? Our mission is to generate a lid-popping fervor for life in you.

OMG THERE IS RICE EVERYWHERE

WHY VITALITY IS WORTH CARING ABOUT, A LOT

Why do we need to prioritize vitality and zest in our lives? Why prioritize vitality over any other noble "live the good life" thing to do, like making meaning or fastidiously filling out a gratitude journal every night? Because vitality plays a massive role in boosting our well-being, in creating a life worth living.

Embarking upon life wholeheartedly with anticipation and excitement, as though it was an adventure ... this approach to living with zesty enthusiasm and energy predicts overall life satisfaction,[1] work satisfaction, and the belief that our work is a calling.

Turkish researchers[2] went through the statistical gymnastics to confirm that subjective vitality acts as the tide that lifts the boats of our subjective happiness:[*] raise your sense of aliveness, and rise with the tides of happiness; ignore your vitality, and get shipwrecked in a low tide of unhappiness and misery. This subjective feeling of aliveness is a big deal for our personal well-being, because the polar opposite sure ain't good ... that subjective feeling of *deadness*.

Zest-filled people are also more likely to believe their lives are meaningful. When we're operating in high-vitality mode, we're more productive, more active, and perform better and with more persistence. Israeli graduate students were surveyed[3] over two different time intervals about creative work involvement and feelings of vitality, revealing that employees with high vitality generate more creative thoughts and contribute more innovative solutions to problems.

The Bridge to Life Satisfaction

You remember Dr. Martin Seligman—Mr. Positive Psychology?[†] Marty has a strong opinion about zest. He's clear from his research[4] that zest is one of the character strengths most highly linked to life satisfaction.[‡] Having recently turned eighty, he's also self-aware enough to know he's not as zesty as he once was. "I just don't have the same kind of vitality and stamina for intellectual things that I did thirty years ago," he told me in a

---

[*] FYI, in the Deep Underbelly of Psychology, the constructs of vitality and happiness are quite distinct, so researchers get persnickety about measuring them in detail through subjective assessments.

[†] The OG!

[‡] Character strengths are positive traits associated with our personalities that influence how we think, feel, and act.

recent Zoom catch-up and then added that his antidote was a hobby that sparks vital aliveness in him: international bridge.

Of course I had to ask what that was about, why bridge brought the youthful zest out of him. He explained, "I'm still improving at bridge. [I'm] at the bottom of the one thousand best bridge players in the world, and I'm moving up and learning more." In other words, participating in activities that challenge us can spark zest and then lead to happiness. Sounds like vitality is a winning hand if we're after lives worth living.

 Positive Psychology Interlude: Zesty Happiness. The character strengths most frequently correlated with life satisfaction are zest, hope, gratitude, love, and curiosity. To what extent do you demonstrate these strengths?

THE HIGHLY SCIENTIFIC VITALITY SPECTRUM

Vitality isn't a fixed disposition; we have the ability to change it.[*]

Let me tell you about a recent client who gave the "all work and no play" ethos a run for its money. I'll never forget what she asked in our first session after we dug into her various work achievements: "Where am I in all of this?" Caught up in the accomplishment juggernaut, she devoted quality time and energy to work—which was fortunately quite fulfilling—but at the expense of other areas in her life. She had lost herself in her career and simply wasn't having fun anymore. She found herself worried about her loss of self, fearful that she had become permanently one-dimensional. How could she spark the fervor of vitality?

One small step at a time. First, she bought a sketch book and started drawing a few times a week, after decades of casting the interest aside. She started taking walks at night instead of watching TV. She made special playlists with her favorite music and started dancing in her living room at night when no one was watching, noting how much she "used

---

[*] This is great news for all of us: the zestless can get zesty, and the already-zesty can get even zestier.

to love to dance." She actively created joie de vivre, with a small bit of intention that grew like a wildfire of life.

Research[5] indicates that fewer than one in five US adults reports high levels of vitality. How do you measure your vitality? Are you living the full width of your life? Where would you plot yourself on this Highly Scientific Vitality Spectrum?

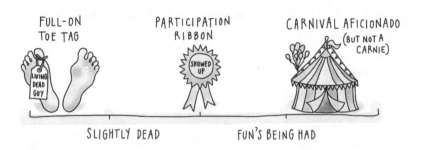

Before you answer, I want to tell you about a client "from toe-tag to riches" story. In our initial sessions together, this client assessed his life on the vitality spectrum above. Like most people, he liked a lot of his life, but there was a glaring area of deadness that was draining his vitality. His career was wearing a toe-tag. He didn't expect every part of his life and job to be like a day at the carnival, but he became startlingly aware (that visceral can't-turn-back type of awareness) that something needed to change with his work, or his work would change him.

So he breathed life into his life again. He zeroed in on where his vitality was lacking, evaluated his options, and made a decision to live rather than settle. In his case, he took time away from work to regenerate some excitement through an eight-week cooking course in Tuscany. Not everyone can afford to press the pause button when work starts sucking, I know, but we all have the option to initiate change in service of letting our respective pots of rice bubble over. Maybe booking a one-week trip to Tuscany would allow for a sufficient boost in vitality for you—while remaining gainfully employed? If a trip isn't in the cards, what about scheduling a local cooking class? What about talking to a career coach about your career conundrum? Or initiating an invigorating project at work, to break out of your rut? Or applying for a completely different role that makes your heart beat fast with electric excitement? Vitality is available to us on any budget.

There are degrees of vitality, as we'd expect—something like the spectrum I doodled for you earlier. Just because we're alive, it doesn't mean we're thriving—as any one of us can attest after a series of ho-hum weeks of work that pass us by, consumed with the angst that the better versions of our lives are out there somewhere (but just not here, now). The psychologists Richard Ryan and Christina Frederick[6] developed the *Subjective Vitality Scale* to help us determine if our health of sprit is alive and kicking or digging its own grave.

Consider the adapted questions below and see how you'd answer on a scale of 1–5, with 1 being "Dear God, No" and 5 being "Hell, Yeah!" Ready? Have at it:

#	Subjective Vitality Question	1	2	3	4	5
1	I feel alive and vital					
2	Sometimes I feel so alive I just want to burst					
3	I have energy and spirit					
4	I look forward to each new day					
5	I nearly always feel alert and awake					
6	I feel energized					
7	I embark upon life wholeheartedly with anticipation and excitement, as though it is an adventure					

Well? Are you alive? And if so, how vitally alive are you?

Now, I know magazine quizzes are way more fun than scientific scales like the one above: in magazines you get amusing answers like "your spirit animal is an iguana" that steer important life decisions. With scientific scales, you won't get a spirit animal. . . . You have to do the heavy lifting and reflect on your answers. But . . . science is a little more, um, empirically legit . . . and since we're talking about *the rest of our lives* here, it might make sense to stick to the proven path of success instead of iguana folklore. So let's reflect: What did your answers reveal to you?

If you answered with a bunch of 3s, you might be feeling decidedly average, dull, and flat. More 1s and 2s indicate some early onset rigor mortis, while a pile of 4s and 5s look like life's getting lived with gusto.

Maybe one question felt like it exposed some necrotic tissue (a hideous metaphor but undeniably apt). You can avoid the dying part of you for a little while, but in my vast medical-drama TV-watching experience, gangrene sets in fast if you don't heal the wound in a hurry. We really must address the parts of you that are dying inside.

For example, if question #4, about "looking forward to each new day," feels rotting and dead, what does that say? Might you need to explore different career options, because *you are allowed to change your career if it's killing you*!? Let this be a vehement encouragement to craft a career (and life) you look forward to waking up for. Please highlight this in all the colors, so it stands out when we get to the action-planning stage.

Maybe question #7 (the one I flagrantly added in of my own volition) caught your eye because you're yearning for an adventure and haven't added too many stamps to your passport in recent years. You're not alone. Like we spoke about in our habit and routine discussion, we can get you in adventure mode, right? We can give you permission to embark on mini adventures (like walking in the rain without an umbrella, pulling out your old Rollerblades, trying Ecuadorian food for the first time . . . you get the idea). We can also get you signed up for bigger adventures like booking that trip to Thailand, registering for that try-a-tri program, or going on a backcountry camping trip, because that might be just what it takes for you to feel astonishingly alive.

Now that you've identified a few cadaverous areas, you might be wondering how to boost your vitality. Let's tackle the "How do I slide myself over to the carnival side of the Highly Scientific Vitality Spectrum?" question in two ways. Up first: what not to do. Followed closely by: what to do.

THE TOP SIX THINGS THAT ARE SNUFFING THE VITALITY OUT OF YOU

Let's be clear on a few things first. I commit every crime on the following list, and often. I say this because I don't want to sound all preachy, like I've got this vitality thing *nailed* and the rest of you are the pitiful walking dead. I suffer from vitality snuffing, and so I research this stuff to help myself first and then come bearing gifts for you to liven things up in your life, too.

This list might irritate you, and if it does, that's good, because it just means we've hit a nerve. You can ignore it and limp along (like trying to ignore sciatica: good luck!), or you can add it to your "Things I Might Want to Do to Widen My Life with Vitality" list (yes, the list you're drafting here and now).

Here are the Top Six Things That Are Snuffing the Vitality out of You, so you can snuff out the things that are doing the vitality snuffing:

#1: Overdosing on screens and social media.
How many hours a day are you in front of a screen, not including the screen you're in front of all day at work?

- 2023 global stats[7] show we're spending 6 hours and 37 minutes per day, on average, online.
- The average American watches 2.86[8] hours of TV per day. Ready to be horrified? Studies show that a single hour of TV watched from the age of twenty-five on reduces the viewer's life expectancy by 21.8 minutes.[9] (By my latest calculations, I will be dead by Thursday.)
- And don't even get me started on excessive social media time.... Worldwide, we're spending an average of 2 hours and 31 minutes[10] using social media per day—which means that we're not only sedentary for that time, but we're also eroding our sense of well-being with every scroll and like. I have yet to find a well-being researcher who's a social media enthusiast.
- One study[11] explored the relationship between Internet addiction, subjective happiness, and subjective vitality and revealed what we all instinctively know to be true: Internet addiction acts like a can

of mace sprayed over our feelings of happiness and vitality. Interestingly, the relationship goes both ways: researchers comment that when individuals work on increasing their subjective vitality, they might experience a decrease in Internet addiction. Research[12] suggests that limiting social media use to about 30 minutes a day may lead to significant improvement in well-being.

> **Math moment!** If you're like most people, you're spending a daily total of 8 hours and 14 minutes[13] in a digital reality (Internet, social media, gaming, etc.). If you have 2,000 Mondays left to live, for example, that's 336,000 hours on your countdown timer. Lopping off a third of that time for sleep, that leaves you with 224,000 hours. Do you really want 114,000 of those hours spent engaging with a screen? Living by proxy? Or would you rather spend half of your waking hours doing something...real?

One of my clients knew screens were her nemesis, so she committed to turning off her notifications, leaving her phone in another room when hanging out with her family, and finagling with the settings in her phone to limit her daily social media time allowance (yes, you can do that). A team I worked with pledged to curb emails after 5:00 p.m. and on weekends, to great well-being-boosting success. A CEO I coach sets a TV timer; she watches a maximum of five hours a week and is sure to prioritize her *Housewives* episodes accordingly.

What if you were to cut out one thirty-minute show, or reduce your social media scrolling by a third, and replace that time meandering through your neighborhood, making a call to a friend, taking that free online galactic astronomy course, or writing a paragraph of your novella?

#2: Not taking your vacation time.
Did you know that 52 percent of us are leaving unused vacation days on the table each year? Like total suckers? I know it's not always easy to stop working. But you know what else isn't easy? Lying on your deathbed, regretting that you spent so much time at work and not enough time living the life you wanted to be living.

A study[14] from the University of Helsinki reveals that if you're taking fewer than three weeks of vacation each year, you're 37 percent more likely to die* compared to those enjoying three weeks or more of time off. (Here's how this tracks: Less vacation = more stress. More stress = more death.) Don't let vacation become a casualty of your work martyrdom. The best way to resolve the fact that you might not be taking enough time off is to plan your time off so it doesn't get to be December, with you forfeiting nine more days and wondering how you let the year slip by.

Vacation mapping is one of the first things I do with new clients for a quick vitality hit. Most busy professionals wait for time off to be convenient, which is like waiting for a bus that will never arrive. Plotting days and weeks off signals to yourself that you can proactively manage your well-being, and it gives you a fighting chance to explore life in ways you don't and won't when you're in the midst of your productive work routine.

Taking time off is a crucial way to restore balance in your life. Commit to being an even more well-rounded human, and set personal boundaries to take every single vacation day you've earned. No one gets to the end with a sense of pride for their bank of unused vacation days.

What days off do you have planned for the rest of the year? (This is not a rhetorical question. If you don't have your PTO mapped out in the calendar, about twelve months into future, you are asking for a de-zest-ified life.)

#3: The belief that more money = more happiness.

If you live under the poverty line, money will radically change your lifestyle and your subjective well-being, big time. If you live over that

---

* Study participants were tracked over a forty-year period; those who took less than three weeks had a 37 percent likelier chance of dying before the end of the study. Ouch.

line, you might still be striving, like a hamster on its little wheel, to earn more money as a way to buy life-widening happiness. Current research[15] notes that income is only a moderate determinant of overall happiness, though. If you're striving in vain to convert money to happiness, you're on the hedonic treadmill that we've already chatted about, and Honey Bunny: you are huffing and puffing to keep up. Buying things will make you happy—initially—and then your unrealistic expectations that these things will keep you happy becomes a recipe for having the life snuffed out of you.

Here are three ways money can actually add to your sense of vitality:

- **Spend money on others.** While personal spending isn't typically correlated with happiness, people who spend money on other people or charities do feel happier—even after controlling for their income. So that feel-good twingle you get when you click "Add to Cart" for a new candle? It'll flame out. That feel-good twingle you get when you give your friend an unexpected candle as a "thank you for being in my life" gift? Longer lasting.
- **Spend money on something you'll enjoy later.** The anticipatory principle is a serious big deal: we love having things to look forward to. Signing up for a wellness retreat that's two months away and excitedly waiting for that first sun salutation on the beach—that's a recipe for happiness . . . more so than purchasing the retreat and departing for it that night. Just knowing you have cake in the fridge, for example, will make you happier if you enjoy it later—like for dessert tomorrow night—more so than if you just demolish it the minute you frost it.* Delayed gratification heightens our enjoyment of being alive.
- **Spend small, more often.** Frequent small pleasures make us happier than the big buys. One big happiness-inducing purchase a year (the bungalow . . . or the yellow diamond . . . or the Birkin!) won't measure up against a bunch of spaced-out, smaller, cheap 'n' cheerful purchases. Novelty jostles that adaptive response. The regular drip of

---

* Okay, but we do have to be honest with ourselves: *no one* of sound mind is making a chocolate cake and then waiting until tomorrow to eat it.

small, special things that make you happy—like a box of stationery here, a beautiful book there—spaced through the year, will tally more joie de vivre points than a fancy new car.

#4: Leading an unhealthy lifestyle . . . duh.

Vitality is all about energy, so it makes sense that a way of living that robs you of energy will quash your vitality in a hurry. I recently corresponded with Dr. Richard Ryan, the world's preeminent researcher on vitality (Yes! The one who created the Subjective Vitality Scale above!), to talk about our common interest in aliveness. He wanted to clarify that "in our work the concept of vitality concerns not energy or arousal per se, but energy available to the self. Vitality allows people to pursue what matters to them, and thus it's essential to a good life." Vitality comes from within, and it's up to us to create the conditions for energy to take charge. Here are four ways to do just that:

- **The Sleep Thing.** Deep sleep clears debris from our brains, and it's referred to as "mental floss" for that reason. Researchers[16] followed a cohort of more than forty-three thousand subjects around for thirteen years and came to the conclusion that if you're under sixty-five years of age and you sleep less than five hours a night, you're asking for a 65 percent higher death rate compared to those who regularly sleep six to seven hours per night.

- **The Movement Thing.** Exercise buys you time on earth: your risk of premature death may decrease by 4 percent for each additional fifteen minutes of daily physical activity.[17] Even a little goes a long way, as just fifteen to twenty minutes of vigorous physical activity each week is linked to a reduction in the risk of dying by up to 40 percent, compared to people with zero activity at all.[18] One more deadly stat: you increase your chance of dying prematurely by 50 percent if you sit for nine hours a day.[19] How can you build more regular movement into your days, even if it's standing during a virtual meeting?

- **The Nutrition Thing.** Studies[20] show that a poor diet directly leads to one in five deaths. . . . So think about it this way: Line up five people in your mind—could be your family, colleagues, friends. One of them will die because they eat like garbage. And let's be honest—the other four people could probably clean up things on their plates a bit too, right? Here's a hard question: Could that one person in five be *you*, because your diet is harming you instead of helping you?

- 💀 **The Water Thing.** Experts say we're not a malnourished society; we're a mal-hydrated society, because we don't drink enough (and what we do drink is either sugary or fake-sugary and our bodies aren't happy with that). Remember when the recommendation used to be eight cups of water a day? Yeah, well with inflation, that's now eleven cups for women and sixteen for men. Research[21] tells us that drinking the right amount of water improves our brain functioning, our mood, and the quality of our sleep.

Are you setting your life up for success with the way you're treating your body? Do you need new "hours of operation"? Do you need to hire that personal trainer once and for all? Might you want to eat an extra serving of leafy greens every week, or maybe drink an extra glass of water or two?

#5: Deadening people.

Hanging around with Debbie Downers and wondering why you lack zest in your life? Debbie Downers are more contagious than the flu. Social contagion is a real thing: social scientists have studied[22] the ways your friends influence your happiness, loneliness, depression, obesity, divorce, smoking habits, alcohol consumption, cooperative behavior, tastes in books, music, and movies...and the list goes on about the ways "social spread" impacts the ways you live your life.

Emotions spread interpersonally, even through multiple degrees of separation. If your partner, family, or friends aren't exactly models of aliveness, my gentle response is to Ditch Them All. Just kidding!*

But back to our autonomy point, we are responsible for our lives and aliveness—which includes being our own well-being and entertainment directors. You can choose to spend less time with the deenergizers and increase your time spent with the sprightly sort. The killjoys in our life do kill our joy; it's up to us to edit accordingly.

---

* Mostly?

This is reminiscent of Shay's circle, isn't it? Identifying who you want in the circle of your life and who belongs on the outside? You don't need to burn bridges with the outsiders, but you can curtail the time you spend with them. One of my clients noticed she was "going with the flow" by spending time with friends and acquaintances she wasn't that energized by, simply because they took the initiative to ask her out for coffees and lunches and drinks. She was passively letting her social life happen *to her* and was finding herself busy with vitality vampires who sucked the life out of her. She started actively spending time with vitality-inducing friends and conveniently didn't have the time for the energy drainers.

> YOU: What if I want to do fun and interesting things, but the people in my social circle aren't interested?
>
> ME: You can invite people in your life to join you if you want, and then you can commit to going solo if they aren't up for it.

One of my clients was frustrated that her partner never wanted to try new things. New places? No. New hobbies? No. New food? No. She said, "Let's try that Ethiopian restaurant," and when he declined, she responded with a well-planned, "I love you, and I hope you order a pizza tonight because I'm going on a date with myself to eat Ethiopian food." She loved it, just as she did the book she brought to read while she pleasantly ate alone.

Another client traveled solo on a road trip this past summer when her inner circle wasn't gung-ho to go. She had a blast visiting museums, taking walking tours, and watching movies in her hotel room at night.

A client from a few years ago wanted to take a pottery class, but his wife wasn't interested. He was torn about whether to stay home or to go alone, but in the end he signed up by himself. He really committed! He bought the wheel and started spinning ~~indented blobs~~ bowls in their basement. Funny enough, his wife gradually caught the spark and gave it a try, too, and while he eventually abandoned pottery to pursue a new fascination, she stuck with it.

Consider these questions: Who do you need to spend less time with, so as not to catch the negativity virus from them? What activities do you need to commit to doing on your own? You don't need to eliminate the vitality parasites from your life (especially if you're related to them *hearty sigh*), but you do need to live your vitally alive life *around* them.

#6: Routines and habits.

Oh, these are deceptive little things, and we waxed on about them in our last chapter. These vitality snuffers are so sneaky and insidious that I'd be remiss if I didn't bring them up again just to drive home the point that they'll diminish your sense of aliveness. (The irony is not lost on me that I'm making a habit out of telling you how deadening habits are. Give me two more minutes of airtime here, and we'll move on.)

Going through the motions of the same workout? Sitting down to the same morning PB+J toast habit? Scrolling through the same stuff you always scroll through? Rehashing the same Sunday brunch routine with your friends? Planning the same-old-same-old potluck lunch with your team at work? All great chances to shake things up in service of revitalizing your moments.

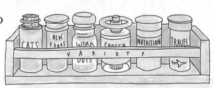

The SPICE of LIFE RACK

Have you jostled a habit since reading the last chapter, just to break out of the trance a bit and be able to discern Monday from Wednesday? What routine do you need to throw a wrench into?

So there you have it...six things to *stop* doing to curb the slow but steady siphoning of your vitality. If one thing grabbed you in that list above, make a note. And since I don't want to be the one to stop you from taking immediate action on a better life today—why not book a vacation day *before* getting to the end of this book when the action-planning party takes place?

NINE "BEST OF THE BEST" WAYS TO WIDEN OUR LIVES

Now that we've snuffed out the vitality snuffers in our lives, it's time to shine the light on the positive actions we can take toward living the liveliest versions of our lives. What do the world's most vibrantly alive people do that we don't? And how can we be more like them? Here are nine of my very favorite research-backed and client-tested ideas:

1. Do things you value.

Positive psychology[23] makes it clear that well-being arises from active engagement in our lives through activities we personally value.

One of my clients who deeply valued creative expression started writing poetry after a twenty-year hiatus. She found an enormous amount of joy from that one change in her life; she felt like she flicked a switch to "alive" mode because she was engaging in something special, just for her, that allowed her to be creative in a way that her accounting job simply couldn't.

Another client valued his health immensely but ruefully admitted he didn't act like it or feel like it—not since kids birthed their way into his life. He made a life-enhancing decision to walk before dinner and eat seven fewer cookies per week.*

What do you value in life, and are you participating in your life to actually honor what matters to you? What activities do you value that might liven you up—like hiking in nature, counseling kids, or helping clients win?

2. Move around, a lot.

Have you ever noticed that zesty people are energetic, enthusiastic, and rarely seated? As though they're all hopped-up on coke? That's the look we're going for. (Active and on-the-go, not cokehead chic.)

My great-aunt Bernice, for example, is remarkably, noticeably alive. At ninety-something, she's on the edge of her seat, ready to live, ready to tap-dance if they offered that class at her senior living center. She's buzzing around (no, not from cocaine—would you stop that?), seemingly defying gravity. We can't all flit around like Bernice, but can we aim for a touch more get-up-and-go in our lives?

Inertia is real. A body on the couch watching reruns remains a body on the couch watching reruns. And a body in motion (walking to the

---

* He had a small Double Stuf Oreo problem.

store, dancing while making dinner, having a walking meeting at work, vacuuming often...) stays alive. Hot tip: when you're feeling like you don't have the energy to get up and move, let that be your indication that the very best thing you can do is *get up and move*. The Vicious Cycle of Inactivity (I know it quite well) is one of the Grim Reaper's bestselling products.

The "where am I in all of this" client I told you about earlier has a childlike level of excitement to go zip-lining, and not just because it's a childlike, fun activity. She was shut out from zip-lining on her last vacation because she didn't have the energy to hike up to the start point—a vitality-zapping moment at its finest. In her new activity-filled life, she's eager to find a zip line with her name on it.

Is your life zippy? If you watched a time-lapse video of yourself on a typical day, would it be full of a lot of movement or mostly a sleeper? Where can you spark momentum and get moving in your life?

3. Copy a lively role model.

Think of someone you know who is super zesty. What is their life like? What makes them seem vitally alive to you?

I'm thinking of Great Aunt Bernice: she's super social, she's physically active, and she's engaged in hobbies and activities. Bernice could never ever be described as dull. I am too introverted to ever be as vitally alive as Bernice, but I keep her in mind when I imagine a model for an ultravital life.

A workshop attendee of mine mapped out a Vitality Profile based on a composite of the three most alive people she knew: "My daughter is amazing at trying new things, so I'm including her traits on the list. My best friend is super active, so I'm incorporating her too. My CEO does an admirable job of aligning her actions with her values, so she makes the cut." This woman's profile provided her with a blueprint of zesty inspiration.

Who can you emulate to ratchet up your vitality, even in the slightest amount? If you can't find anyone in your close circle, is there a celebrity, entrepreneur, or other success story that you look up to who seems to have five thousand hours in a day? Their biographies or podcast interviews might be a good place to start. Mimic the way someone else lives their life if you like the way they're living it.

4. Adopt a play mentality.

Many people with off-the-charts "health of spirit" know how to *play*. They know how to leverage the oodles of scientific studies[24] that tell us play is so much more than just having fun. Play increases brain functionality, improves memory and critical thinking, stimulates creativity, decreases stress, and keeps us feeling young. Just so we're clear about what play is: it can include ritualistic things like board games or sports where you follow the rules.... imaginative play like drawing, playing charades, or taking improv classes.... It can involve body play where you move or defy gravity, like riding roller coasters, trampolining, or surfing...and anything that brings you back to your childhood, like scavenger hunts, snowball fights, giant Jenga games, or building forts.

Play is serious stuff. One of the leadership teams I work with starts every meeting with ten minutes of playtime—creatively working on brainteasers, having a quick round of Pictionary, even the odd round of Twister. They approach the remaining fifty minutes of the meeting with more energy, openness, and enthusiasm.

If you are inclined to view play as a frivolous use of your time, you might need to update your self-talk track—that voice in your head that judges everything you say, do, don't say, and don't do—and tell it that it's okay to take time out of your week for R+R. Where might you be able to fit in a bit more silliness and play?

5. Grease the social skids.

Consider the energy gained by being around humans you like or find interesting (so, *not* the Debbie Downers we've already ix-nayed from our lives).... That's what we're after: positive energy from others.

Positive Psychology Interlude: Other People Matter. One of the early researchers in the field of positive psychology, Chris Peterson, was asked to sum up positive psychology in two words or less. His answer? "Other people." He later elaborated: "Other people matter, and there may be no happy hermits."

Leading researchers have concluded that good relationships with others may be the single most important source of life satisfaction and emotional well-being, across different ages and cultures. One study's[25] findings were staggering: people with social relationships realize a 50 percent increase in odds of survival.* (This study aggregated data from 148 independent studies, looking at three hundred thousand people who were followed around for an average of 7.5 years; the evidence is a tad empirically rigorous.)

Researchers[26] connect the dots between interpersonal connections at work and vitality. Cultivating "high-quality connections" on the job—relationships that revolve around mutual positive regard, active engagement, and trust—energizes us worker bees and generates the enthusiasm to take action on whatever the mighty mission is at hand. One leader I work with has created a "coffee chat" culture, not just because he loves cappuccinos but because he sees the ROI (return on investment) after team members get to know one another over informal thirty-minute conversations. It's hard to hold a grudge against Mindy in marketing for dropping the ball on your project when you've seen pictures of her kids playing T-ball. Seventy-nine percent of employed people with high vitality overwhelmingly "feel connected with people" at work, compared with just 12 percent of low-vitality workers.[27]

By middle age, we typically have about five close friends, and that number slowly decreases as we age. As adults we spend less than 10 percent of our time with friends, which isn't a lot of time considering that having friends reduces our risk of dying. As we get older, we tend to deprioritize friendships, and as we learned in our regrets chapter, we often lament the time *not spent* with these special people. I smell opportunity, and I know you do, too.

In some of my workshops, I ask attendees to pull out their phones and go through their contact lists, identifying the people who actively light them up. Most people admit they don't spend as much time with the "energizers" as they'd like. Who is on your "light me up" list?

Who can you connect with today, even if it's to make a "let's get together" date (in person or otherwise)? What drifted friendship might

---

* Compared to people without buddies, across the study period.

you want to rekindle? Who can you text *right now* to say something loving, like I love you, or Thinking of you and I'm glad I can call you a friend, or even just a series of eggplant emojis?

6. Use your ESP (extrasensory perception).

The definition of vitality includes both psychological and somatic factors. Said simply, being alive is a totally sensory experience, and being ultra-alive means that we stimulate all of our senses on a regular basis.

I worked with a woman who was feeling lackluster in her life—kind of bored, in an "I've lost my zest" kind of way—so she clued into what her favorite things were, according to all of her senses. She had been overlooking many things she liked—like the smell of the trees in the forest preserve where she used to hike, the taste of the oatmeal cookies she used to bake, the feel of faux fur in a pillow that was one of those "display only" props in her living room. She organized her list of things that made her happy and alive*—by each sense—and picked a few things to amplify in her life. For example, she set a date to drive to the forest preserve with a friend and hike, and she now goes every month or so, sometimes after work for even twenty minutes. She bakes cookies regularly (giving many of them away so she gets the balance of smelling them, trying them, feeling generous, and not becoming a cookie). And the faux fur thing . . . I love this one: she went onto fabric.com, ordered about five different colors of faux fur, and made pillows out of all of them—pillows she uses, to *feel*, not just for display. She's experiencing more of her senses and feeling that much more alive as a result.

One woman I know (who may or may not be the lovely editor of this book) takes her dog on walks and touches the bark of trees for an instant stress remedy; "I just put my hand on it, feel it, and look at the green of the leaves. Instant calm." Well-being studies show that spending time outdoors, especially in green spaces, is one of the fastest ways to jack up our health and happiness—in large part because it activates so many of our senses. The great outdoors improves our mood and mental health; lowers stress, heart rate, and blood pressure; and encourages us to move our bodies.

---

* You have one of these from your pre-mortem, on page 43! (Friendly reminder.)

Spending only twenty minutes in a park—even if you don't exercise while you're there—is enough to improve well-being.[28] A client of mine who lives in Manhattan takes her dog on a walk through pure chaos until she gets to the park (which she affectionally refers to as the "rat zoo")—where she can walk, sit, breathe, slow down. Even that little slice of nature centers her, and she returns home to work with a new lease on life. She's working this into as many days of her week as she can muster.

What senses do you need to activate? When was the last time you tried a new flavor—garam masala, maybe? Have you deeply smelled the air in your favorite place—like that spot by the lake or outside your favorite bakery? Have you deliberately felt the softness of a flower petal or your pet's ear, or looked at a stunning piece of art or architecture or even just a crowd of people?

7. Become constantly curious.

No surprise here after our habits chapter! Joie-de-vivre-type people are consistently curious. They want to know what's going on in the news, their neighborhoods, with climate change, in art, what Taylor Swift is up to, and what's going on in other people's lives (in ways that don't elicit restraining orders). Wondering about things is good for us. Seeking information keeps us fresh, current, and alive.

Check out what researchers[29] have to say on this matter: "People who are regularly curious and willing to embrace the novelty, uncertainty, and challenges that are inevitable as we navigate the shoals of everyday life are at an advantage in creating a fulfilling existence compared with their less curious peers." But you already knew that from our snow-globe-shaking conversation. I want for you to have a fulfilling existence amid the shoals of everyday life.

Where are there chances for you to find out answers to new things? To grow and expand your perspectives? Read an autobiography of someone you'd normally not care to learn about? Watch a news channel that leans in a different direction from your usual leaning? Take a class in something you're not good at, because you're confident enough to be unconfident? Take a different route than your habitual one? I went down a cobblestone alley in Chicago recently and found this delightful little historic passageway with old fire escapes and stairwells and doorways to who knows where Capone might've shot people. I was swept up in the experience...something I wouldn't have done if I'd just stayed on the usual beaten path.

If you need a little jostling of your routine, return to the Anti-Autopilot Assessment (page 193) to help identify where the blood is being drained from your body. How might you bust out of autopilot and get curious?

8. Assertively—bordering on aggressively—pursue life.

I mean actively, not passively. Vitality requires—demands—us to get up, get out, try things on for size. The flames of passion don't set themselves: they require kindling, and you're going to have to light that fire yourself, camper.

I learned this one the hard way, years ago, when I felt stuck in that job I wanted to leave but was afraid to figure out how. I kept hoping for something to happen, for another magical job to land in my lap, and for some reason no one swooped in to pluck me from my office and plop me in a mystical land of career happiness. I had to take action myself, which in my case meant doing some serious work on investigating new careers. I took the long route but ultimately proved that vitality can be cultivated. It's in the risk of being willing to fail and flounder that we so often find the thing that lights us up.

Where do you need to shift from passive to active mode in your life? Where might you need to stoke the fires of passion? Where might you need to acknowledge fear and make a decision to move forward anyway?

9. Intentionally live a life of leisure.

Vitally alive people don't wait for permission to take up a new hobby or pick up the pieces of a dormant hobby they left behind. They don't have qualms around whether to take a break. Let's not confuse this with work ethic: high-vitality people can be worker bees, too—but they work hard and play hard, making time for their leisure pursuits. Unapologetically.

Researchers tell us the amount of time we devote to leisure has been shown as one of the more robust correlates of life satisfaction, and the concept of time affluence—the feeling that we have enough time to participate in the activities that truly matter to us—also positively relates to subjective well-being.[30] Serious leisure seekers who effectively balance challenge and skill get to revel in the optimal experience known as flow . . . the immersed psychological state associated with highly engaging activities. On an average day in 2021, adults spent 5.3 hours[31] per day in leisure and sports activities, like watching TV, socializing, or exercising. We've already covered that the TV swallows up 54 percent of that time, so even if you don't curb your boob-tube time, how do you want to spend several hours of your precious day when you're not sleeping and working?

What would your life look like if you increased your leisure time by even 9 percent? Where can you amplify your time off in your life? How can you schedule your life to take more time off in the first place? What hobby needs to enter your life?

So there you have it: six ways to arrest the deadening and nine ways to juice up your vitality. That's a lot of verve, and my recommendation is to let the wave of research-soaked liveliness wash over you and see where it all nets out as our conversation continues.

I'm going to expand on the "life of leisure" concept for a moment with you here, because it's an easy-pickings situation with significant life-widening potential. See if these discussion points about hobbies and celebrations resonate with you?

HOBBIES FOR ADULTS? DEFINITELY! ABSOLUTELY! NECESSARY!

Ask any adult about their hobbies, and chances are they'll get that distant, wistful look in their eyes—a look best described as ambiguous grief. The rite of passage into Responsible Adulthood indubitably killed the hobby.

We shelved the books we used to make time to read and sometimes even take a stab at writing. We closed up the violin case and packed it up in that tight-lidded container under the stairs, far out of sight and even further out of mind. We donated the figure skates, thinking resignedly that "someone will have so much fun in these"—just not us, though. No time for triple axels in Responsible Adulthood! We sold the pasta roller in a garage sale. We let the paint tubes dry up and the paint brushes get all frayed on the edges.

You get the idea.

I get it—many of our hobbies had to shift to the back burner because we didn't have time. We got busy with fifty-plus-hour workweeks, climbing the corporate ladder, all things kids and their pet turtles, mowing the lawn, and oil changes. We prioritized other things and lost sight of how fun and recreation are necessary components in a life well lived…that people with hobbies pop up in study after study[32] as having less stress and depression and are more satisfied and engaged with their lives (like eighty-year-old Marty playing bridge like a zesty twenty-year-old).

It's time to bring the hobbies back to life.

The books? They're still there, waiting to have the dust blown off them and their spines cracked open as you settle into chapter 1 with a big cup of hot chocolate. Your old draft is waiting for you too (unless it's on an old floppy disc, in which case good luck with that).

The musical instruments are right there where you left them, or they can be purchased all over again because I'm not sure if you've heard the news that Amazon delivers everything now? So many ice skates, pasta rollers, cameras, violas, sketchbooks, bowling balls, swimming goggles, sewing machines, tarot cards, cross-stitch stuff, beer-making everything…all ready to Add to Cart and land on your doorstep before the weekend.

In the spirit of memento mori, pull up your life countdown timer. How many Mondays are left on the docket for you? In light of your dwindling years, months, weeks, and days, what passions do you want—no, *need*—to pursue? Oh, look who suddenly has time for macramé! Does the act of putting your mortality in perspective help you reprioritize what matters in life and reshuffle your activities to reflect the way you really want to spend your time?

It's time to ignite the embers of hibernating hobbies. Here's how:

- ☻ **Reincarnate an old hobby.** You got to green belt in karate in 2003 and yearn to return? Slam dunk. Stop reading, and go online to investigate local karate classes.
- ☻ **Dream up a new hobby from scratch and dabble in it.** Curious about knitting? Buy a starter kit. Wonder about geocaching (don't we all)? Read up about it. Interested, even mildly, in cake decorating?

Let YouTube do the heavy lifting and learn about the joys of fondant; then go make a celebratory single-tiered cake for yourself. One of my seventy-five-year-old clients challenged herself to trying one new thing a month in a veritable Hobby Sampler Platter. She landed on horseback riding.

- ☠ **Spend smart.** Spending money on things that support your hobby can help you like your life a little more...because spending money on experiences makes us happier. Way more people report getting happy from an experience they purchased—like a Blogging Bootcamp Weekend or a How to Roll Sushi Once and for All cooking class—than people who bought material goods. With experiences, we can anticipate them and savor them after the fact.

- ☠ **Copy someone else's hobby.** Your friend won't stop droning on about making her own soap, and the idea doesn't revolt you? Try it. Your partner is into ax throwing, and you want to risk your life too? Give it a go. You're likely to like things that people you like, like. Use their hobbies as inspiration.

- ☠ **Just register already.** Commit to something before you talk yourself out of it. Years ago I made an appointment for an archery lesson and showed up only because I'd made the appointment and didn't want to bum the old war vet of an instructor out by no-showing on him. I loved it! For like four months. But I will be better off when the zombie apocalypse hits.

- ☠ **Abandon underwhelming hobbies swiftly.** Be careful not to listen to the voice that says you have to "follow through" on your hobby because you paid a lot of dough for top-of-the-line golf clubs or whatever, because "it's the responsible thing to do." Hobbies are supposed to make us feel happy, not obligated and trapped. Donate the soap-making stuff if it's not for you, and find something new you look forward to doing. Oh, and maybe you need to skip the judgment about a waxing and waning commitment to your hobbies. You are allowed to like a hobby and then lose interest in it. It doesn't make you flaky or fickle. It makes you curious and open to experience if you're always up for something new. (Just maybe don't get the best bow and arrow that money can buy if you tend to fizzle on your interests in a hurry.) (Not that I'm speaking from personal experience.) (But I am.)

☻ **Carve out time.** Even an hour a week—that's all it takes to spend time on an activity that might spark joy, take your mind off the circus going on around you, maybe make you feel like you've accomplished something or made something or scored something (like maybe that elusive 1914 stamp for your collection). What about carving out *more* than an hour or two? A former client sends me texts and pictures of his days off where he travels to attend heavy metal concerts—a major source of glee amid his busy corporate life. What's that you say? You don't have an hour a week? I am suspicious but understanding. If an hour a week sounds impossible, what about fifteen minutes?

☻ **Be not afraid.** Many achievers don't love the idea of working through the kinks when rekindling a hobby. If it's been twenty years since you golfed, you are going to suck a bit when you visit the driving range for the first time in two decades. You won't play the piano with the same dexterity; you won't run as fast; you won't sketch with as much ease.

☻ Remember when Steve Jobs said, "Stay hungry. Stay foolish. Never let go of your appetite to go after new ideas, new experiences, and new adventures"? Staying foolish means actively choosing a beginner's mindset and reveling in the nonmastery. Speaking of mindsets...

Coaching Chestnut: Choose the Growth Mindset. Widening our lives requires us to shift from a *fixed mindset* (where we believe failure is an embarrassing limit of our abilities) to a *growth mindset*[33] (where we believe failure is an opportunity to learn and grow, even if it looks like a shit show at first).

I am sometimes reluctant to pull out the paints with my art projects because I'm not in the mood to *not* win the imaginary art contest I'm competing in. I need to stop myself in those moments of being fixed and narrow and ask myself if I'd prefer to favor growth and width...and then I need to actively choose growth and width. Where might you be stuck in a fixed mindset today, a tad scared of what failure says about you?

Our time is finite, but our energy and experiences can be expanded while we're above ground. Hobbies have never been easier to get into, if we're willing to give ourselves permission to make the time, see that there is a well-being ROI, and live a little wider. Let's find fun, engaging, captivating, challenging-but-not-buzzkillingly-hard hobbies. Let's go gongoozling (which is really a thing) and then revel in our handmade vitality.

HOW MAKING UP PREPOSTEROUS CELEBRATIONS MAKES LIFE BETTER

Did you notice that I just said "revel"? Of all the things associated with widening our lives a little more, festooning our lives with celebrations might be among the most fun. Who doesn't like to eat, drink, and be merry?

Let's up the revelry ante. I'm proposing that we combine the life-liking factors of celebration and positive anticipation by unabashedly making up reasons to "live it up." I'm also suggesting we do this on a regular basis, in an unabashedly contrived way to widen our lives with vitality.

For example, I celebrate the 333rd day of the year—partly because I am a superstitious piece of work who loves the number three but mostly because I want a day to look forward to, an excuse to plan a day of fun, and a day to live out the cockamamie fun plans I've dreamed up. (On a recent Day 333, I devised a day that started with a run that ended *exactly* in front of Do-Rite Donuts, where a bag of preordered sprinkle-covered fried dough was waiting for me. The rest of the day was mapped out, and yes, it did include so-bad-they-were-good movies from the '90s, on the couch, with ramen for dinner.)

Lives worth living rarely happen to us. We have to engineer them, and once we get past the disappointment of that truth, we can really get on with living like we mean it.

You, too, can enjoy the wonders of made-up holidays. Here is a random assortment of fabricated fun days:

- **The longest day of the year.** The first day of summer is the longest day of the year, which means we can either savor or squander the extra two seconds of daylight bestowed upon us by the people who made up astronomy. Plan a whirlwind of a day from the moment the sun rises until it sets (or just do it at your own pace, like a normal person).

- ☻ **The shortest day of the year.** Don't throw shade on this unpopular day. When most people have plunged to the depths of sunless despair on December 21, why not throw a "The Days Are Getting Longer" barn dance?* Glass half full this life!

- ☻ **Monday Nite Date Nite.** It's a thing around our house, because Mondays are Mondays and The Husband and I need something to look forward to on the saddest day of the week.† We giddily say, "Cheers to MNDN!" with our glass of whatever leftover wine is on the go, have the easy meal we've plotted in advance (hello, gluten-free fish sticks, thank you for swimming your way back into my life), and hunker down for a date night befitting people who have been together for twenty-six years (a lot of HBO followed by a frisky finish of HGTV).

- ☻ **First-date anniversary.** Celebrate the shit out of that day! The seeds of love were planted! Re-enact the date if you're up for it.

- ☻ **Half birthdays.** Surprise someone with a half cake and a half-assed present!

- ☻ **Half lifetimes.** So this one kind of went over like a lead balloon when I took The Husband out to dinner on the exact day he turned 38.1, because that year the average life expectancy for men was 76.2. I had a hard time finding him a "half-life" birthday card, but I made do. He was a little weirded out by what I believed to be a thoughtful gesture. Choose your recipients of this celebration wisely.

- ☻ **Leap days.** For a woman obsessed with getting extra time in life, February 29 is four times as exciting as a yearly birthday. It's a total bonus day every four years and therefore must be exalted! Guys: the next leap year on a Monday will be in 2044. Should we meet in Death Valley for a celebration of extra life? I'm so excited! Let's definitely not die before then.

- ☻ **Celebrations of small wins.** I love having big reasons to celebrate, but they are too few and far between. Why not celebrate the milestones, the wee little accomplishments? A client of mine was slogging away in grad school, and after each seven-week class she completed,

---

* No barn? A more moderate shindig will do!

† I can admit it, even as the self-anointed Queen of Mondays.... They're the fucking worst.

she had full-on Champagne cork-popping celebrations at home. Her kids even made a Bristol-board sign with a countdown to her degree. Imagining those special evenings got her through the late-night research papers.

- ☠ **Random weekdays.** Why not celebrate the third Tuesday in February? Or just a random Thursday in an otherwise unremarkable week? Barry, a mentor of mine who used to coach cancer patients and knew a thing about memento mori, once said, "Don't save all your good 'stuff' for only special occasions (i.e., Sunday go-to-meetin' clothes in the old days); today itself is a gift, so remember it is special; use the real silverware, put on the nice sheets, drink that 1990 vintage red Bordeaux." The bottom line here? Every day we're alive is kind of a special occasion.

- ☠ **Silly days.** I doodle a calendar every year full of goofy but notable "not to miss" days, like how the first Thursday of April is National Burrito Day, and July 31 is Uncommon Instrument Awareness Day—maybe an opportunity for you to hold a celebratory jam session with your fellow piccolo players?

Studies[34] tell us that having something to look forward to (whether it's a week at a cabin, a scuba-diving class, or banana splits for dessert) greases the skids to well-being. We also know that savoring celebratory moments (like special anniversaries or National Grilled Cheese Sandwich Day) builds optimism and resilience, especially when we express gratitude.[35]

Cooking up excuses to live with more aliveness is more than just fun—it's scientifically good for us. And given the consistent absurdity of life, we all need a good dose of something ridiculous to look forward to. (National Grilled Cheese Day is on April 12. I will use Manchego cheese. And your cheese of choice will be . . . ?)

YOUR VITALITY CHALLENGE

I realize it's unconventional to get a homework assignment at a vitality party, but, dude—you knew what you were getting yourself into about six minutes into the pre-mortem. But this will be a fun project, so no one will be feeling sorry for you here.

Your official challenge is to do something life widening between now and the next fourteen days of your life (a.k.a. two Mondays). It could be any of the ways we spoke about jacking up your vitality—maybe you'll kickstart a new hobby? Maybe pick up an old hobby? It could have to do with an anti-vitality-snuffing idea—maybe a TV detox from Monday through Thursday? Maybe you'll ~~kick~~ gently edit Negative Ned out of your life? You might initiate a full-blown adventure, or even just a partially blown one? Maybe you'll go hog wild and celebrate that your birthday is "exactly eight months from today"? You might try that Intro to Pole Vaulting class? Or you might eat a rutabaga. This isn't a life commitment; it's a gesture to show yourself you can add some zest-on-demand in your life.

WRAPPING UP THIS VITALITY PARTY

This is it, Team Vitality. We made it to the end of the "ways to start living as though you gave a shit you were actually alive" chapter, and I'm not going to lie to you: I'm feeling a little hyped up over here.

Might you become the most vitally alive person you know? The lively person others emulate? Maybe. Maybe screw that, because there's no pressure to become that crackerjack role model. You don't have to live a jazz-hands kind of life.* You just need to ask yourself how you might tap into the vitality do's and don'ts we've covered to stay out of the dead zone.

Vitality accounts for how we feel about our ability to make our own choices and be in control of our lives. As humans we have an intrinsic

---

* Or a "double dream hands" kind of life—that's a dance move I just got wind of. Such vibrancy on the dance floor!

need for autonomy, and our degree of living-like-we-mean-it-ness is related to how much we feel like we're in the driver's seat of our lives. We have the ability to make decisions big and small—like what town to take a road trip to or how we'll spend our twenty-minute lunch break—that can add to or detract from our positive sense of aliveness. We can choose to spend ten minutes or two hours on social media. We can choose to binge-watch *Ted Lasso* or go for a walk after watching one great episode. Sometimes we lose sight of our Life Captainship. We are in so very much more control of our vitality than we think, and in a short-term life, we want to captain that ship.

Pulling the thread of memento mori through to our vitality conversation, let's get clear on how remembering we're going to die can actually boost—rather than bust—our sense of aliveness. Remaining consciously aware of our mortality can motivate us to improve our vitality and action orientation in life. (Yes, that's why I keep reminding you to calculate your remaining Mondays.) The little jolt we feel where we're startled by the reminder of death is typically followed by feelings of intrinsic motivation to better ourselves, to get the show of life on the road. That jolt leads to feelings of vitality. And isn't that what we want in our quest to feel maximally alive?

For those of you with a mild case of existential anxiety (so, all of us): a willingness to fully participate in our lives tends to relegate the fear of death to the

background. By dialing up the vitality, we benefit from a dialing down of anxiety. You might recall from our Deathly Denial conversation in chapter 4 (page 93) that there's a strong correlation between our fear of death and our sense that our lives are unlived; the more we fail to live with width, the more profound our death anxiety becomes. Spun more positively, the more we dive in and live our lives with gusto, the less we will experience anxiety about the sucks-to-be-true inevitability of death. Shall we sign up right now for the widening, then?

 "Vitality! That's the pursuit of life, isn't it?" Katharine Hepburn was right. We're here to pursue that rapture of being alive. Go blow the lid off your pot!

CHAPTER 9

LIVING DEEPER WITH MEANING: PLUNGING THE DEPTHS OF PURPOSE

 We dread a meaningless life as much as we dread the terror of death.

—PAUL WONG

Now that you've stuffed your life full of vitality at the all-you-can-eat pleasure buffet, you're ready for a little more substance, aren't you? (It's not that I'm saying vitality is all about empty calories—you must never, ever quote me on that—but meaning does contain a wee bit more nutritional value for our souls.)

We're cozied up on the couch here today* to talk about deepening your life with meaning. We will dive deep into what a meaning-full life looks like and why it's worth including in your version of a life worth living. Most of us have a sense that a "mile wide and an inch deep" kind of life might not feel all that fulfilling, so after a handful of pages, I'm hoping you're sold on the pursuit of a life that's multiple miles wide *and* just as many miles deep. We'll then get you contemplating your own sense of meaning (or lack thereof), leaving with a list of possible actions worth taking to further deepen your existence.

> YOU (looking unexpectedly sheepish): I really binged at the vitality buffet in our last chapter. I feel like I'm splashing around the shallow end of my life, without a lot of time spent in the deep end. Is there hope for me?

---

* We may or may not be "recovering" from our vitality party. It was an open bar.

ME (looking very uncomfortable in a wetsuit): Darling, we're about to go deep-sea diving into the depths of meaning. Of course there's hope! Now suit up. I can't be the only one standing here in such an unflattering outfit.

LIVING DEEPER WITH MEANING

You make your life deeper when you infuse it with meaning—a heavy hitter in the world of well-being. This includes feeling like you have some sense of purpose in your outstanding Mondays, connecting any of the dots in the universe to come up with some kind of cohesive reason why you are here and why you are creating new spreadsheet tabs at work. Deepening your life also involves making connections to others, doing what you do best, having an orientation to something bigger than yourself, belonging, helping, giving... all great things.

Think of this on a vertical scale that ranges from feeling meaningless on the bottom end (empty, pointless, and hollow), all the way up to feeling meaning-full (oozing with purpose, direction, and a sense that you're here on earth to do things you care about).

To what extent do you feel like you're living with purpose today? Does your work feel fulfilling, beyond earning a paycheck and getting to buy shoes with nice names on their soles? Do your days feel rife with meaning or conspicuously shallow? If you suspect you might land on death's doorstep feeling like your life was expansively wide (go, vitality!) but superficially deep, here's your invitation to work on the meaning part... to ultimately rest in peace with depth.

Positive Psychology Interlude: I think we need to clarify something before we go any further. Well-being researchers—as well as philosophers and great thinkers over the years—highlight a distinction between a *happy life* and a *meaningful life*.

There is the hedonic approach, which favors pleasure and all-out happiness, through positive emotions and pretty much everything we talked about in our discussion about vitality. Think: life-widening stuff... using your senses to experience the glories of life like bacon, exploring a new city, getting a great massage, or more bacon...feeling good in general.

The second branch is the eudaimonic approach, which can be seen as more of a way of being than a lifestyle. Eudaimonia is about finding meaning, reaching our potential, contributing to our communities...living a life of good character. Psychology researchers note that the pursuit of meaning and engagement tends to boost sustainable life satisfaction more so than the sole pursuit of pleasure. In this chapter we're hunkering down in Camp Eudaimonia.

THE MEANING OF MEANING

Meaning is what gives us depth in our lives, the counterweight to the hedonic-pleasure-zest-filled life.

Meaning provides us with a sense of significance, underscored by a belief that our lives are inherently valuable. We tend to want to know what our lives are all about and how they fit into the grand scheme of things and the world around us. Meaning can answer these questions for us.

The Holocaust-surviving psychologist Viktor Frankl (Yes! The author of the most excellent *Man's Search for Meaning*) referred to the "will to meaning" as the center of human motivation. "The question can no longer be 'What can I expect from life?' but can now only be 'What does life expect of me? What task in life is waiting for me?'"[1]

Let's both catch our breath for a moment.

A meaningful life includes a sense of responsibility to find out what our lives are expecting from us—what our futures are expecting from us.

Are you also enchanted by this notion? I have 1,821 Mondays left in life (give or take); are those Mondays gathering a quorum, flip charting the "Things We Expect from Her before She Bites the Biscuit or It'll All Have Been a Spectacularly Meaningless Dumpster Fire of a Life"?

How do we know what our lives expect of us? How do we know what tasks in life await us, other than dusting, reheating dinner, and printing out Amazon return labels? And how does all this connect to meaning? And why are there so many questions?

Meaning, one of the pillars of well-being, isn't just sought in the aftermath of a traumatic event, like Frankl surviving the horrors of the Holocaust. Our desire for meaning is a fundamental part of being human, helping us to make sense of even the most mundane everyday occurrences (like why our teenager is behaving the way he is or why Tom got the promotion we were hoping for).

Determining what our lives "expect from us" is precisely what makes life meaningful. The exploration of how we might be able to make a difference...the blood-sweat-and-tear-stained effort toward achievement of things that really matter to us...the seeking of our next calling...the practice of looking up at the sky with incredulity and trying to connect to something bigger than us...the asking (usually forlornly and late at night with a sloppy second glass of pinot noir in hand), "Am I doing what I'm supposed to be doing, like really?"...All these things form the foundation of meaning.

It's not so much about cracking the code of what life expects of us—as though there was an official, gratifyingly correct answer. It's the act of *figuring it out* that creates meaning in life. For most of us, this ascertainment is an ongoing pursuit. Times change; we change; our priorities change. Isn't it a relief to acknowledge that you're not always supposed to know what your life expects of you in the moment? That it's enough to be actively pursuing that answer, with the intention of finding it? You don't need to know in the moment, but you *do* have to commit to sniffing it out, exploring, iterating, piloting, growing in the direction of the sun.

Meaning rarely lands in our laps; we have to make it.* Courageous action is what conquers the threat of meaninglessness.

NERD NOTES: RESEARCH THAT MAKES THE CASE FOR MEANING

- ☻ Research[2] consistently shows that having meaning and purpose in life increases overall well-being and life satisfaction, improves mental and physical health, builds our resilience and self-esteem, and decreases the chances of depression.
- ☻ People who reveal they're suffering from a *crisis of meaning* (i.e., a notable lack of meaning and frustrating emptiness in life) experience negative well-being and mental health.[3]
- ☻ Happy people with an absence of meaning show similar gene patterns as those with adversity stress responses.[4] Meaninglessness appears to be stressful on an otherwise jolly mind and healthy body.
- ☻ People with high purpose and meaning in life have commensurately accepting and positive attitudes toward death; the degree to which we fear or accept death is intrinsically linked to the degree to which we've found meaning and purpose in life.[5]
- ☻ Those who believe their lives have a greater sense of purpose and meaning are able to bypass the typical death anxiety response.[6] In other words, existential meaning inoculates us against existential despair and even existential crisis. Purpose-led people with life-threatening illnesses, for example, find even more depth in life, realize increases in self-esteem, and often experience personal transformations as they make new meaning in their limited time left.
- ☻ A meta-analysis[7] that collated the data of more than 137,000 people, over ten studies, found that for every one-point increase on a six-point scale measuring purpose in life, adults with heart disease have a 27 percent decreased risk of having a heart attack over a two-year period. For older adults, a one-point difference in purpose can mean a 22 percent decreased risk of having a stroke.

---

* See "Giving Two Shits" in our introduction (page 12). The shits keep piling up.

💀 Survivors of traumatic events often shift from having concerns about the meaning of life to the work of *making* meaning in life. For those of us fortunate enough to have evaded trauma, we can reflect on how we are making meaning, too. Are you making it or waiting for it?

Surely you're sold on the purpose of purpose and meaning, how it can deepen our lives in the window of time we have left to do the deepening? Let's transition from the *why* into the *how*...

ELEVEN RESEARCH-BACKED WAYS TO MAKE MEANING IN YOUR MONDAYS

I've put together a cornucopia of my very favorite ways to deepen your sense of meaning in life. You are undoubtedly nailing some of these already, while other meaning-making methods might ruffle a few of your feathers. Please remember that feather ruffling is usually an indication that something is resonant and worth considering on your path to a deeper way of living. Make notes on both what inspires *and* what irks you.

1. Clue into your impact.

People who extract the most meaning in their lives tend to grasp the impact of what they are up to. Working as a veterinary assistant, for example, or fundraising for the new hospital wing, or helping a friend through her breakup—understanding why we're showing up doing what we're doing helps us connect with a bigger purpose and find satisfaction in what we're up to.

I worked with a leader in a mortgage brokerage firm to systematically connect the dots for each and every team member about why their roles mattered in the grand scheme of things. No one was left feeling like a cog in the wheel, because even the most junior analyst could see how their small step in the process led to the rewarding outcome of families moving into their dream homes.

An account executive I worked with at an advertising agency mustered up the courage to ask for specific feedback and testimonials from several of her key clients. "It was meaningful to learn that what I'm doing makes an actual difference," she said after receiving glowing reviews. "We joke here at the agency about the trifling deodorant ads my team comes up with, and now I see the impact of our work. Our campaigns have a direct relationship on our clients' revenues, which helps them give people raises, promote people, give other humans a good living. Lavender Meadows deodorant isn't so silly after all."

Reflect for a moment on the impact of the roles you play in and out of work. Is there a ripple effect of your work on other people or outcomes?

2. Adopt a giving mindset.

It's no surprise we make meaning when we set aside our self-centered interests to serve someone or something outside of ourselves. Volunteers consistently experience more meaning and purpose in their lives compared to those who don't volunteer. One study[8] out of the United Kingdom found that volunteering elicited positive changes in one's well-being and even went so far as to calculate that volunteering makes us as happy as receiving a bonus of £911 ($1,120) per year.

There is such a thing as a "helper's high," but it goes deeper than that delicious hedonic feeling. Helping and giving connect us in some way to other humans, which paves the way for meaning. Relationships and well-being are joined at the hip.

Many people I work with fall into the "all or nothing" trap—believing they need to sign up for arduous and frequent shifts at the soup kitchen to make a meaningful dent in the world. They simply don't have time for that kind of commitment, so they give up on giving as a route to fulfillment. Research,[9] perhaps relievingly, shows that random acts of kindness provide a notable win-win scenario, too: both the giver and the receiver benefit from a well-being boost . . . even though we consistently underestimate how much the recipient will appreciate the gesture.

One woman I worked with who was feeling particularly egocentric after a string of successes made a "casual kindness" list and proceeded to tick off a box per day for a month. She brought flowers to an elderly neighbor, bought a coffee for the person in the drive-through line behind her, mailed out-of-nowhere "thinking of you" notes on pretty stationery to friends and family, dropped off donated towels to the dog shelter, took a new junior colleague out for coffee, brushed the snow off a stranger's windshield, complimented her son's teacher in front of the principal, left a ginormous tip for a lovely server, and so on.

How might you be able to help someone today?

3. Boost your self-awareness.

Research[10] consistently shows that people who really know themselves—their true selves, what they value, what motivates them, what makes them tick, what ticks them off, what they are really talented at and capable of and fearful of—tend to believe life is more meaningful.

Authenticity can seem as elusive as Bigfoot. Can one really put one's finger on who one is at the core? Can this really be a wellspring of meaning? Yes, and yes.

This exploration of "getting to know you" is some of the most gratifying work I get to do with clients—and not because I get to know them (although that's never not lovely)—because people get to know themselves, warts and all.

I'm thinking of one client who came to terms with his real self rather than just the version he presented to the outside world. He drew a mind map on one of those giant sticky notes of what mattered to him in life (achievement, integrity, and financial security), what his fears were (being found out as a fraud*), what themes were resonant in his life (growth and exploration), who needed to be in his life (his husband and their Dalmatian), what sparked him in a good way (recognition and small wins within a big project), what set him off in a bad way (pretty much anything his mother said to him), where he needed to grow (not caring what people thought of him as much, being less defensive), and so on... This excavation allowed for a radical acceptance of his fabulousness and his opportunities for development.

---

* Of the imposter-phenomenon sort, not the embezzlement sort.

Are you willing to look deeply into the mirror (and not just to tweeze), to get to know that person you really are deep down? What motivates you and *de*motivates you?

4. Be willing to compromise on the hedonic high.

We often experience meaning at the expense of happiness. Some of the most meaningful things we do are decidedly unhappy endeavors at times, but we self-sacrifice for the good of the cause (parents everywhere—I see you).

One of my clients looked after her mother for a year before she passed away, and although it was one of the most exhausting challenges of her life, it also made her life feel exponentially more meaningful. She keeps a photo of her always-cooking mom in her kitchen as a poignant reminder that life is fleeting and special.

Another client I worked with was a family crimes prosecutor, which could never ever be described as a happy-go-lucky, fun-loving job—but her life was rich with meaning. This suited her for several years until she yearned for something different in her life, something a little lighter. She transitioned to providing legal counsel for a nonprofit.

I recently worked with a dynamo of a woman who completed an Ironman triathlon, which meant that her life was swallowed up whole by training for a race that included a 2.4-mile swim, a 112-mile bicycle ride, and a marathon 26.22-mile run. Was she giddy during her three-hour-long Sunday training runs, while her son was playing baseball without her in the stands to cheer him on? Was she elated while participating in the grueling race during a cold, torrential downpour? No. And yet preparing for and participating in this race was one of the most mean-ing-inducing activities she has ever known. She regularly draws on this story of perseverance to pull through when thrown life's curve balls.

Are you open to a trade-off every now and then of width for depth?

5. Bolster your belonging.

Why do you think people are most likely to mention "family" when asked what provides them with a sense of meaning? The sense of belonging that people experience from being a part of a family unit or from a close personal relationship leads to feeling valued (i.e., the opposite of loneliness—which is a massive epidemic in our society and carries the same health risk as smoking fifteen cigarettes a day[11]).

Positive relationships reassure us that we belong, that someone cares if we show up for choir practice, that someone notices if we're alive or dead. Meaning is not something we make in a vacuum, all alone in our basements. Meaning largely exists because of other people.

Positive Psychology Interlude: Can we please talk about *mattering*[12]—one of my favorite concepts that I all but insist my corporate clients eat up? Mattering refers to our universal need to be noticed; it includes the experiences of *adding value* and *feeling valued*. Think of these as complementary elements on a scale we want to balance over time.

Adding value is all about doing work that feels meaningful, with a sense of autonomy and mastery…the belief at the end of the day that we've proudly left it all out on the field. Bravo, us!

Feeling valued is all about being acknowledged and recognized for our work, feeling like things are fair and that we belong. Belonging is crucial: even if we're delivering grade A work, if we don't feel like our team members or clients or family care about our hard work—or us—things don't feel so hot, do they? Many of the most capable clients I work with are doing some of the best work of their lives, and they go squirrelly because they don't feel like it matters to anyone.

How balanced is your mattering scale these days? Are you bored because you're unable to contribute work that "means something"? Are you feeling unnoticed and therefore unmoored because you don't feel valued? Awareness of where your scale is off-balance can help you either find a way to do more work that has oomph or communicate what you might need more of from your team, boss, or family.

I coached a client during The Plague who was burning the midnight oil at a new job, churning out epic amounts of quality work. He was invigorated by his accomplishments, but he didn't feel like he was part of the team. Working remotely made him feel like the permanent new guy, despite best efforts to connect. It didn't help that his colleagues seemed to prefer working individually and were largely uninterested in *teaming* as a verb. After several months of trying to fit in—of trying to be noticed, which never feels motivating—he realized he needed to resume his job search and find a workplace where he mattered. He found a new organization that valued belonging... and him. He felt like he mattered, and with that, he also found deeper meaning.

6. Consider a spiritual infusion in life.

Finding a connection to something bigger than yourself can be profoundly impactful on your ability to find meaning and a path toward the good life. Spirituality and religiosity have been found to be positive predictors of people's subjective well-being in more studies[13] than we have time on earth to discuss.

Spirituality can be considered a connection to the essence of life, originating from a relationship with oneself, others, the humanities (like art, music, or literature), nature, and/or the transcendent. Spirituality may or may not include organized religion, which has been shown to help people form coherent views of their lives and the world, especially during stressful circumstances.

Research[14] tells us that people who attend weekly religious services—regardless of denomination—strongly agree their life has meaning... 67 percent in one study, compared to 36 percent of people who never attend religious services. It's not that atheists don't find meaning—they just find proportionally more of it in hobbies, other activities, and finances.

Religion has been shown to both alleviate and inflame fears of death.[15] It can facilitate the belief and hope of immortality through the portal of an afterlife or alternate plane of existence, yet it can also trigger incremental anxiety for those who fear they aren't living up to the expectations of an unforgiving doctrine or God.

Spirituality enables us to discover a sense of significance in our lives. I led a CEO peer advisory board for five years, and many of the entrepreneurial leaders longed to shift from "a life of success to a life of significance." For many this was achieved, in part, by connecting with a spiritual realm. I'll never forget my trepidation around hiring a meditation expert to speak to the group at one of our monthly meetings; I worried the CEOs would roll their judgmental eyes at something as fuzzy as a "spiritual intervention." I was fantastically wrong. This group of hard-charging, KPI-focused chiefs hung on every word this presenter had to say. Many hired the speaker for one-on-one meditation and breathing work, to help spiritually center themselves and provide what one eloquent leader called "inner peace in an otherwise clusterfuckish reality."

I've noticed that many clients yearn to return to their spiritual or religious roots, that they've let their practice fall by the wayside as they prioritized other phases of life. Many are hesitant to talk about it, but it's there, like a quiet but persistent spiritual whispering. I think if it's whispering to you, then it matters, and you might benefit from checking it out and seeing if a return to religion or a spiritual practice is right for you.

To what extent do you have an overarching aim for your life, and what role does spirituality play toward that aim? Might you want to reconnect with a religion that once anchored you in meaning? Might you want to dabble in a new ideology to feel that connection with something beyond yourself and your worries and woes? Perhaps a walk in nature might achieve this for you?

7. Become a savorer.

People who are reflective about what lies ahead into the future, or contemplative about hard times they conquered in the past—these people tend to welcome more meaning in their lives.

Savoring is what we're talking about here, and it's about fully feeling, enjoying, and extending our positive experiences. It's associated with a boosted sense of well-being and increased engagement, meaning, positive emotions, and gratitude . . . I call it the low-hanging fruit of a well-lived life.

Savoring the moment is about mindfully engaging in whatever is happening right here, right now—relishing the bright flavor of the lemon tart you're eating one bite at a time, reveling in the art on the gallery wall that you happen to find captivating, delighting in the look on your toddler's face as she blows bubbles, savoring This Very Moment.

We can also savor the past, which is a gift we so often don't give ourselves. When was the last time you walked down a pleasant memory lane, looking at old photos or memorabilia, evoking the laughter or positive glow from that trip to Jackson Hole? Or your wedding day? Or New Year's 2000? Or that incredible presentation you gave last year? Or that email from the president of your company that said you're "a gem"?

 Coaching Chestnut: I recommend keeping a Warm + Fuzzy folder in your inbox to save the emails that make you feel like a billion bucks (or even just twenty bucks). If it makes you smile because of a compliment or kind words, file it away to reread later for an instant warm glow of meaning.

And lastly, we can pre-savor, which means actively anticipating great things on the horizon. It's lovely to look forward to a yacht tour of the Mediterranean, but for the rest of us who don't get regularly chartered around the seas, we can still pre-savor a girls' spa weekend, attending your son's well-prepared-for piano recital, wearing your stunning new shoes out to that upcoming cocktail party, or even planning what you're going to put on your ice cream sundae this Sunday night.

8. Go challenge chasing.
Meaning-filled people love a good Gordian knot. They love the art and science of untangling a problem or working at their upper limit of capability. It could be tackling the tasks that no one else wants to deal with in the office, creating a household budget (again, that no one else in their right mind wants to deal with), finishing an online course, nailing a Van Halen guitar solo, flashing a 5.11+ route at the climbing gym, or putting a 1,500-piece puzzle together.

9. Embrace suffering, loss, and discomfort.
No, those words weren't all typos (*heavy sigh*). People with significant meaning in their lives have typically undergone struggles that rocked

Positive Psychology Interlude: We really need to talk about flow[16] again, the glorious state of psychological absorption when we're immersed in highly engaging activities. It's that prized state of immersion in an activity that's not too beyond your skill set to make you feel like a born loser and just challenging enough to not make you feel like you were lobbed a softball. We usually think of it as a life-widening, hedonic, feel-good state of being, but meaning-full people live in flow, a lot. They're learning and growing while avoiding boredom and anxiety...riding the wave of that sweet spot between challenge and skill that churns out meaning.

Meaning can come from experiences that happen to us, like trauma, deaths of loved ones, or memento mori contemplations (these are called "push" experiences); or meaning can come from actively pursuing activities and moments that add substance to our lives (the "pull" model). Just another way of saying we don't have to wait for life to happen to us—we can "pull" meaning into our lives every day.

The act of deliberately discovering the world around us sows the seeds for meaning to take root and bloom. The "discovered life" involves us being curious serendipity seekers, willing to explore and find activities that light the flame in our furnace, willing to immerse ourselves in the pursuits that open up the faucets of flow.

What activities get you into flow? Do you seek out enough challenges in your life to keep you engaged and motivated?

their world and caused them to put the pieces back together again (hello, Humpty Dumpty). Crises precipitate a search for meaning.

This counterintuitive embrace of adversity ranges from the benign to malignant. Loss of a loved one, bankruptcy, debilitating illness, rehab stint #3, near-death experiences, getting pink-slipped from a dream job...meaning appears to emerge from the full gamut of unfortunate events that life reliably throws at us.

Meaning can be made from the growing pains we feel when we're learning or developing in pursuit of being better versions of ourselves— like the weekends spent working on an advanced degree, when you could be out enjoying all the bottomless mimosa brunches that life has to offer.

Traumas—small *t* and capital *T* alike—can also yield meaning. As we spoke about in chapter 5, 30 to 70 percent of people who experience traumatic events experience post-traumatic growth,[17] the phenomenon that involves rising to a higher level of functioning as a result of a major life crisis.

I used to work with people who had lost their jobs and were trying to figure out their next career chapter. So many of us intertwine our identities with our jobs, don't we? It can be devastating for achievement-oriented professionals to be exited from roles that define who they are as humans... even if they wanted to leave the job in the first place, because *we just want to be the ones doing the leaving.* The roller coaster ride of being let go from said shit job, getting the interview sweats, being rejected from so-close opportunities that looked promising; job searching is not for the faint of heart. And yet the process of finding a new job is often a soul-searching endeavor that is undeniably enriched with meaning. Most clients emerged with a heightened self-awareness ("Here are the amazing things I have to offer"), more humility, a broadened perspective on "what went down" at their last job, a newfound appreciation for employment, and a healthy acceptance of the impermanence of pretty much everything.

Think of any misfortunes you've experienced in life. When you brush aside the rubble of the trouble, was meaning born amid those ashes? Existential struggle invariably leads to existential health.*

10. Pursue awesomeness.

Living deeper, through the engagement of eudaimonic† activities, is associated with greater connection to our values, meaning, and what are known as "elevating experiences"[18] that ignite senses of awe, transcendence, and inspiration.

---

* Don't worry: you aren't necessarily void of character if your life hasn't been forged by fire thus far.... You just might need to build meaning in other ways.
† Quick refresher: *eudaimonic* is the deeper side of well-being, in contrast to the frolicsome side of *hedonic* well-being.

Have you had an elevating experience? Have you experienced a sense of awe, maybe visiting Stonehenge or witnessing breathtaking talent—like a figure skater who triple salchows her way to an epic gold-medal performance? When was the last time you lost yourself in something that seemed colossally bigger than you, as mysterious as that sounds? Getting swept up in *awe*some experiences gives us that distinct feeling we're a part of something vast, that the world isn't just these bodies and heads of ours we're usually so myopically focused on. Awe can help us contemplate the myriad factors that made this moment possible.

 Coaching Chestnut: Awe in Space. Have you heard of the overview effect?[19] It's the view of Earth from space that astronauts are fortunate to experience. NASA astronauts have repeatedly commented on how no level of training could have prepared them for the magical, awe-inspiring experience of being simultaneously removed from yet connected to our planet from their spaceships. This is known as perceived vastness, and it's often accompanied by feelings of self-diminishment. This self-transcendent state can help us become less focused on ourselves and our trivial worries and more connected to other people. Self-diminishment, in this way, is saturated with meaning.

Researchers[20] sent sixty older adults out on fifteen-minute walks over an eight-week period. Study participants were randomly assigned to either a "control walk" (with no special instructions) or an "awe walk" (asked to walk in new locations, to take photos, and tap into their sense of wonder). The awe walkers experienced increases in joy, greater feelings of social connection, greater smile intensity (Yes! That's a thing!), and greater feelings of being part of something larger than themselves during their walks (as made evident in what the study researchers called "self-size"; the awe walkers included increasingly less of themselves and increasingly more of the background scenery in their photographs over the course of the eight weeks).

How can you tap into your sense of wonder, awe, thrill, and the mystery of being alive? Where can you go to be in the presence of vastness, so as to encourage a sense of self-smallness? The good news is that you don't need a lofty budget of time or money in the event that you can't get to the Grand Canyon or the moon in person; looking at photos or videos of wonder-full things can still spark awe and meaning.

11. Generate generativity.

This aspect of meaning oozes with self-transcendence and has been shown to be the most significant predictor of meaningfulness of all.[21]

Generativity refers to our innate human desire to create or be involved with things that will outlast us after we're dead and gone. It's Erikson's seventh stage of development, better known as *Generativity vs. Stagnation*; generativity is all about contribution to the world for generations to come; stagnation is all about anchoring into an "I'm okay being stuck in my stale comfort zone over here" self-absorbed mindset.

People who are inspired to create and do things that will endure beyond their death—like mentoring kids, creating art, starting a company, or donating money to a local library that will serve others for years into the future—these people bathe in meaning at times in life where the rest of us are often wondering what it's all for.

Generativity is the gift that keeps on giving for those who give the gift and those who benefit from the endowment, or the trees planted, or the life-changing self-help book that wakes them up to life. The *generater* wins from an immortality project (hark back to our deathly denial conversation), and the *generatee* wins from the figurative and literal gifts bestowed upon them.

One of my favorite keynotes to deliver is aimed at helping people determine what they want their legacy to be. The conversations always start out the same way: attendees think they need copious amounts of cash to leave a "proper" legacy. Au contraire! You can be remembered through the examples you set for others, the values you demonstrate, the stories you tell that might endure for future generations, the innovative ideas you come

up with, the processes you invent at work, the hand-carved chess pieces that get handed down to your kids and their kids and their kids, the tree you planted in your backyard (hello, Johnny Appleseed!), and the list goes on as deep as your imagination will take you.

How might you live a life of consequence? How might you create something generative in your own life? What pathways can you help forge for others? Might this contemplation cause you to edit your obituary or eulogy 2.0 drafts?

LIVING ON PURPOSE

As a new coach way back in the day, the fastest way I learned to turn off new clients was to preface their introductory Discovery session with "So, what's your life purpose?" Deers. In. Headlights. (I'd like to apologize to the first seventy-five clients I worked with.)

Purpose is so often laced with the pressure to find it (like the other *p* words *passion* and don't even get me started on *potential*—a surefire way to spark a panic attack), so let's depressurize for a moment. You don't have to be clear on your purpose right now—you're very allowed to have your mission be murky or even totally see-through because it just isn't evident yet. Our goal is to get you a little bit clearer on some of your reasons for living.

Purpose is baked into the definition of meaning; it refers to more of a "deliverable" kind of goal. Purpose can be a long-term life aspiration, goal, or a direction that we're consistently working toward, like "educating kids," or "curing ALS," or "being an amazing aunt".... It usually involves a contribution to the planet in some way, toward a cause that matters in some way to you.

Educating kids as a purpose in life, for example, might deliver the big bang of meaning through connecting to others, feeling that you've somehow made a difference in the lives of the hundreds of students you've taught, feeling like you've shaped a future generation.

Psychologists[22] have found that that finding a direction for life, and setting overarching goals for what you want to achieve, can help you actually live longer—regardless of when you find that purpose. So the earlier someone comes to a direction for life, they say, the earlier these protective effects may occur.

Researchers[23] have also shown that *not* having a purpose in life is almost two and a half times likelier to kill you than having a reason to wake up in the morning. (Okay, so I said, "no pressure," and now I've told you you're going to die in a hurry if you don't have your purpose nailed down. Life: it fucks with us!)

Only 40 percent[24] of Americans report having a clear sense of purpose though, which means that 60 percent of us are dangling precariously over the edge of meaninglessness. People who do feel their lives are already full of meaning report a consistent search for more...and this might be you right now—always interested in taking things up a notch.

Let's be clear: our purpose doesn't have to be a magnanimous thing that impresses people. No one has to even know what it is (unless you work with a nosy coach). Some clients I work with *do* want to do ostensibly big things, like "lead a team that revolutionizes health care"—that's one woman's mission in life. I recently finished working with a client who landed on "being a great parent" as his purpose. And I'll never forget a client who wrestled with it for a while, pressuring herself to pick something big—as though she was going to be graded on her purpose—and she was so excited to finally realize her purpose was "to be the bright spot in people's day." She's the type who you totally want to run into. (And should we give her an A?)

Think of your life purpose as the reason you are on this planet. It's not necessarily about your current job or your profession.... It's something you're meant to accomplish—like a gift you are meant to bring to the party of life. When you're doing the thing that's on purpose for you, you feel fulfilled and as though you're reaching your full potential. When you're not living on purpose or doing things that are in line with your purpose, you feel dead inside.

A woman I worked with was at a loss about this whole meaning subject, to the point she was feeling actively worried about it. "Is my life meaningless?" she wondered out loud. When we reviewed the different sources of meaning in the Meaning-Making Assessment you'll complete in a few pages, she had a little epiphany that nature was a massive source of meaning for her. Being outdoors made her feel most alive, and there was something self-transcendent about it that made her feel part of an enormous galaxy of life and purpose. She joined a hiking club and is making plans to live mostly off the grid when she retires, now that she knows this is such a wellspring of meaning for her.

MEET MICHAEL: AN UNEXPECTED PATH TO PURPOSE

Michael Kutcher is no stranger to health adversity, and speaking with him recently, I ate up every word about the hardships that crystallized his purpose in life. He was diagnosed with cerebral palsy (CP) as a young child and experienced inexplicable heart failure when he was thirteen. Given that his heart had grown to be four times its size, he was told he had three or four weeks to live. That's when things got intense. He went into cardiac arrest, and his life expectancy was further abbreviated to just forty-eight hours. Michael's life was miraculously saved thanks to a last-minute heart donor.*

We know meaning can spring from adversity, but what was Michael's specific portal to purpose? It's not like as a young teenager he woke up from his heart transplant operation with a clear mission; if anything, he proceeded to live out of fear as a young man who believed his heart had a ten-year expiration date. He was scurrying to live: buying a car, getting married, having a kid, buying a house . . . trying to live before what he believed was an imminent death. This does not sound purposeful, does it? And yet it was a gradual breeding ground for meaning.

"I found my purpose when my brother outed me on a *Nightline* interview in 2010. He told the world I had cerebral palsy." (Michael's twin brother's name is Ashton—yes, that one—and Michael wasn't out in the open at that point about his disability.) Like many life-changing moments, they emerge from discomfort. About a month after the *Nightline* interview, Michael received a request to speak at a CP fundraising event. He reluctantly agreed, having never spoken about the topic before and all too recently being "outed" . . . and yet the light switch flicked on

---

* PSA: *Have you filled out your organ donor card yet?!?*

for him. He realized he could use his newfound notoriety as a platform to be an advocate for CP, to help reshape perspectives on what he refers to as "diffabilities."

"I know my purpose. And my purpose here is to help you come to your senses." He wants audience members to think, "What the hell am I bitching about my job for? What am I complaining about my kids for? I've got some personal struggles of my own, and they suck, but here's this guy who's literally died three times, has a disability, and he appreciates life, and he's positive."

Could there be an unexpected path to purpose right in front of you, that you might be overlooking because the path is narrow or overgrown with weeds? Might Michael's story inspire you to look at the causes that you care about or opportunities around you in a new light?

A MEANINGFUL THOUGHT EXPERIMENT

Imagine for a minute that it's the year 1903...so you haven't been born yet. The people who made you probably haven't been born yet either. So it's more than a hundred years ago, and all sorts of things in the universe are conspiring for you to be born.... People are meeting, dating, copulating, whatever it takes for you to get to have a life. Why will you be lucky enough to get to have a life? Why will you be born? What gift will you have to offer?

Maybe the flashback isn't doing it for you, and you're more of a futurist. Imagine it's 2133, and you've been dead and gone for a nice long while—may you be resting comfortably in peace. From that distance of time away, imagine looking back on your life. Why did you get to have a life? What purpose did you serve while you were on the planet for four thousandish Mondays? What impact did you have, big or small?

THE MEANING-MAKING ASSESSMENT

It can be powerful to either say "bingo!" to what you find meaningful in life or...whatever the opposite of bingo is. There is no right or wrong on this "sources of meaning" assessment,[25] so go with your first instinct when answering the questions.

	A LOT OF MEANING	Mucho meaning	Mild meaning	No meaning, thanks	NOT A LOT OF MEANING
1	I'm all about faith, religion, and prayer.				Atheism is my middle name; I'm not explicitly into religion.
2	I have a close connection to what I see as sacred and a reality beyond what is known.				I'm not into unknown realities, and sacred for me isn't about spirituality.
3	I'm an active crusader for human rights and anything that improves our community.				Social commitment isn't a big thing for me.
4	Being in harmony with nature is like oxygen to me. I need to be in it.				I prefer almost no contact with nature, thank you very much.
5	Discovering my authentic, true self is a noble pursuit. I'm all over figuring out who that person is!				Authentic self? I don't really need to get to know the real me.
6	I'm a health nut.				I won't win any awards for maintaining or improving my health.
7	Doing things that give me a feeling of lasting value is so meaningful, like having a park bench named after me or building a legacy.				I couldn't care less if my name lasts beyond the day I die. No need to outlive myself!
8	Seeking novelty, risk, and change are totally important to me.				Change and newness are overrated. I like things the way they are.
9	I am motivated to be my own person, unique from everyone else.				I don't need to be a snowflake who is independent from others. I'm fine to blend in.
10	I like it when I can lead and exert influence over others or situations.				Following is comfortable to me. Why dominate when others are willing to lead?
11	Personal growth is such a high value of mine.				Goals and development have never really motivated me or meant much.
12	Achievement is a biggie in my world.				Success isn't all it's cracked up to be.

	A LOT OF MEANING	Mucho meaning	Mild meaning	No meaning, thanks	NOT A LOT OF MEANING
13	I absolutely want to be in the know, absorbing information. I'm super curious.				Why bother with so many questions? It's too much work to stay on top of all the info.
14	Creativity is a state of being for me, whether it's making something or imagining it.				I don't put a lot of value in fantasy and originality. I don't need to make stuff.
15	I honor tradition in many aspects of my life.				To be honest, I find traditions pointless. Who wants to do the same thing every holiday?
16	I really value practicality in life, being effective at what I do and being useful.				Practicality just sounds boring, doesn't it?
17	I know what I like at restaurants and seek it out again and again. They sometimes know my order when I walk in the door.				I rarely order the same thing twice when I go out to eat.
18	Being moral in my character and actions has been a theme for me since my first fable books as a kid.				Morality and I have a sketchy relationship. Sometimes I skirt the edges of right and wrong.
19	Reason is important to me, having a good, logical argument.				Being rational isn't that important. Logic isn't always the be-all and end-all.
20	Fun is where it's at! No really—where's the party?!?!				Fun and recreation are for children or simpletons.
21	Being a part of a community makes me feel whole and like I belong.				Communities are annoying.
22	Love really is what makes the world go round. I wish we had so much more of it.				I have never understood why people go on and on about love. It's very touchy-feely.
23	Feeling comfortable and prosperous is like medicine for the soul.				I think that comforts in life make you soft and vulnerable.
24	Caring for others and being cared for are basic human needs.				Care is nice, sure, but optional. Food and water are essential. Care is a luxury.

	A LOT OF MEANING	Mucho meaning	Mild meaning	No meaning, thanks	NOT A LOT OF MEANING
25	Being attentive to others' needs, and even my own, is part of my basic operating manual.				I have been accused of being inattentive. I can admit it.
26	Having everyone get along and be in sync is my preferred state.				Harmony schmarmony. Let's use conflict to motivate us all to be better.
27	Overall, my experience of life is meaningful (significant, coherent, and directed).				Overall, my experience of life is frustratingly empty, kind of without a point, and void of meaning.

Making Sense of Your Assessment

1. What was it like to complete this questionnaire?
2. Highlight the areas you feel extrameaningful. Are there ways you might want to extract even more meaning from these purpose-filled pockets in your life?

#	AREA OF LIFE I'M EXPERIENCING A LOT OF MEANING...	WAYS I COULD WRING EVEN MORE MEANING OUT OF THIS ASPECT OF LIFE...

3. Highlight the areas you indicated the *least* amount of meaning, and choose whether you'd like to *do* anything about those aspects of your life...remembering that you don't have to make meaning in *all* areas or in *any* particular area at all. Brainstorm ideas here to come back to later.

#	AREAS OF LIFE WITH NOT SO MUCH MEANING . . .	DO I WANT TO DO ANYTHING ABOUT THIS RIGHT NOW?	IF YES, WHAT ARE IDEAS TO BOLSTER MEANING AND PURPOSE?

4. Go eat a brownie.

THE MERGING OF VITALITY AND MEANING

Here is where the worlds of vitality and meaning join together to create the Astonishingly Alive life. When we fully engage in a host of meaning-filled activities—whatever that looks like for you—we fully appear in our lives. This commitment to getting a "life participation" ribbon alleviates the nagging anxiety of lack of meaning and, more viscerally, allows us to confront our own mortality with peace of mind and acceptance. This decision to really take part in our lives is what connects the dots between vitality and meaning; by playing full out and not sitting on the sidelines of our lives, we turn up the dial on vitality and consequently turn up the volume of meaning.

When our lives are colored in with both absorbed enjoyment and meaning, it's known as "vital engagement."[26] Said differently, you have both a quantity of joy-inducing things in your life and a depth of meaning; you're squarely in that tippy-top right quadrant of the graph back on page 54. It's living an Astonishingly Alive life, my friend.

THE OODLES O' FUN EXISTENTIAL DREAD QUIZ

Because we all love multiple choice questions about our existence!

As we start to round the bend in our time together this chapter, let's put some of our "meaning matters" conversation in context with the bigger picture of life. See if you can identify the Big Five existential concerns[27] we humans typically encounter:

A. Life, identity, meaninglessness, change, spotty Wi-Fi
B. Death, in-laws, meaninglessness, identity, uncertainty
C. Death, isolation, muffin top, freedom, eternal damnation
D. Death, meaninglessness, isolation, freedom, identity

If you answered A, B, or C, you are permanently excused from class (but I'd like to hang out with you afterward anyway). If you answered D, let's raise a glass to you.

It is believed we need to come to terms with these five inescapable parts of the human condition to reach our full potential. An absence of meaning leads to an existential vacuum, which sucks the life out of our days, which we've covered inside out here together. You likely noticed another topic on the Big Five list we've already been wrangling with: *death*.

In our quest to live like we really do *mean* it, death awareness can create even deeper meaning and gratitude for the lives we're fortunate to get to live. Yet another plug for memento mori.

It's not difficult to follow the breadcrumbs of meaning back to memento mori. The existential psychotherapist Irwin Hoffman notes that we create our realities and meanings "in the teeth of the constant threat of nonbeing and meaninglessness"[28] (a real ray of sunshine to brighten your day).

Welcoming the truth that we are going to die helps us *not* waste our lives on meaningless activities. Viktor Frankl stated that death is not just an ingredient in a meaningful life but also a driver—a point that holds significant weight coming from someone who lost his parents, brother, and pregnant wife at Auschwitz. By deliberately tackling the tough existential questions, we create opportunities for greater meaning.

Knowing we are going to die can enrich our experience of being alive; recognizing this fragility-of-being can help us make life choices that align with what matters, with what we find meaningful. Making "matterful," meaningful choices is what adds the depth we are looking for in our lives.

YOUR MEANING CHALLENGE

Your official challenge is to embark on a meaningful journey within the next two weeks of your life (a.k.a. two Mondays). It could be volunteering.

It could be planning a challenging task with your teenage daughter, like researching your family tree. Maybe you tune into an online religious service. Perhaps you map out your ideal legacy. You could call an elderly relative and make a substantial connection, beyond what's going on with the weather. Maybe you sit at the coffee shop and make a list of "The Top 10 Things I Value in Life," really upping the ante on your self-awareness. You might choose a challenging task that sweeps you up into the flow zone. Maybe you sit with a journal and write about the impact you've made at home, at work, in your community—in ways both big and small. It could be seeking out an awe-inspiring experience. You might choose to record three things you're grateful for each night for the month. There is no wrong pathway to meaning; remember that it's the *pursuit* of purpose that does the mighty job of creating depth in this life you get to live.

MEANING CHALLENGE

☐ EMBARK ON A "MEANINGFUL JOURNEY" IN YOUR NEXT 2 WEEKS.

☐ GO DEEP!

 Congratulations for being willing to wring the meaning out of your life. For a wry wrap-up, let's let the Nobel Prize–winning philosopher Albert Camus drop the mic: "The literal meaning of life is whatever you're doing that prevents you from killing yourself." Okay then! Another Monday down, not dead yet. Sounds meaningful to me.

CHAPTER 10

THE PAINT BY NUMBERS PART: SPECIFIC ACTIONS TO LIVE IN VIVID COLOR

 Tell me, what is it you plan to do with your one wild and precious life?
—MARY OLIVER

Look at you, all rosy-cheeked over there! You're starting to look awfully alive, if I do say so myself. You're intoxicated with information and ideas about breadth-busting vitality and depth-plunging meaning—and like any intoxication worth its while, you're slaphappy, but your head is spinning. Here, have some water.

This was to be expected. How could you not feel a bit dizzy after all we've been through? You've been guzzling inspiration for several chapters straight, and now things are swirling. You've survived (and dare I say thrived!) through nine chapters of personal excavation, and now you're chomping at the bit to Do Something Already with all that we've covered. Well, chomp no further! My goal is to arm you with practical, actionable takeaways to implement today (because although you're looking fabulous, there might not be a tomorrow).

What kind of life sounds like the one you'd like to live from today until you're dropped off at the crematorium?

A. A black-and-white life
B. A life in color

C. A technicolor life

D. A pyrotechnic life

If you answered A, then I don't even know how we made it to chapter 10 together. I'm going to assume you got confused or you've been over-served? I'll go get you a Tylenol.

If you answered B, we can work with that. Keep reading.

If you answered C, woo hoo, you!

If you answered D, I can't tell if you're showing off or just fucking fabulous . . . so stick around, amigo!

We want the vivid color version of life—the full-tilt technicolor dreamcoat variety. We want the iridescent, luminous, kaleido-scopic rainbow kind of life. We want astonishing. We want to live like we mean it. All we ever wanted was everything! And so we didn't show up for the "paint by numbers" chapter with a palette full of gray and brown paint, did we?

OKAY SO I SNUCK IN SOME BLACK

YOUR VIVID LIFE

YOU: Wait, did I just show up at art class? I don't have a beret.

ME: Worry not; this *paint with vivid colors* is just a metaphor I'm going to work to death for a good cause . . . for *you*.

I'm a fan of a step-by-step, paint-by-numbers approach, because easy steps cut overwhelm off at its bastardly knees. This means we'll do a round-up of our discussions so far—like a highlight reel of what it takes to live like you mean it—and you'll get to pick what's next.

ADVICE TO MAKE IT THROUGH CHAPTER 10 LIKE A CHAMP

Tip 1: Pour your favorite drink. (I'm thinking of a White Russian, but you do you.)

Tip 2: Situate yourself somewhere comfortable (hopefully in soft, elastic-waisted pants).

Tip 3: Have your notes handy (maybe a few pages pinned up on your wall, some pages on your lap, some on the floor—a full-out *Beautiful Mind* scenario).

Tip 4: Read through the upcoming tips, tricks, and suggested ways to live like you mean it with an open mind. Some of the ideas will feel perfectly designed for you—almost panacea-ish—while others will beg to be scoffed at and crossed out on the page. But try not to dismiss the ones that don't immediately call your name—remember, we're trying to instigate change here.

Tip 5: Highlight and sit with the ideas that strike you. Get excited! Get appropriately nervous! Get in the mood to pull your favorite idea(s) together in the Grand Finale Postmortem (the next—and last—wrap-up chapter).

Tip 6: Go eat a brownie.

PAINT BY NUMBERS STEP #1: TAP INTO TIME, YOUR MOST LIMITED RESOURCE

If we take care of the moments, the years will take care of themselves.

—Maria Edgeworth

Our entire conversation about memento mori has been rooted in the notion of finitude, that our time is limited to give-or-take four thousand Mondays. So in my ongoing pursuit to reach through these pages and grab you (lovingly) by the throat and (gently) throttle you, in a clumsy but well-intended attempt to remind you that time—your most valuable asset—*is running out so pretty please make the most of it*, it would be careless of me to not spend a few of these precious minutes talking about the saving *and* savoring of your time.

I get giddy about any opportunity to mark the passage of time—any kind of calendar, egg timer, hourglass, observation of the longest day of the year (and the less popular shortest day of the year), any way to highlight what was and what will be—all in service of the idea that time is ticking, unapologetically, and that it will pass us by because it's a ruthless mf-er like that. And I say that (mostly) without bitterness because I've accepted that Time Is the Boss around Here. Time is relentless in its passing: it gives no second chances; it stops for no one; it offers zero do-overs to do life *for real this time.*

I respect the consistent way time chugs on, all 86,400 seconds in our days, all 168 hours from one Monday to the next, all 52 Mondays in each year of our lives. Time marches on through our epic achievements and our catastrophic failures, our mundane moments, our worrisome hand-wringing. The engine of time steams on through births, inaugurations, unrequited love, mergers and acquisitions, pandemics, and all ten episodes per glorious season of *The Great British Baking Show.* It's up to us to decide how we spend that time, each precious passing moment—savored or squandered.

I'm using my time to help you make the most of your time (*pause for accolades*), by pointing out **eight ways to savor your Mondays before you go.** Answer the questions after each point and see which ones are worth carrying forward into your actual action plan.

1. Capitalize on the Fresh Start Effect.

Salient temporal landmarks provide the motivation for aspirational behavior. Translation: fresh starts motivate us to get our shit together. There's a reason we're inspired to pursue goals at the onset of key landmarks in time—like committing to become A Way Better Person on January 1 (fresh start for the year), going back to the gym on a Monday (fresh start for the week), quitting smoking on September 1 (fresh start for the month), or looking for a new job on the first day back from a vacation (fresh start back from the land of Tequila Sunrises).

So what do we do with this? When the fresh start of January wears off by February 21 and you've found yourself neglecting the Vitamix and on the verge of canceling your health club membership . . . wait. Find another fresh start, and ride that wave. Get back on the horse the very next Monday or kick off again at the fresh start of another month or season or phase of the moon. We are going to get derailed—we just need to regoal. Mondays are like reset buttons you get to press every week, keeping you motivated and committed to accomplishing the things you believe matter in some way.

What's an example of a goal you're in hot pursuit of these days? Can you preidentify fresh starts when the fire to pursue your goal goes from hot to lukewarm?

2. Use the Fast Finish Effect to your advantage.

In a recent email chitchat with the author Daniel Pink about the limits mortality places on time, he referred to the Fast Finish Effect,[1] which salutes our inclinations to exert more effort as a deadline nears. The approach of a new decade inspires us to take action: when we reach the last year of a chronological decade (29, 39, 49, 59, and so on), we get our shit together (either that or shit hits the fan). One study[2] revealed that a significantly incommensurate number of firsttime marathoners are at an age that ends in a 9. These "9-enders" were also shown to run 2.30 percent faster in marathons compared to the two years before and after.*

As we face important endings, we have the chance to respond adaptively to our internal search for existential meaning. What endings are in store for you that might trigger healthy action? What finish lines can you fathom to persist toward your goals?

3. Get to know both Chronos and Kairos.

The ancient Greeks offered this world so much more than baklava. Chronos refers to how we traditionally understand the notion of time—the qualitative measure of seconds, hours, days, weeks, and so on. Chronos's tirelessly ticking clocks keep us on time for chiropractor appointments

---

* It's at this point that we're going to gloss over similar research that busts male 9-enders for exuberantly and disproportionately participating in an online extramarital affair dating website. Endings can be motivating; it's up to us to use our motivation as a force for good instead of evil.

and give us the structure to conveniently calculate our remaining Mondays.

Kairos, more poetically, refers to the qualitative measurement of the opportune moments in our lives. Say what? "Opportune" or right moments might look like knowing when to bid adieu to an unfulfilling job, knowing when to go in for that first kiss, knowing when to pick the tomatoes in the garden, knowing when to embark on an adventure, knowing when to put the pen down, knowing when to reach out for help for your life-zapping eating disorder.

I spend most of my hyperorganized time in the realm of Chronos but miss some of the signals and senses about Kairos. Are you also swept up in managing your life by the hour, so much so that you miss the call of Kairos's fortuitously timed moments in life? How can you slow down and tune into those right moments that just might be right in front of you... maybe even now?

4. Imagine a fabulous old age.

Researchers[3] tell us that how we *think* we'll be in old age is a reliable predictor of how we'll *actually be* in old age. If we vividly imagine the kind of person we'd like to be far into our future and optimistically believe we can become that version of ourselves in our old age, we'll not only influence our aging outcome, but we'll live longer.

They[4] say that people at fifty who envision themselves positively when they're older (like as an active, social, healthy person) live seven and a half years longer than those who are Negative Nellies about the future (like those who expect to be couch-ridden, chronically sick, dependent on others, cranky, and shooing kids off their lawns).

Reflect on who you hope to be when you're old—at whatever age "old" means to you.[*5] Can you consciously imagine yourself as a vibrantly alive person as you age? Maybe you want to be connected to a strong network

---

* Millennials believe the average person becomes old at fifty-nine (proof that youth is, in fact, wasted on the young), whereas Gen Xers define old age as sixty-five. Baby Boomers and beyond believe the magic number is seventy-three, which is consistent with research that explores how older adults push their perceptions of age transitions out to help make themselves feel younger.

of friends and family...deeply engaged in challenging hobbies...getting an impressive number of steps in each day...learning and growing and taking classes...What else is possible for you?

5. Make time as tangible as possible.

We take time, like the Mondays you have ahead of you, more seriously when we understand it with precision. We're more inclined to think abstractly about events that we perceive as psychologically distant or far into the future (e.g., "retirement is a far-off figment of my imagination, so I'll just plan for it later"). Scientists[6] have made it clear that details become fuzzy or absent altogether when we construe larger psychological distances, whereas details become more concrete when we perceive events and possibilities to have smaller psychological distances.

Here's the problem: perceiving the amount of time until your next big life event, for example, as fuzzy and void of details, is like raising your hand and volunteering to squander your time. How can you unfuzz the details to start being more intentional with your time rather than letting the months and years all bleed into one? Visual calendars help. What plans can you actively make to help shrink that psychological distance of time? Here are a couple to get you started:

- Booking all of your vacation time off through the end of the year...so you don't forfeit it.
- Marking off how much time you have until a big anniversary and exactly how you'd like to celebrate the auspicious occasion...so it feels special and doesn't pass you by.
- Setting vividly visual financial milestones toward your retirement in the calendar...so you're excited about a vibrant future rather than a vague expanse of time that'll just get pilfered away.
- Creating an interactive Google doc to plan a big weekend getaway with your buddies that's far into the future...so you pre-savor it and get as much joy from the event rather than letting it approach and feel like "just another weekend at the cottage."
- Counting down the Mondays you have left in life...so your time doesn't slip through your fingers. (Oh! We've already covered that one.)

How can you make your decades ahead feel more concrete and less abstract? More like invigorating sprints? Setting intentions and plans are a heck of a great start. How might you slice and dice some of those lofty goals into milestones, to make your time feel tangible and front row center?

6. Understand your desires will change over time.

Socioemotional selectivity theory[7] proves what we intuitively know to be true: our perception of time horizons significantly impacts our motivation and goals. As we age and perceive time to be limited, we tend to favor goals related to meaning and emotional satisfaction. When we're bright-eyed and bushy-tailed in our younger years, we perceive time to be more open-ended and nebulous, and we typically pursue goals that veer toward knowledge acquisition and novelty-seeking. This explains why sixty-three-year-olds are into volunteering with friends at the food bank, while twenty-three-year-olds are into backpacking across Europe with questionably long stays in Amsterdam.

When time feels open-ended, we prioritize more vitality-filled goals. When time feels limited, we prioritize more meaning-filled emotional goals. Since time is such a pliant, moldable construct, it's possible to manipulate our perceptions of our horizons to balance the vitality and meaning in our lives. We can make time feel more expansive if we keep learning, growing, and seeking novelty.

If you're on the older side, how can you use novelty to stoke the fires of vitality? If you're on the younger side, how can you reflect on your diminishing number of Mondays left to help add more meaning and emotional nuance to your life?

7. Get rich on time affluence.

Time affluence, as you might remember from our vitality chapter, refers to our perception of having enough time for our duties and desires, so we don't feel overly hurried as we finish that PowerPoint deck and take Kimmie to the orthodontist.

Having too little leisure time leads to increased stress, whereas people higher in time affluence report[8] spending more time engaged in personal growth activities, connecting with others, and participating in physical fitness activities.*

So how do we find that zest zone? How do we feel a little more time rich when most of us are feeling time bankrupt?

The good news is that across seven studies[9] with over six thousand participants, it became clear that spending money to buy back time spikes our satisfaction with life. Paying someone to shop for our groceries and deliver them? A great idea if it saves us ninety minutes. Paying someone to clean our place? A great idea if it saves us several hours (not to mention our fresh manicure). There are brigades of people who can trim our hedges, do our taxes, skim the leaves out of our pools, paint our sunrooms, and build our websites. We are probably smart and capable enough to slog through those tasks on our own, but unless they bring us joy, outsource our hearts out whenever we can afford it.

But what if we can't afford to buy time? We're not all in the position to outsource the polishing of our rare silver coin collection so we can spend more time on the yacht. We get creative; that's what we do. We time-stack. If we want to carve out a spare three hours on a Saturday morning, we find a way to stack our tasks and activities in a "kill two to-dos with one stone" effect. Invite a friend to our bootcamp class, and—presto—we've saved an hour by stacking our social fix *and* workout time. Doing laundry while going camera-free in a banal Zoom meeting and—ta-da—another hour saved. All of a seeming sudden, we have an extra few hours to do whatever we darned well please that makes us feel more alive. Now, I want to be very clear that my goal here is not to get you to stack time so you can answer more emails, take on another soul-sucking renovation project, or spend all night making allergen-free cookies for the bake sale you got strong-armed into. My goal is to help you find free time to do something that truly adds value to your day.

8. Getting ruthless with protecting your time.
Maintaining time affluence also requires fastidious protection of our calendars, saying things like, "Sorry! I can't make the committee meeting

---

* These time-rich people are very easy to hate. Too bad they're too busy enjoying life to care if you hate them.

tonight, so I'll catch up with Raj later on the highlights," or as the ballers out there advise, "No is a complete sentence." I am not comfortable responding with a one-word "no" and then walking away after someone has asked me for help—but the spirit is noted: we don't need to overapologize and overexplain why we can't sell raffle tickets this weekend.

Building in unstructured, "white space" time can also create the feeling of time richness, largely because it's a breeding ground for creativity. It's tough to conjure up ideas, solutions, and dreams when we're focused on finishing the Quarterly Bullshit Report at work. Blocking off and honoring an hour a week for ideas, strategy, and life planning creates an oasis of calm control that can permeate through the rest of our time-starved frenzied schedules.

When can you carve out a small block of time for white space?

Before we shift off the topic of time, can I encourage you to pause and review these seven points about time? Of these seven considerations, which one feels most pertinent to you in your life right now? Why is this one worth focusing on? What do you have to gain by paying attention to this notion of time?

PAINT BY NUMBERS STEP #2: DIAGNOSE THE DEAD ZONES

Phew! This step is pretty much colored in already, because you've taken all the assessments along the way. After sixty-eight questions in the Astonishingly Alive assessment (page 32), fifty-two questions in the Anti-Autopilot assessment (page 194), twenty-seven questions in the Meaning-Making assessment (page 256), and a bunch of other quizzes along the way, *you know you by now*. But we must color things in with an even finer paintbrush! It's one thing to say you're "Meaningfully Bored," and it's another thing to zero in on *where* things have lost their oomph.

Where does each realm of your life sit on the Dead or Alive Scale, as of this moment?

☠ Work/Career Life
☠ Family Life
☠ Friend/Social Life

- Significant Other Life
- Health/Fitness Life
- Spiritual Life
- Recreation/Leisure Life
- Financial Life
- Personal Growth Life

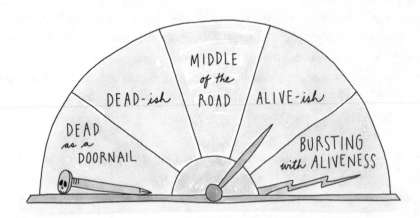

Which parts of your life are on fire with aliveness? Keep. Up. The. Good. Work!

Which domains of your life are worth undeading? You don't have to undead all the dead zones, and certainly not at once. It's okay to put some of the dead zones on ice for a while—yes, like a body being chilled at the morgue—if you're not ready to deal with it just yet (like if you have a new baby and a new job . . . maybe it's just fine to have a dead zone in your leisure life for a beat).

Now that your dead zones are ~~glaring~~ staring at you in the face, you're better equipped to design a plan to bring them back to life. Onward . . .

PAINT BY NUMBERS STEP #3: YOUR REGRETS ROUNDUP

Remember your morphine-infused deathbed visualization back in chapter 6—that little party we had? Here is your chance to corral and record your pre-grets in one colorful place. List all things big and small, and

MY PRE-GRETS LIST:

remember to focus on the things you'd regret *not doing* if your time was up, not the regrets of commission.

Looking at your list above, do you see any connections between your dead zones and your potential regrets? It's likely your pre-grets tick and tie with the parts of your life you'd like to focus on.

Of all the pre-grets on your list, which ones give you the biggest pangs? Are these worth intervening, so as to redirect and prevent the regrets?

PAINT BY NUMBERS STEP #4: GET OUT YOUR SNOW GLOBES (TO SHAKE UP)

You will recall that we hated on habits in chapter 7, and we decided they do not have a seat at the table* of our decidedly alive lives.

---

* Well. Habits and routines do have a place, but on the laundry-folding table, not at the lovely dinner table that we've set with the nice china, because, #yodo.

Since novelty and variety are crucial for a thriving human experience, you spent time thinking about routines and patterns you wanted to interrupt—just enough to shake things up, stave off boredom, and live a psychologically rich life.

What are the habits and routines you'd like to jostle every now and then? How do you plan to do the jostling?

Let's get a little more action oriented when talking about boosting your curiosity and adventure.

Go Get Curious

- **Make a list of things that interest you,** then set aside dedicated time to learn more about them. Look up MOOCs,* podcasts, TED talks, articles, interviews, coffees with experts, whatever it takes to feel more knowledgeable about your subjects of interest. Give yourself permission to get lost online for the finite period of time you can afford.
- **Design your own curriculum.** One of my clients picked one topic per month to delve into and created summary notes (and even PowerPoint slides!) to capture his key takeaways. Maybe pair up with an equally curious friend and present your findings to one another each month? Or to your team at work?
- **"Take notice" around your community.** Imagine it's your first time in your neighborhood, and see your environment through fresh eyes. Find something new in your backyard, on your street, at the corner store, around the park, and so on. What have you been taking for granted or overlooking?
- **Take a different route** when driving to the office / dropping the kids off at swim practice / taking your evening bike ride. It's easier to be curious in new environments.
- **Fully investigate a future experience:** plan a weekend visit to a new city, or reservations at an avant-garde restaurant, and research ahead of time what you'll do or eat. What's the history of the city you're visiting, and what's its claim to fame? Where's the best place to eat

---

* Massive open online courses: Free! Amazing! Education!

breakfast there? For the restaurant, what's the chef's story? What does their wine list look like? And why did they name it Charlie's Cornichon Emporium?

Adventure Inducers

Now that your curiosity antennae are up on alert, you're ready for adventure—without necessarily having to pack your bags. Wondering how to create remarkable excursions so life feels more like an adventure and less like a wretchedly slow and monotonous spiral toward our inevitable death? Aren't we all? Make note of the points that tempt you.

- Make a habit of saying "hell yes!" instead of "um, no thanks" (unless Tom asks you to stay late to fix the printer). "Hell yes" means breaking up with inertia and saying yes to things that might initially feel a little uncomfortable but end up being full of something interesting and *alive*. Yes to tiki bar invitations! Yes to that eight-pack of Intro to Dance classes! Yes to blind dates! Yes to that high-profile project at work! Yes to visiting your high school bestie in Detroit! Yes to going out on a Friday night when the couch beckons! Yes to sneaking backstage! Yes to the eel! Yes to nude painting classes!* Rid yourself of any guilt surrounding saying no to things that deenergize you or bust your boundaries, but ask yourself which opportunities are sitting in front of you that might just need a resounding response of "yes."
- Carve out adventure-inspiration time. Best-kept secrets are no longer secretive in the Age of the Supercomputer. Our parents had to go out and seek adventure-in-the-raw, but we get to plan our sojourns!

---

* I was thinking you'd be painting the nude guy, but I suppose if you're up for a size large dose of adventure, you could be the nude model?

(Wait—maybe it was cooler to hit the road with just a station wagon and a folded-up map?) Check out *Atlas Obscura* for a horde of excursions that are waiting to delight you (like my client who went with them to Vietnam for "A Culinary Adventure from Hanoi to Saigon"). Google will also do a decent job of serving you up some fresh "things to do near me" ideas. Or afar. When might you fit in time to explore possible ideas? Even fifteen minutes over lunch?

- ☠ **Keep a list of "Adventures to Embark on before I Die."** Think of this as a catalog from which to draw when you're jonesing for something out of the ordinary. *Not* capturing your ideas in advance guarantees you'll come up empty for ideas on a Saturday morning when faced with forty-eight hours of time in front of you. Keep at least a dozen things on the list, ranging from the "economical and entertaining" (like attending a pay-what-you-can meditation class at the local community center) to the "big and brash" (like taking a sommelier course . . . in Barcelona). After researching ideas and options, what dozen things are on your list?

- ☠ **Find an adventure buddy.** It's not as easy to get going on a remarkable afternoon of spelunking . . . alone. Make a pact with a friend who also wants a more adventurous existence that you'll take turns planning a monthly escapade. Who could be a part of your adventure squad? How many people do you want to invite into the club? Do you want to make membership cards?*

- ☠ **Embrace "slow adventure."** It's the slow cooking of the travel and adventure world! Not into the adrenaline-packed bungee-jumping excursions? You might favor immersive experiences that slow the pace down and get in deep with nature and the environment and the culture and the peoples of an area.

- ☠ **Strike the planning/spontaneity balance.** Plans fuel ideas, but they can feel strangle-y if we fanatically follow them hour by hour. One of my most organized clients planned to *not* plan a vacation (other than lodging—phew), and she loved the spur-of-the-moment decisions she and her partner made. Are you willing to (*shudder*) *turn the car around* to check out the cute little antique store you just drove by in

---

* I'm kidding but not really.

that one-horse town, on your way to your *real* destination? Are you willing to (*shudder again*) pull off the highway to check out the state capital—on a whim—as one of my clients did while driving through Springfield to Chicago? One day I want to show up at the airport with a packed bag, have The Husband look up at the giant digital screen of upcoming flights, pick a random destination, and then fly there for a good old-fashioned "TBD" long-weekend adventure. What would it take for you to set an adventure intention and then let the wind blow you where it may? What kind of mindset do you need to adopt to "take the road less traveled"?

☻ **Watch out for serendipity.** You know—those delightful happy accidents—like getting lost in the Boise countryside without a GPS signal, thinking your trip is a total bust, but then stumbling on the best farm stand of all time. Adventures are messy in nature because they involve traipsing over uncharted territory, so we need to reframe "oops" moments as chances to tap into fortuitous luck. Are you ready to adopt the mindset that things going wrong might be another version of things going right in disguise...that just might help you uncover unforeseen treasures?

☻ **Take a daycation!** No, not a staycation, a daycation. Why not fly to South Beach *for the day*? Take the 6:00 a.m. flight, buy a pool pass at a fabulous hotel (because you can do that), lounge and eat lunch for a few hours, and hop on the last flight home. The Husband and I did this on the last day of our 2021 sabbatical, and I have to say, it'll make our life highlight reel. Where can you escape to for a day, even if it's on a train or by "free is affordable" foot?

Like most things we long for in life, adventure needs to be ferreted out. It will not knock on our doors at 7:30 p.m. on a weeknight, interrupting the passive pleasures that lull us into "what day is it again?" trances. We need to get up the gumption, then get up and go.

Approach life as though it was an adventure—like a Continental love affair! That balls-to-the-wall approach to life can make up for its boundedness with intensity and sizzly passion. How can you orchestrate adventures that are both ginormous and wee—some seemingly inconsequential (like asking the server to surprise you with your order*) and some downright elephantine and even preposterous (like sending a text to your friends to "meet me in Belize in February, because I'll be working remotely there for the whole month!"). Don't you want to get to the end and look back on a life of remarkable moment after remarkable moment? What's one remarkable moment waiting for you to kickstart?

 Cover the earth before it covers you.
—DAGOBERT RUNES

PAINT BY NUMBERS STEP #5: WIDENING YOUR LIFE WITH VITALITY

Can I ask you to blow the dust off your notes from chapter 8? While you're flipping back, refer to chapter 2 when you plotted the entirety of your life on page 53—where were you on that x-axis of vitality?

You'll recall from my research that a majority of people identify as "Meaningfully Bored," with a desire to expand their vitality. Widening our lives with zest-inducing activities is a great place to start in an effort to live like we mean it because it's typically easier to do than seeking out meaning...and as discussed, vitality activities can help pave the way toward meaning.

Maybe you identified a need to Go for Gusto and dedicate real time, energy, and attention to your positive sense of aliveness...or perhaps you're already feeling zesty but you're always game to shift even further to the right of the spectrum. Regardless of how vitally plugged-in you feel today, here are a few ideas to widen your life:

- **Hark back on the times you felt anywhere close to the "rapture of aliveness."** What were you doing then? Who were you spending time with? What was your mindset? What activities might you want to pick back up?
- **Give yourself permission to try new things.** Explore what interests you, while acknowledging it will feel fumbly at first—like learning

---

* I officially dare you to do that! (And if you do it, I'll do it too.)

conversational Portuguese, taking a knife-skills class, reupholstering that chair from the flea market...anything new and decidedly out of your comfort zone. Blue eyeshadow, maybe?

- **Keep track of the new things you've tried.** It's amazing and motivating to look back on a list of things you've "given a go"; it can also help hold you accountable to try one new thing a week, for example. How often do you want to introduce newness? Where might you record your "Vitality Victories"? Some teams I work with share weekend photos with one another to keep an encouraging and gently competitive spirit of go-for-it-ness in the air.

- **Retry something you used to like as a kid,** like trampolining, baking, or ~~shoplifting~~ playing piano.

- **Barrage yourself with the following positive emotions**—one emotion per week will do: joy, love, gratitude, hope, serenity, interest, pride, amusement, awe, and inspiration. Vitality often emerges with the pleasure of these emotions. Which one jumps out at you first?

- **Consult your "Things That Make Me Happy" list.** Commit to doing at least one thing—big or small—on your list each week, like texting a long-lost friend or dancing in your jammies at night.

- **Quickie checklist from chapter 8**...because we all love a chapter summarized in a bullet point list, don't we? Put a checkmark beside the ideas that still resonate with you:
  - Do things you value
  - Move around, a lot
  - Copy a lively role model
  - Adopt a play mentality
  - Grease the social skids
  - Use your ESP (all of your senses)
  - Become constantly curious
  - Assertively—bordering on aggressively—pursue life
  - Intentionally live a life of leisure
  - Prioritize hobbies
  - Make up and participate in preposterous celebrations
  - Less screen and social time
  - Take. Your. Vacation. Time.
  - Relinquish the idea that more money = more happiness

- ☠ Consider a healthier lifestyle
- ☠ Avoid deadening people
- ☠ Strangle your habits and routines

What specific things would you like to do to widen your life? Make a list of your "Top 100 Ways to Widen My Life" ideas here. (Or 10 ... I'd be happy with 10.)

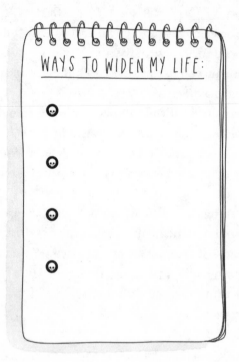

PAINT BY NUMBERS STEP #6: DEEPENING YOUR LIFE WITH MEANING

Here we are with the counterbalance to all that fun and fizz: *meaning*. Skim through your notes from chapter 9, and see what felt particularly resonant. On the Astonishingly Alive zones, where were you on that y-axis of meaning?

Whether the dot you placed was below the midpoint (i.e., you're feeling a little empty and lacking in purpose) or off the top of the grid (i.e., so deep you're drowning in meaning), these ideas to further deepen your life might just make your master plan for life:

- **Consider the times you felt like life was more meaningful.** What was different then? Why reinvent the wheel—what can you do now to reactivate some of that meaning?

- **Rate your current level of purpose for waking up each day on a scale of 1–100.** What might it take to notch it up just two points?

- **Think of someone you know with a strong sense of meaning.** What do you notice about them? Are they plugged into purpose in or outside of work? Committing acts of service? In the midst of deep relationships? Devoted to something? Spiritually infused? Generous with their time, dough, and smiles? What do they do that's worth emulating?

- **Deflate the pressure to have a "big enough" purpose.** Purpose and meaning are so very relative. You don't have to start a global not-for-profit to have your purpose "count." It can be your purpose to make people feel included in whatever circles you populate, for example.

- **Let's pretend you passed away** (RIP—it was one hell of a wake, by the way). How do you want people to remember you? How can you readjust your life to leave that kind of legacy?

- **Get others' input.** Ask a trusted family member or friend where *they* observe meaning in your life. Their answers might provide a fresh perspective . . . or they might inspire you to make a shift. Whom might you want to ask?

- **Consider reading** Viktor Frankl's *Man's Search for Meaning.*

- **Quickie checklist from chapter 9** . . . again, we all love CliffsNotes! Flag the points from our chapter on meaning that are worth coming back to:
  - Clue into your impact (where you are already making a difference)
  - Adopt a giving mindset, riding the volunteer's "helper's high"
  - Boost your self-awareness
  - Be willing to compromise on the hedonic high
  - Bolster your belonging
  - Consider a spiritual infusion in life
  - Become a ponderer—savoring the past, present, and future
  - Go challenge chasing
  - Embrace suffering, loss, and discomfort
  - Pursue awesomeness (awe and wonder)
  - Generate generativity for generations ahead of you

What bubbled up for you in the Meaning-Making Assessment on page 255? Any areas feeling particularly shallow? They might be worth filling up first. Conversely, if there's an area in your life that's already showing mountains (or even just murmurs) of meaning, you might be energized to dig further into those activities. Make your "Top 100 (or 10) Ways to Deepen My Life" list now.

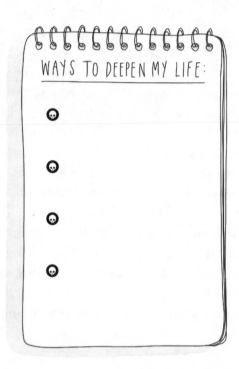

Last question: It can be easy for us to tell when we've widened our lives with incremental vitality, because the feeling of fun and engagement is somehow more tangible, more pinpointable. How will you know when you've deepened your life with more meaning? What will that feel like?

PAINT BY NUMBERS STEP #7: HAVING SOMETHING TO LOOK FORWARD TO (BECAUSE IT CAN'T BE DEATH)

Some of the lowest hanging fruit out there in the world of positive psychology has to do with anticipation; it's the ripe and ready strawberry of happiness.

Having something to look forward to, both small and big, makes a difference in our life satisfaction. It could be something like an afternoon snack—like what one of my clients gets excited about every day—because she has carved this time out to pause from work, enjoy fresh-popped popcorn, and do a word game. She actively looks forward to 3:00 p.m. every day, and it adds a jolt of joy to her afternoons.

Anticipation Activators

- **Block off your vacation time as far ahead as possible.** Planning vacations and staycations and daycations(!) . . . all that preparation and suspense is almost as delightful as the time off itself. Research[10] shows the buildup to a getaway is often more enjoyable than the vacation itself (because sunburns and lost passports and bickering kids happen on the trip, not in our heads before we go). What days are you taking off for the next twelve-ish months? And what might you plan on some of those days, to arduously anticipate?

- **Plan events into the future.** Broadcast to your social sphere in March that you'll be hosting Friendsgiving this year (if that's the kind of thing that floats your boat), and lick your lips as you pre-savor every side dish you plan to serve. One of my clients looks up the goofy holidays for an excuse to have fun—like how National Hot Dog Day is the third Wednesday in July. He has a hot dog party and looks forward to it all year, as do the invitees. What can you plan for and savor the shit out of until that date arrives?

- **Anticipation might be hiding in plain sight.** Anticipation isn't about always having a costly and epic trip on the horizon or a big annual event you have to plan and bake all sorts of pies for. To the contrary, it's often more about thinking about *what's already there* in your life and waking up to the great things in the hopper

SAVE the DATE

NEXT JUNE 2ND

NATIONAL DOUGHNUT DAY

→ OKAY, THIS IS SOMETHING TO LOOK FORWARD TO, RIGHT?!

you might have been taking for granted. Upon reflection, one client realized that time with her grandson on Fridays meant more to her than she knew, so she started actively pre-savoring the visits. The Husband and I loosely map out our dinners for the week, and when we've earmarked pizza for Thursday night, for example, I am aflutter all week long, excited about what toppings I'm going to pick out. What little things can you look forward to? Pepperoni and mushrooms, maybe?

- ☠ **Create an anticipation plan.** I ask clients to ensure they have something to look forward to in the next 7, 30, and 365 days. One woman in particular has done a bang-up job of crafting her life to maximize anticipation. She looks at her calendar and maps out visits with friends, birthday celebrations, or work milestones to keep excitement on the horizon at all times. Take out your calendar now, and check for anything worth pre-savoring in the next week, month, and year. If nothing is there, that perfectly illustrates how we have to be the ones to build the good stuff in. So...what are you going to build in?

Take a moment to think about how you might engineer your life to look forward to events, experiences, get-togethers, meals, holidays, Amazon packages—ideally things that correspond with the parts of your life that might be in the dead zone as of late. What small, medium, and large things do you want to see on your horizon?

Building Bite-Size Bucket Lists

The Bite-Size Bucket List makes the biggest life anticipation list of all—the traditional Bucket List of things we want to do before we die—fabulously manageable. Most of us know we'll never live long enough to experience and accomplish the things we'd love to stuff into our four thousand Mondays, but it still stirs a tad bit of heartburn to see a daunting Bucket List of Things I'll Never Get Around to Doing because I'll Either Die First or Not Get Off My Behind to Actually Make Happen. Bite-Size Bucket Lists work better because they nudge the dreaming into doing; they're scoped for sweet sanity.

I make countless Bite-Size Bucket Lists to capture the Things I Want to *Do* With My Life, in an attempt to actually achieve some of those things (because if it's not written down, it's just a dream withering on the vine without a plan). Every long weekend, summer, winter holiday break, and vacation, The Husband and I get a piece of paper out of the printer and draft "The List of All Things [Whatever the Thing Is]." By way of example, we're working on "The List of All Things Staycation" right now, because we're doing one of those here in Palm Springs soon—and the risk of waking up and letting two days off work feel like just another unexceptional weekend is menacingly great. We need a list of ideas to keep us on track and to make sure we do in fact get to the World Famous Crochet Museum in Joshua Tree—a tiny little wagon that houses a curious abundance of crocheted alligators that have no business being in the desert. I cannot fucking wait.

These deceptively simple lists are massive difference-makers for how I choose to live like I mean it—dreaming up and planning around seasons / trips / weekends / birthdays / National Tortilla Chip Days* / random Wednesday mornings—and I'm certain if I didn't make these Bite-Size Bucket Lists I'd have died (on the inside) long ago from Routine Overdose.

When we don't want to miss out on our lives—not because we're degenerates but because that's just what we're prone to do—we need to take our lives by the reins. Sit down and dream up your own Bite-Size Bucket Lists. Be sure to capture minute details, so you're creating action items to accomplish *and* little bullet points to anticipate. Examples:

- **Things We'll Do in the Best July Ever** (e.g., "sleep outside in the backyard," "catch fireflies with the kids," "go strawberry picking")
- **List of All Things Amazing Week Off on Vacation** (e.g., "eat breakfast in bed every morning," "visit the Mayan ruins," "run 5k on the beach, in a row")
- **Top 20 Ways We'll Crush the Winter Holidays** (e.g., "have a reading marathon," "bake Grandma's Mystery Elf Bars," "check out the light show downtown")
- **The List of All Things Fall: Weekend Edition** (e.g., "organize a neighborhood pumpkin carving contest," "stay overnight at that cute country inn," "go rock climbing")

---

* February 24—this bitch does not mess around.

- **Best Career Year of My Life List** (e.g., "initiate twelve mentor sessions," "take the CPA exam," "make one presentation per quarter")
- **Things to Do until My Next Birthday** (e.g., "do Pilates thirty-six times," "write my book proposal," "travel to San Antonio")

What are the parameters of your first Bite-Size Bucket List? You can have several on the go at the same time, of course.

If you are also inspired by the good old-fashioned Big Bucket List, I am not here to stop you from drafting that size-large list of things to squeeze in before you die. What might be on that list? Could that list inform the bite-size lists?

PAINT BY NUMBERS STEP #8: MAXIMIZE MEMENTO MORI

Well, duh.

How has your memento mori mojo been going since we first spoke of it however many Mondays ago? How about a quick bit of math acrobatics: How many weeks has it been since you calculated your number of Mondays left? And if you subtracted those weeks from your original number of Mondays, what's your new Life Countdown Total? It's okay if you're not as smitten with the idea of death as me, but we do want you at least *slightly* smitten. And if "smitten" doesn't sit with you, then we very much want you to respect death—can we agree on that? A healthy dose of respect for the Reaper?

We spent the 2010s extoling the virtues of YOLO before decisions big and small,* and now it's time for YODO, friends and family. We spoke in chapter 3 about little reminders of The Big Reminder—the little tools and talismans to help keep the mighty "remember you must die" message at the forefront. In addition to the laundry list of ideas we chatted about

---

* We were so innocent back then, weren't we? And then the '20s came roaring.

there, what memento-mori-esque things can you keep in your passive sight line?

- ☠ I just ordered a custom-embroidered pillow on Etsy that reads, "YOU ONLY DIE ONCE" (but of course). How about getting your own pillow embroidered with a reminder that "YOU ARE DYING!" in a colorful, cheery font?

- ☠ Perhaps you write, "YOU ARE A BEAUTIFUL CORPSE-IN-THE-MAKING" on a Post-it note and stick it on your bathroom mirror for a confidence booster with unexpectedly meaningful undertones?

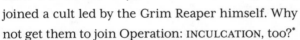

- ☠ Trip over your skull-inspired decor, keychains, coins, outfits. Make memento mori in-your-face enough that people who visit your home/office/purse raise an eyebrow and wonder if you've joined a cult led by the Grim Reaper himself. Why not get them to join Operation: INCULCATION, too?*

- ☠ Watch Steve Jobs's Stanford commencement speech—the one he delivered about a year after being diagnosed with pancreatic cancer. It's worth a before-bedtime watch tonight if you haven't seen it yet.

- ☠ Pull out a fresh page of paper, and draw a straight line. The starting point on the left is your birth, and the ending point on the right is your death. Draw an exclamation point on the line to indicate where you are in the grand scheme of your life. Think about that exclamation point as you go about your day.

- ☠ When you need a little egging on in life, try this sentence starter: *"Life's too short* not *to..."* For example, "Life's too short *not* to give my own

---

* Whoa—let's slow down on the cult thing. But you are allowed to buy this book for thirty of your closest friends and see what catches fire for them?

business idea a go," "Life's too short *not* to hire that matchmaker," or "Life's too short *not* to go on that birding trip in Honduras." Try filling in the blanks now: *"Life's too short* not to _____*."*

☻ When you need a helpful prompt to curb counterproductive thoughts or actions, try starting sentences with *"Life's too short to..."* For example, "Life's too short to worry about this birthday party being perfect," "Life's too short to keep hanging around with Gillian, who's really more of a frenemy," or "Life's too short to care about Tom's latest promotion." Fill in the blanks with this version: *"Life's too short to* _____*."*

☻ And your "best for last" paint-by-numbers question: You are still counting your Mondays, right? How many do you have left?

I have to say, you did a nice job of painting by number across these eight steps. Some of the topic areas might have warranted broad brushstrokes, because maybe you've nailed the pre-grets thing or you're already living with width in life, for example. Great! Maybe some steps required painting with detailed, pointillistic care, because you know the depth in your life needs a little TLC, for example. Also great! Some of your paint-by-number canvases look like perfect Bob Ross-esque mountainous landscapes, organized and clear, while for others your canvases look like paint factory explosions—a lot of scribbles and question marks. Zero worries—you will get to prioritize your needs and wants in our wrap-up chapter.

Temporal scarcity is in full effect; our time is almost over (in the book—not in life)! We have one last chapter together, and I don't know about you, but I'm pretty bummed that our time's coming to an end. How can we make the most of it? How can we savor it? Should we plan a party? If you bring the limes, I'll bring the tequila. We're going to make it the best postmortem shindig of all time.

CHAPTER 11

THE POSTMORTEM: THE GREAT BIG "SO NOW WHAT?" BEFORE YOU BITE THE BISCUIT

 Death is our friend precisely because it brings us into absolute and passionate presence with all that is here, that is natural, that is love.

—RAINER MARIA RILKE

This. Is. It. We made it to the final chapter of our "Living Like You ~~Give Two Shits~~ Are Astonishingly Alive before You Cease to Exist, because It's Really Just a Matter of Time" odyssey-adventure, and I'm not going to lie to you—I'm feeling feelings over here. I don't want our time to come to an end. Maybe you're feeling feelings about this postmortem, too?

YOU, swallowing hard: Postmortem?
ME: I'm sorry, is that a question?
YOU: (*unresponsive*)

Right! A postmortem is an examination of a dead body to determine the cause of death—but that sounds way less cheery than what I'm going for here in our last chapter. To the best of my knowledge, you are not dead yet—so there will be no autopsies, at least until further notice.

We're gathered here today to put a pretty black bow on this Existential Exhumation of yours, this excursion we've journeyed on together for the last ten chapters. You just barfed a lot of color onto your canvas in the paint-by-numbers chapter, and we need to take those ideas and craft them into a plan that feels invigorating and doable. The plan won't be Reaper-proof, of course, but it will act as Reaper Repellant.*

So how is this postmortem going to go down, especially if autopsy is off the table? Think of it like any good funeral: one part poignant reflection, one part inspiration, one giant part "So Now What," one part hugging, and another part whatever's-in-your-flask.

Can I encourage you to take ten deep, slow breaths before we dive in? This is your life we're planning here, and we want you in the right headspace, in possession of all your faculties (minus those swigs from time to time). Keep an open mind as you prepare to give the rest of your life a real go . . . before you go.

Coaching Chestnut: Forgetfulness vs. Mindfulness of Being. The philosopher Martin Heidegger[†] asserts[‡] that we tend to veer down one of two avenues in the way we live our lives: we're either *forgetful* of being or *mindful* of being.

Forgetfulness of being is less about misplacing your keys and more about "leveling down," living in a world of things, becoming consumed with the whirlwind of life and concerned with the *way* things are . . . rather than *that* things are in the first place.

In glorious contrast, the mindful state of being includes an all-consuming awareness of being alive, of the fragility of life, and how acutely responsible we are for the way we live our lives. This is where change exists in all

---

* Every day you live with width and depth makes you less desirable to Grim, who prefers his meat tenderized by time spent in the dead zone.
† Remember we spoke about Heidegger back in chapter 4—the "life should be an ongoing adventure perfused with unshakable joy" guy?

its potency—where the potential to live astonishing lives is possible—in this mindfulness-of-being mindset.

Let's get you into the mindful state of being as you map out your next life steps: full of intention and agency.

THINGS I KNOW TO BE TRUE ABOUT MYSELF

 Abraham Maslow once said, "If you plan on being anything less than you are capable of being, you will probably be unhappy all the days of your life." We're here not just to prevent unhappiness but to help you become everything you're capable of being.

Think about what you've reflected on so far—what you hope for, what you dream for, what you're great at, what you value, why you're here on our planet. When you imagine yourself fully actualizing those things, what does that look like? How would you describe yourself at your best, as a fully optimized person, fully flourishing? And I mean literally—what does this version of yourself act like? Look like? Sound like? Live like?

◉ My most important values in life are:

_____

_____

◉ My biggest strengths to lean on are:

_____

_____

◉ My purpose/meaning in life could be described as:

_____

_____

◉ I feel most alive when:

_____

_____

☻ The things I am most proud of (that I did, said, thought, etc.) while reading this book are:

_____

_____

☻ The limiting beliefs I have let go of (e.g., about myself, life, others), that I no longer believe, are:

_____

_____

☻ The positive beliefs (e.g., about myself, life, others) that I now do believe are:

_____

_____

☻ The things I am doing differently in terms of vitality in my life, as a direct result of this book, include:

_____

_____

☻ The things I am doing differently in terms of meaning in my life, as a direct result of this book, include:

_____

_____

☻ Something that surprised me about myself during this book is:

_____

_____

☻ Things I know to be true about myself at this point:

_____

_____

I know I encouraged you to let your ideas germinate while reading these many pages together—without pressure to Take Immediate Action Today—because we knew this wrap-up was coming. But I also know you likely made a few real-life tweaks, because life just begs to be lived. So are there any highlights that stand out for you, where you feel particularly proud of any growth you've made?

THINGS WE MUST KEEP IN MIND ON THE ROAD
TO ASTONISHING ALIVENESS

Potholes be damned! Pitfalls are a feature of the human experience. We can't erase them, but we can manage them, so they don't derail us. Keep these fair warnings in mind...

☻ **Self-imposed pressure is a thing.** I work with a lot of people who judge themselves for not living wider and deeper, for having a certain degree of lacklusterosity. Maybe you're the type to be hard on yourself, too?* Here's the thing: the only one judging you is you. And if you've been living a Squander-Filled Life thus far (instead of the Squander-Free Life we're aiming for), firmly planted in the Dead Zone (or taking several day trips there), all of that is water under the bridge. Sometimes days and weeks and even months feel like write-offs, and if that's the case for you, then Write Them Off. Let them go. All you have is today, and hopefully an assortment of Mondays ahead of you to take action. Today is your chance. Yesterday is just a bunch of photos in your phone and memories you can barely hold onto, and tomorrow—well. Don't even get me started on tomorrow. Make a choice about *today*.

☻ **You are going to get off track with your Like My Life a Lot More plan...all the time.** This is not because you are a loser at life but because you are a busy, successful, well-meant person who oh-so-humanly gets swept up in the current of life's minutia. You will need to deal with password-resetting bullshit and other people's inconvenient problems and last-minute assignments from Tom that get in the way of the life you yearn to be living. Having a blueprint for what you know matters will help you get back on track more often than you fall off track.

I'm looking right at you. Yes, you.

- **Small doses of aliveness add up to an Astonishingly Alive life.** Living your life wider and deeper is about the small things, adding up over time, to make a life worth living. You might be into big 'n' ballsy life moves—like the woman I worked with who woke up one day and quit her job, moved to the Florida Keys, and put all her energy into opening up a creatively fulfilling Etsy shop. If bold moves are your thing, be bold! But please know that for the rest of us, it's about incremental, volitional decisions to be more alive, every moment of every day. Skipping a book club meeting to read in the bath for some necessary alone time might be the small-scale alive-inating decision for you. Deciding to drink a big glass of water when you wake up and then seven more in the day is an important, relatively-small-effort vote for well-being. Small changes compound without you taking notice until reaching for a glass of water first thing in the morning becomes a healthy workout routine five days a week. Our lives are really just five-minute fragments of time—192 of these sweet little segments within our waking hours each and every day—patched together to make a life. How can you best manage your five-minute increments?

- **Life Done Right means something different for each one of us.** Your version of an Astonishing Life might involve working more *or* working less...saying yes more *or* saying no more...taking more courses to learn *or* taking fewer courses to actually apply all that you've been learning...socializing more *or* socializing less...dropping your mundane habits *or* picking up healthy habits...spending some of your hoarded cash on experiences *or* saving money for peace of mind...setting goals *or* eschewing goals in favor of dreams...You get the idea here; I know you do. Living like we mean it is entirely dependent on the perspective of the person living that life. A great life for you this evening might look different this time next year, which encouragingly means you're growing and evolving.

- **Be wary of the myth of Living Large.** I'm a fan of living with fervor—living with intention, in ways that leave us feeling like we didn't squander the shit out of our time. But as we've discussed, this doesn't mean we need to Live Large, like gazillionaires jet-setting and caviar-ing around the globe. Happiness isn't contingent upon larger-than-life voyages and front-row seats and tasting menus and—wait! These are all fun and fine! Don't not do them (if you can afford them)! Just remember that Living Large isn't the only pathway to the good life.

- ☠ **Kill the comparison.** The wind can be taken out of our aliveness when we compare our experience of being alive with someone else's. Scrolling through the Fun Facade on social media isn't for the faint of heart, especially when others are attending so-hip-it-hurts barista jams (WTF?) or cavorting on private jets with all-you-can-eat caviar on board (ew). If you can't find a way to feel inspired by other people's carpe diem sprees, maybe curtail the screen time? Comparison-ignorance really is bliss.

- ☠ **Let's bury fear, not our plans.** For some of us, we're scared of the thing we really want, so we cleverly launch Operation: Sabotage. (Cue every frustrated entrepreneur who can't find time for liftoff.... Fear of rejection and failure are paralyzing, and this girl knows a thing or two about that deadly fear duo.) We solemnly say, "Someday I'll _____," and then avoid the very thing we want, because it's 390 times easier to play not to lose than to play to win. The Graveyard of Hopes and Dreams has a waiting list, and your name must never make that list. It's okay to be secretly afraid to reach our goals / put ourselves out there at acting class / attend a networking luncheon. Think about a time when you were scared but did it anyway. You do hard things all the time. *Permission granted to press the "Refresh" button.*

- ☠ **"Go confidently in the direction of your dreams.** Live the life you have imagined." This Henry David Thoreau quote has always been a favorite of mine, maybe because I'm always working on feeling more confident...maybe because I love the idea that we can give ourselves permission to live the lives we've imagined. Are you feeling particularly permissive about what you have imagined for yourself? This book has been a massive imaginarium (the big aquarium you've been swimming around in, imagining all sorts of possible realities for yourself). Think of the many notes (or mental musings) you've made along the way about things you'd like to do, ways you'd like to live, who you want to become.... You have no shortage of content. I urge you to summon up the confidence, energy, and courage to live the life *you've* imagined.
- ☠ You might recall filling out a "spice your life up" permission slip in chapter 7. If you're like most people, you might need to flash an even larger green light to make changes that feel more substantive. Where do you need to give yourself permission to press the "Refresh" button in your life?
  - ☠ You get to move to the coast (pick a coast, any coast!).
  - ☠ You get to respectfully leave a loveless and/or lifeless relationship.
  - ☠ You get to leave a going-nowhere job.
  - ☠ You get to have another kid without a partner.
  - ☠ You get to retire from the company you tirelessly built (or sell it or give it to someone).
  - ☠ You get to drift away from a friendship that fails to fill your soul.
  - ☠ You get to leave the church (or whatever institution isn't right for you anymore).
  - ☠ You get to renovate your kitchen even if your siblings are strapped for cash.
  - ☠ You get to roll off the board you've been serving on for years.
  - ☠ You get to go back to school for that degree—at any age, as long as you have your marbles.
  - ☠ You get to make over any part of yourself if it makes you feel confident and happy.
  - ☠ You get to start that freelance stuff on the side.
  - ☠ You get to go for a forty-five-minute run/walk when your kids are whining about why you're not there to make them Hot Pockets.

☻ You get to do whatever the fuck you want. (Within reason, because there's the law.)

Now is the time to fall in love with yourself for being the kind of person who does things worth loving and leaves things worth scrapping.

I want you to be careful with yourself. It's too easy to let your life pass you by, to go with the flow, to not put your talents to good use, to not share what's extra special about you with the world, to not eat more bacon or cheese or chocolate,* to not visit the corners of the earth you've Googled countless times, to get to the end and feel like you led a seven-out-of-ten life when you could've reached an eight or nine *or maybe even a ten* some of the hours of some of the days.

You might want to spice things up a bit in your life with minor tweaks here and there, or you might want to go on an epic, life-overhauling journey of self-transformation. As we've just covered, I'm not here to say that it has to be serene and soothing or radical and adventurous. You get to pick what kind of life you want. What *do* you want to pick? Oh, the perfect segue...

YOUR "PICK + STICK" COMMITMENTS

The rubber is meeting the road here, friends! Here is where you will Pick the One Thing (and maybe a few subsequent Next Things) to get a move on, and then Stick the landing by scheduling the thing you picked into your life...so it doesn't become a dormant dream that wilts your life force (because we all know that sidelined dreams are the stuff that cancer of the soul is made of).

Before we do the Picking + Sticking, I'm going to ask you to make a mental agreement with yourself—something along the lines of:

☻ "I am worth it."
☻ "I want to really live before I die."

---

* Okay, so as someone who has high cholesterol, I get that we need to be responsible with our hearts...but as someone who has also starved herself, we must also live a little while we're still alive. Are you with me?

☠ "I have ___ Mondays left and it's up to me to make the most of them."

☠ "I don't want to be complacent with my life."

 Coaching Chestnut: Complacency Is the Silent Killer (okay, that and high blood pressure). Complacency extinguishes the flame within you and leaves you wondering what you did with your life—that life that once held so much possibility and potential. Complacency ferments into regrets, and as we know, regrets are fantasy fodder for the Reaper. We must kill complacency before it kills us. Every day you take purposeful action to live, rather than merely exist, is a win for you and a loss for Grim. *Today is a winning day*, because you are actively planning how to maximize your time. I'm very excited about what's in store for your complacent-free life.

PICK YOUR "ONE THING"

What choice do you need to make about your life today?

After all your reflections and assessments, are you called to widen your life with vitality or deepen it with meaning? That can help you start to narrow your focus.

I know your style: you're going to want to take ~~the world~~ your life by storm. Your temptation after reading my astoundingly inspirational words might be to pick thirty-three new things, and while I identify with you and your desire to overachieve, Ms./Mr. Hot to Trot, it'll be more sustainable if you pick one thing and actually stick to it. One Thing. Maybe just a small thing. Surely you've heard the old proverb "He/she who chases many rabbits catches none"? Once we put aside the horror of catching rabbits (because we know the proverb ends badly for bunnies), it reminds us to take a deep breath and focus. Prioritize. Simplify.

I worked with a "Meaningfully Bored" woman who was gung ho to boost her sense of vitality. She dove into the life-widening endeavor with exuberance...into a pool of overwhelm. Thinking it would be "too type B" to pick just one thing to start with—like playing a rousing game of pickleball on Tuesday evenings—she picked eight things. *Eight.*

She signed up for French class, planned a pączki-baking day with her sisters, painted her living and dining rooms in Viva Magenta,* switched her workout routine from evenings to mornings, arranged to have her saxophone sent from her parent's home, booked a trip to Savannah... I'm not even done with the list, and I'm exhausted. She tuckered herself out, too. "I haven't even opened up the FedEx box yet," she confessed, weeks after the sax had arrived (sitting in the middle of her very bright pink living room). This is a cautionary tale of what *will not* happen to you. It's all about pacing.†

Our lives appreciate it when we make small gestures, because the small things are like sweet, simple peace offerings for when we've been neglecting our lives a bit. We need to prove we can be trusted to live like we mean it...by visiting the contemporary art museum, for example, as a start. Or harking back to our conversation about getting curious and looking up the origins of the phrase "gung ho." We get to pat ourselves on the back after walking through the exhibits (Yay! A life-widening excursion!), learn a new fun fact, and *then* we can move on to proving we are also capable of following the meditation app three mornings a week.

When you've shown you can do the One Thing that shifts you further into the Astonishingly Alive zone—like going for a zippy walk twice a week before dinner—then you can layer on more, as your *Next Thing*. This is all about realistic, sustainable action to live like you're alive. It would be wretchedly ironic if your pursuit of aliveness led you to overwhelm so strong that it froze you into rigor mortis.

Even if you have a radical life overhaul in mind—like if you just listed all your furniture for sale on Craigslist to finance your "anywhere overseas" move—you can still play the One Thing + Next Thing game. Your step(s) will just be larger than most.

So let's get you laser focused on your One Thing. Of all the things you have identified as areas to grow, develop, change, or to make your life incrementally better, what stands out to you?

---

* Yes! The flashy 2023 Pantone color of the year!

† This client's story ends well: she cooled her jets, recalibrated her life-widening plan, and now plays her saxophone within a reasonably scheduled week.

YOU (a little breathless with a thin glaze of sweat on your brow): I have
a lot of thoughts and dreams and colors in my notes. Any advice on
how to pick my One Thing out of a bunch of options?

ME: The burden of choice! It's a deluxe problem I'm thrilled you are facing.
But I know it can feel like a dessert buffet: *Which one to choose?*

Let's talk more about dessert.

Culminating all your One Thing options is like taking 750 ingredients
out of the pantry, putting them on the kitchen counter, and figuring out
how to make kitchen-sink brownies.* So you have all sorts of ingredients—
in this case, all sorts of mini goals and intentions and dreams and hopes
and pre-grets, and maybe a few half-baked plans you've already come
up with between chapters 1 and 10. Look at all those sweet and savory
options!

You might feel overwhelmed with all the breathtaking things you
said you wanted to do, like visiting all 195 countries before you die. That's
perfectly okay. Here's where we get you to prioritize what to put in your
brownies, so to speak. Nothing will be shelved forever; we're just going
to prioritize what's most important to you for *now*. To further kill this
metaphor, some ingredients work well in a brownie, and some don't play
well with others. Chocolate chips, peanut butter, almonds, maybe a pret-
zel thrown in if you're feeling frisky—they could all be combined to make
a great dessert. But that turkey jerky you were thinking of chopping up?
Maybe hold on to that for another brownie, another time.†

Take a look at your ingredients splayed out on the counter (i.e., all of
your summary notes from chapter 10). Intuitively you'll put some things
away, for consumption at a later time. Now reflect on these questions:

- ☻ Keeping in mind that your time is irrefutably finite, what item(s) do
  you feel called to fit into your remaining Mondays?
- ☻ What ideas make you feel most excited and alive, just imagining them
  coming to fruition?

---

* Please tell me you know what I'm talking about—when you put a bunch of ingredients into a brownie (everything but the proverbial kitchen sink), so you end up with
a medley of all your favorite bits? Very excellent.

† Scrap that—you're the boss of what goes into your brownies.

- What items frighten you in a good way—because you know they're gold mines for the "I did the tough thing" kind of astonishing aliveness?
- Is one of those things an easy slam dunk and therefore worth accomplishing out of the gates to ride the Momentum High?
- Is your burgeoning One Thing actually composed of wee components, worth breaking into smaller, more attainable chunks?
- Is your One Thing aligned with your desire to widen and/or deepen your life?

These are your indicators. They're the clues to look for, to include in your ~~brownie~~ life. Examples include...

- Maybe you're inspired to book that scuba-diving trip to the Great Barrier Reef.
- Maybe you want to rekindle that friendship that went south for no great reason.
- Maybe your One Thing is to finish that watercolor painting in the back of the basement.
- Maybe your thing is to eat something green every single day.
- Maybe you're going to seek out a confession booth so you can start going back to church.
- Maybe you're called to apply for that fashion design program.
- Maybe you're going to ask Tom for a well-deserved raise.
- Maybe your One Thing is to finally try that South African bobotie recipe.
- Maybe you're inspired to travel to Philly for no other reason than to catch your favorite band in concert.
- Maybe you're moved to initiate couples counseling.
- Maybe you're going to make that appointment to freeze your eggs.
- Maybe your thing will be to negotiate a four-day workweek.
- Maybe you want to book that silent meditation retreat.
- Maybe you want to surprise-visit your eighty-six-year-old dad who is not expecting you and is very understanding about you being busy and all, but he'd love to see you and you'd love to see him too.*

---

* Okay, so maybe this one's personal.

What's worth zeroing in on between now and
your next Monday, in an effort to look even
more alive out there? Capture your One
Thing here:

And in the spirit of anticipated success, because you are going to nail this One
Thing, what would a few Next Things look
like? (These are the runner-ups to the One
Thing, the other ingredients you will throw
into your brownies.) But, repeat after me,
"These are *Next* Things, I will not try to start
them all today."

YOUR ONE THING

DAMN IT'S GOOD

Amazing job! Maybe now you'd like to tran-
scribe this list onto your refrigerator whiteboard as a remind of all the
goodness you have to look forward to?

Remember when we kicked this book off, we agreed that an astonishing life was characterized by giving two shits? Roger. At this point in our
adventure, giving one shit means coming up with your Pick list. Killed it!
Giving two shits will now involve the Stick part ... because as they say, a
dream without a plan is like a G&T without the G.

STICK YOUR "ONE THING"

Check you out ... You have a lofty list of what makes you feel happy and
alive, Bite-Size Bucket Lists, options galore for both widening and deepening your life, and a newly prioritized One Thing to focus on. There are
no shortage of ideas on your list! So now what? The plans and ideas and
intentions definitely won't happen *to you*, without you having to put in
a wee bit of effort to make them happen. What's the difference between
people who live like they're dying* and people who die with all their ideas
stuffed inside them?

The road to hell is paved with good intentions; I know this is true
because I've paved several miles of it myself. I have to work hard at taking
action with many of my dreams, because I'm inclined to dream them

---

* Live like they're dying in the good way, not like the palliative care way.

and then get sidetracked with the comings and goings of my life...and then lament that I never did the One Thing. You know what the secret is, the secret to doing Any of the Things? The secret to living like we mean it—other than memento-mori-ing all over ourselves? The entirely unglamorous secret? Brace yo-self:

It's your calendar.

Planning things in your calendar makes things possible. It sounds face-stabbingly boring, I'm fully aware. But how else can you make intentions move from ideas to actual actions? How else can you make your One Thing a reality? How else can your Bite-Size Bucket List items transpire from bullet points on the list to actual visits to the fudge factory? How else can you tick things off your Ways to Widen My Life list and not get swept up instead by the tasky bits of life that will otherwise consume you—like roaming the aisles of Home Depot looking for fridge filters? You pick One Thing, and then you schedule it.

Of course there's a fine line between an intentionally planned schedule with breathing room for spontaneity and a militant, stifling, minute-to-minute agenda, right?* But you know you can fit more of the *right*

---

* You know I will come over with my sidekick Grim if you overschedule your life into a monotonous, robotic routine.

things in—the things you've deemed that *matter*—if you plan them and then plot them in your calendar, right?

If you like to read sci-fi novels by the fire with a cup of rooibos, the book will not call out to you to get back to chapter 3. The tea kettle will not start whistling on its own. The window of time to indulge in this sweet snippet of life will not present itself to you. You need to do the unexciting thing of planning it. Booking it into your calendar . . . making an appointment with yourself.

Let's say you've identified friendship-bolstering as a top-tier priority.

Option 1: Identify friendship-bolstering as a top-tier priority. . . . Then do jack shit to bolster any of your friendships (because inertia will always be a compelling choice when you're busy and tired).

Option 2: Identify friendship-bolstering as a top-tier priority. . . . And *schedule something friendship-like into your calendar*—like a Friday afternoon FaceTime catch-up chat with Natalie, or trivia night at the pub with the guys next Thursday, or June 19 as your White Mountains hiking trip with that one couple you don't hate. Simply scheduling time together is a major difference maker between friendships that are dead or alive.

Want to work out more? Block off two or three chunks a week in your calendar to get active, or schedule in a session with Brock the Trainer every Wednesday morning. Want to get an exciting project off the ground at work? Preserve blocks of time in your workday, instead of letting people railroad you into their meetings. Is the idea of personal growth calling you by name as of late? Register for the course and carve out actual time to complete the modules . . . like my client who set aside one hour before bed twice a week to become a Certified Nutrition Coach. Want to dream up and make an astonishing life happen? Block off a few hours here and there to live with width and depth.

Vitality and meaning aren't going to come looking for you, knocking on your door and forcing you to pay attention to them. You are hereby required to make the space for the things you want to do, and that happens by making sure Saturday from 3:00 to 5:00 p.m. is *yours*, for example.

One of my clients started blocking off chunks of time in her calendar for her "alive" time, color coding them in her favorite bright aquamarine blue. She said if her week-at-a-glance wasn't speckled with the color of the ocean, she knew she had some adjustments to make.

The only way I know to not end up with a bunch of garden-variety days passing me by is to put a smidgeon of thought into how to make those days fun and/or meaningful. Where might you benefit from planning a special day, or weekend, or date night, or time alone?

Take a look at your calendar right now. Where does your One Thing fit it? Where can you prioritize what makes you feel happy in your days and weeks and months? What can you schedule in before the next Monday of your life?

THE MOST PERILOUS PROCRASTINATION OF ALL: DON'T WAIT TO LIVE

 Let us prepare our minds as if we'd come to the very end of life. Let us postpone nothing.
—SENECA

You are at a critical juncture at this moment. You have identified what most other *Homo sapiens* will never be in tune with: the answers to the test of life—pardon me, the answers to *your* test of life. *You now have the freaking answer key for how to ace the rest of your life.* You know what you want and need to do next. There are zero mysteries about the One Thing you will do next, and there is no question about the Next Thing after that, just as there isn't any confusion about the Next Thing after that thing.

And yet.

Life is going to do what it does best—it's going to go to hell in a handbasket in small, medium, and large ways, and you might be tempted to do your One Thing(s) *later.*

You might also get The Chickenshits—losing your nerve to apply for that grant, ask out Jayne in accounting, get fitted for the right running shoes, cold-call that big account, get bangs.

So please consider this my impassioned plea-turned-pep-talk.

Make a move. Do it before you don't. Your life will be patient (too

NEWSFLASH

DO IT BEFORE YOU DON'T

patient) with you if you defer your plans until "next summer" or "when work dies down," because it is a total softy and just wants you to feel okay about issuing raincheck after raincheck. But this is why we've chosen death as our motivational speaker; life just doesn't have the same urgency. Don't put your joy on the back burner. Don't wait for the eleventh hour to start living. (I'd be remiss if I didn't jog your memory that you might not get to even the eighth hour.)

Leaving life "till the last minute"—like you might do with submitting your work expenses and paying your credit card bill—is one way to live, but if you've made it through to chapter 11 with me, we both know it's not the life you want to live.

 The philosopher William James said, "Procrastination is attitude's natural assassin. There's nothing so fatiguing as an uncompleted task." We are not here to procrastinate/assassinate your life. In your quest for zest, we want you taking action on being alive, not living a put-it-off existence where your One Thing gets sorted into a Things to Maybe Do Some Other Time folder.

YOU: So what is it you're trying to say?

ME (on my knees, in a loud, preacher-like voice that came out of nowhere): *Do not mothball your life!*

Do any of these statements sound familiar?

- "We'll travel to the Croatian coast when we retire."
- "I'm waiting for things to die down at work to build my workshop."
- "I'm going to start dating after I feel better about my body."
- "I plan to start writing when the kids go off to college."
- "I'm going to take walks at lunch once the weather changes."
- "I'll book the trip when I'm through mourning for Jay."
- "We'll crack open the good wine for the next big celebration."
- "I'll stop working on weekends when I'm through this acquisition at work."

- "One day I'm going to volunteer at the animal shelter."
- "I'll start informational interviewing for a new job when I have a little more experience."
- "After I feel fit, I'm going to start wearing shorts again."
- "I'll visit my aunt next Thanksgiving."
- "I want to go back to temple soon—maybe after the busy holiday season."
- "After I get the promotion, I'll register for that online course."
- "It would be great to mend my relationship with my brother—maybe in time for the holidays."
- "I'll book that family trip to Mount Fuji and Tokyo when our schedules settle down a bit."
- "I'll write my haiku book when I arrange a sabbatical from work, one day."
- "When I have more time, I'll pick up Mandarin classes again."
- "I'd love to get into beekeeping someday."
- (Okay, someone needs to stop me here because I will go on until we *both* die.)

It's normal to take our lives for granted. We defer "the good life" until later because we think later is a guaranteed event in time. Surprise! You could die next weekend, and where did your plans to visit the Croatian coast go? *Right there in the casket with you, Gladys.* You've made your haiku book contingent on a sabbatical? *Maybe you'll die before Tom ever approves your sabbatical, Nestor.* It's true: I sound hostile when I talk about putting life on ice.

Want to play this game with a lighter touch? Okay, let's. You wanted to build a workshop? If you wait too long, your rheumatoid arthritis might flare up and get in the way of woodworking your little heart out. You wanted to wait to start the course after getting the promotion? What if the course is what will help get you promoted . . . and maybe the promotion isn't in the cards for you? Does that mean no course for you? You wanted to wait for tranquil schedules before going to Tokyo (*insert giggle at how we delude ourselves into thinking schedules will ever mellow out*)? What if you do wait for "the right time" to get to Tokyo—when you are sixty-seven—and you can't do the things you imagined because hiking

Mount Fuji requires a certain level of fitness that you no longer possess? Or what if Mount Fuji blows the fuck up before you get there, because it's an active volcano? I can't even handle that idea for you.

Where might you be deferring your aliveness in such a way that you'd sorely regret it from beyond the grave? Henry David Thoreau said, "Nothing must be postponed...Now or never! You must live in the present, launch yourself on every wave, find your eternity in each moment. Fools stand on their island of opportunities and look toward another land. There is no other land; there is no other life but this."[2]

Wait, what? There is no other land? There is no other life but this? But what about the land we gaze at through our binoculars on the clear days—that island where we're for sure going to be more fulfilled and educated and successful and loved and wide and deep, with way better abs? Some of us have been living warm-up lives, lives in training with a distant, hazy view to Astonishingly Alive Island, where the best years of our lives will ostensibly play out.

That's a bunch of bullshit.

Don't wait.

Use the good dishes tonight. Start drafting your calligraphy business website today. Start chapter 1 today (because you never know when your last chapter will sneak up on you). Set up an online dating profile tonight, regardless of how you feel in your jeans. Register for that Delicious Dim Sum class today, even if you're under water at work (because the work will always be there waiting). Open the good wine on a random weekday in March because you're just so darned delighted to be alive.

What are you waiting for? Go do your One Thing—before inertia, injury, illness, ennui, Tom, or getting hit by lightning gets in your way. Don't. Wait.

THE BIG END EXERCISE

Are you willing to do one last exercise with me—just for old times' sake? (Of course you are. You are now living an Astonishing Life of Yes, and it would be unseemly to say No after all we've been through.) Humor me with this one.

Well, it happened: you went the way of the dinosaurs. Holy crap, you died! You always knew this day would come, and as always, you were right. So here you are, looking back on your life, being interviewed by a middle-aged woman from Four Thousand Mondays about how you really *did* live an astonishing life.

1. What parts of your life were you most proud of? And why?
2. What regrets did you avert, because you made careful course corrections to prevent them?
3. What edits did you make—big and small—for when maybe your life had lost its way?
4. What were specific examples of how you lived wide with vitality? (Take liberties here to imagine things you maybe haven't done yet.)
5. What were specific examples of how you lived deep with meaning? (Again, liberties galore.)
6. What made you love your life? What made it special, upon reflection?
7. Who and what did you love in your time on earth?
8. What advice do you have for people who are still alive, for them to live like they mean it?
9. In the grand adventure that was your life, how do you want your story to be told now that you're gone?

Parting thoughts from the great beyond? Are there nachos there? (Please tell us there are nachos there.)

BUT BEFORE YOU GO . . .

Look what you did, you book-finisher you! Look how full of life you look! You're ready to unleash your Astonishingly Alive self out into the wild, and we're throwing you a party to celebrate you!

You have navigated through countless words, ideas, reflections, emotions, and existential angst on this adventure—and you somehow culminated it into a Next Step of Highest Priority. You've committed to action. You're taking responsibility for your one kick at the can of this life. I hope you feel proud.

And there's the Grim Reaper, polishing off the good stuff at the head of the table. He's particularly proud of you for not trying to kill yourself on your blind date . . . and also for being such a diligent student through all these chapters. He's raising a glass to you—oh!—to *remind you that you're still going to die.*

To paraphrase Hemingway,[3] all good stories end in death.

What do we have to gain by inviting this morbid Reaper into our daily lives rather than shirking him or meeting him at the didn't-see-him-coming end? I have found no better way to stop living as though we have all the time in the world than to focus on memento mori. Remembering we are going to die is the sharpest way to bring everything that matters into focus.

Counting how many Mondays we have left[*] acts as the swift kick in the behind we need to show up and participate in our lives. Just like Key Lime Slime-Flavored Twinkies—which are gone before you know it[†]—you are Limited Time Only.

---

[*] Yes, temporal scarcity! You get an A.
[†] Thank goodness.

Death acts as a powerful and healthy reminder to live. Reflecting on our impermanence inspires us to appreciate the lives we're fortunate enough to still have; it encourages us to get curious and ask, "What's possible next?" In the face of our most existential adversity, we're called to make the very most of our lives in the four thousand Mondays we've been given.

Not a single one of us is getting out alive; we're all headed for the same place. (No . . . not the McDonald's drive-through, but would you get me a large order of fries if you're making a pit stop?) It's precisely because we're temporary—because we don't know when the Reaper will show up to escort us out the back door—that we can live like we've got something to lose.

In this finite whirl-of-an-existence, you can either hit the snooze button on your life or live like you mean it, making choices to live wider and deeper into the Astonishingly Alive zone.

I hope you live a long life—a ten-out-of-ten-till-one-hundred kind of life—but that's me talking tipsy at your party. What I really want for you is a squander-free life that looks exactly like the one you've been fathoming for yourself through all these pages—as wide as you want, as deep as you want, as astonishing as you want. I think you want a lot, and I want all of that for you, too.

Living the life you've imagined is entirely possible when you stop taking it for granted. Tomorrow isn't a promise; it's a premise. You only live—and die—once, so go live a life you'd be proud to look back on from your eventual deathbed. Let's carpe the fuck out of our Mondays, my friend.

Now . . . have you scheduled your One Thing? No? Go do it.

Then go eat a brownie.

ACKNOWLEDGMENTS

Thanks to the Grim Reaper for taking an extended coffee break and giving me the time to finish these pages. (I already dedicated the book to you, Grim, so I'm done with the sucking up for now.)

Thank you to Laura Mazer, a.k.a. Agent I'm in Awe Of. Laura, I feel so extraordinarily fortunate that you agreed to join forces with me on this mortality-as-a-motivator ride. (I knew we'd get along just fine when in our first email exchange you told me, after I apologized for maybe being too giddy, that "Composure is for people who are unencumbered by joyful enthusiasm. They can have it!") I want to be supersavvy, generous, and full-on exuberant while inexplicably serene at the same time, like you.

Thank you to Thea Diklich-Newell, a.k.a. Voracious Editor Extraordinaire. Thea, you are impossibly smart (on the verge of intimidatingly so, if you weren't so lovely), impossibly effective (you somehow used a scalpel, rather than a well-warranted cleaver, to whittle my wordiness down), impossibly sagacious (will you edit this word out? It's a test!), impossibly thoughtful (consistently careful with my creative feelings), and impossibly cool (as evidenced by your enigmatic tombstone tattoo). Thank you for sprinkling your Harry Potter–inspired magic (i.e., serious talent) all over these pages.

Thank you to the crackerjack team members at Voracious / Little, Brown:

- To Katherine Akey and Lauren Ortiz for leading the mighty marketing and publicity missions, respectively. I appreciate your patience with my rookie questions, your encouragement, your creativity, and your behind-the-scenes blood, sweat, and tears. (I really hope there wasn't a lot of blood or tears. Sweat is fine though.) You both make your work look effortless and I *so* know it's not.

💀 Thank you to Pat Jalbert-Levine for shepherding the book through its various phases along the conveyor belt of The Labyrinthian Publishing Process—like copyediting, design, and typesetting. Kudos to the team—Matthew Perez, Carol McGillivray, and Emily Baker—who worked to make those crucial steps happen. I love you detail-people so much! I loved learning from you that it's *shit disturber* and not *shit-disturber*! *Because hyphens matter.*

💀 Thank you also to Kirin Diemont for your artistic input (because I was shitting my pants about doing the cover while trying not to look like I was shitting my pants about doing the cover).

💀 Thank you to Ghenet Harvey for producing the audiobook, to Finlay Stevenson (world-reigning Pronunciation Champ) for directing the heck out of it (and me, lovingly), and to Sebastian Zetin and Jerry Maybrook at The Media Staff for making All the Tech (and sourdough bread) happen.

Thank you to the team at DEY. (Rimjhim, Andy, and Jessica) for helping to spread the word about *You Only Die Once*. It's a joy to work with people who are masters of their craft who also happen to be downright joyful to be around. You're the real deal, and I appreciate every connection made. Cheers to a round of White Russians, on me.

Thank you to the people whose stories I told in these chapters. Your experiences inspire us to widen and deepen however many Mondays we have left. Thank you also to the bevy of researchers and experts (dead or alive!) I have quoted and referred to. Your work deserves to be amplified, to be brought *even more* to life.

Thank you to my friends and clients—for your infectious rah-rah spirit, curious questions, and cheery emoji-filled texts and also for making sure I hadn't, in fact, perished amid this YODO-writing-drawing hoopla.

Thank you to my dear 86-year-old dad who says he's "playing with house money" at minus 416 Mondays. I am astounded by your support, Dad. I knew you cared, but your interest and involvement in this book— from encouraging me to write my query letter alllllll the way to mailing me cash money for the copy I preordered for you online—made me feel like a billion bucks to know I made you proud. (I know you fall asleep while reading books, so I don't expect you to actually slog through these 352 pages. I love you even if you just use it as a doorstop.)

Thank you to Andy, our senior cat who should have three paws in the grave by now. You hindered my productivity by commandeering my lap—which should have been designated for my laptop—but you did make me happy, so let's call it even.

Thank you to The Husband, who all this living wider and deeper is really for. I simply cannot wait to grow old and die with you, after living squander-free lives we'll hopefully be able to remember from the retirement home. All we ever wanted was everything, and I already have that with you after 1,400 Mondays in your company. Let's rage against the dying of the light together.

NOTES

CHAPTER 1

1. Cantril, H. (1965). *The pattern of human concerns*. Rutgers University Press.
2. Deaton, A. (2008). Income, health, and well-being around the world: Evidence from the Gallup World Poll. *Journal of Economic Perspectives, 22*(2), 53–72. https://www.aeaweb.org/articles?id=10.1257/jep.22.2.53
3. World Happiness Report. (2023). *World happiness report 2023*. https://worldhappiness.report/ed/2023/
4. Sheldon, K. M., & Lyubomirsky, S. (2021). Revisiting the sustainable happiness model and pie chart: Can happiness be successfully pursued? *Journal of Positive Psychology, 16*(2), 145–154.
5. Gallup. (2023). *State of the global workplace: 2023 report*. https://www.gallup.com/workplace/349484/state-of-the-global-workplace-2022-report.aspx
6. Hamarta, E., Ozyesil, Z., Deniz, M., & Dilmac, B. (2013). The prediction level of mindfulness and locus of control on subjective well-being. *International Journal of Academic Research, 5*(2), 145–150.

CHAPTER 2

1. Kaplan, D. M. (1984). "Thoughts for the times on war and death": A psychoanalytic address on an interdisciplinary problem. *International Review of Psychoanalysis, 11*(2), 131–141.
2. National Institute of Mental Health. (2023, July). *Major depression*. https://www.nimh.nih.gov/health/statistics/major-depression

CHAPTER 3

1. United Nations. (2023). *Population division*. https://www.un.org/development/desa/pd/
2. Roser, M., Ortiz-Ospina, E., & Ritchie, H. (2013). *Life expectancy*. OurWorldInData.org. https://ourworldindata.org/life-expectancy
3. Covey, S. R. (2020). *The 7 habits of highly effective people*. Simon & Schuster.
4. Dweck, C. S. (2006). *Mindset: The new psychology of success*. Random House.
5. Kurtz, J. L. (2008). Looking to the future to appreciate the present: The benefits of perceived temporal scarcity. *Psychological Science, 19*(12), 1238–1241.
6. Singh, R. R. (2012). *Death, contemplation, and Schopenhauer*. Ashgate.

7. Schumacher, B. N. (2010). *Death and mortality in contemporary philosophy*. Cambridge University Press.
8. Duckworth, A. (2016). *Grit: The power of passion and perseverance* (Vol. 234). Scribner.
9. Emmons, R. A., & McCullough, M. E. (Eds.). (2004). *The psychology of gratitude*. Oxford University Press.
10. Moon, H. G. (2019). Mindfulness of death as a tool for mortality salience induction with reference to terror management theory. *Religions, 10*(6), 353.
11. Inforum. (2023). "Doug died": Fargo man has the last laugh. https://www.info rum.com/newsmd/doug-died-fargo-man-has-the-last-laugh

CHAPTER 4

1. Becker, E. (1973). *The denial of death*. Macmillan.
2. Proulx, T., & Heine, S. (2006). Death and black diamonds: Meaning, mortality, and the meaning maintenance model. *Psychological Inquiry, 17*(4), 309–318. https://doi.org/10.1080/10478400701366985
3. Yalom, I. D. (1980). *Existential psychotherapy*. Basic Books.
4. Snape, J. (2023, September 14). "My ultimate goal? Don't die": Bryan Johnson on his controversial plan to live for ever. *The Guardian*. https://www.theguardian.com/society/2023/sep/14/my-ultimate-goal-dont-die-bryan-johnson-on-his-controversial-plan-to-live-for-ever
5. Iverach, L., Menzies, R. G., & Menzies, R. E. (2014). Death anxiety and its role in psychopathology: Reviewing the status of a transdiagnostic construct. *Clinical Psychology Review, 34*, 580–593.
6. Cicirelli, V. G. (1998). Personal meanings of death in relation to fear of death. *Death Studies, 22*(8), 713–733.
7. Gesser, G., Wong, P. T. P., & Reker, G. T. (1988). Death attitudes across the life-span: The development and validation of the death attitude profile (DAP). *OMEGA—Journal of Death and Dying, 18*(2), 113–128.
8. Lavoie, J., & de Vries, B. (2004). Identity and death: An empirical investigation. *OMEGA—Journal of Death and Dying, 48*(3), 223–243.
9. Singh, R. R. (2012). *Death, contemplation, and Schopenhauer*. Ashgate.
10. Holcomb, L. E., Neimeyer, R. A., & Moore, M. K. (1993). Personal meanings of death: A content analysis of free-response narratives. *Death Studies, 17*(4), 299–318.
11. Juhl, J., & Routledge, C. (2016). Putting the terror in terror management theory: Evidence that the awareness of death does cause anxiety and undermine psychological well-being. *Current Directions in Psychological Science, 25*(2), 99–103. https://doi.org/10.1177/0963721415625218
12. Taylor, S. E., & Brown, J. D. (1988). Illusion and well-being: A social psychological perspective on mental health. *Psychological Bulletin, 103*(2), 193.
13. Kesebir, P. (2014). A quiet ego quiets death anxiety: Humility as an existential anxiety buffer. *Journal of Personality and Social Psychology, 106*(4), 610–623.
14. Cicirelli, V. G. (2001). Personal meanings of death in older adults and young adults in relation to their fears of death. *Death Studies, 25*(8), 663–683.

15. Sinoff, G. (2017). Thanatophobia (death anxiety) in the elderly: The problem of the child's inability to assess their own parent's death anxiety state. *Frontiers in Medicine, 4*(11). https://doi.org/10.3389/fmed.2017.00011

16. Boyatzis, R., Smith, M. L., & Van Oosten, E. (2019). *Helping people change: Coaching with compassion for lifelong learning and growth*. Harvard Business Press.

17. DeWall, C. N., & Baumeister, R. F. (2007). From terror to joy: Automatic tuning to positive affective information following mortality salience. *Psychological Science, 18*(11), 984–990.

18. Gilbert, D. T., Pinel, E. C., Wilson, T. D., Blumberg, S. J., & Wheatley, T. P. (1998). Immune neglect: A source of durability bias in affective forecasting. *Journal of Personality and Social Psychology, 75*(3), 617–638.

19. Grant, A. M., & Wade-Benzoni, K. A. (2009). The hot and cool of death awareness at work: Mortality cues, aging, and self-protective and prosocial motivations. *Academy of Management Review, 34*(4), 600–622.

20. Greenberg, J., Solomon, S., & Pyszczynski, T. (1997). Terror management theory and research: Empirical assessments and conceptual refinements. In M. P. Zanna (Ed.), *Advances in experimental social psychology* (Vol. 29, pp. 61–139). Academic Press.

21. Yaakobi, E., Mikulincer, M., & Shaver, P. R. (2014). Parenthood as a terror management mechanism: The moderating role of attachment orientations. *Personality and Social Psychology Bulletin, 40*(6), 762–774. https://doi.org/10.1177/0146167214525473

22. Cozzolino, P. (2006). Death contemplation, growth, and defense: Converging evidence of dual-existential systems? *Psychological Inquiry, 17*(4), 278–287. https://doi.org/10.1080/10478400701366944

23. Rosenblatt, A., Greenberg, J., Solomon, S., Pyszczynski, T., & Lyon, D. (1989). Evidence for terror management theory I: The effects of mortality salience on reactions to those who violate or uphold cultural values. *Journal of Personality and Social Psychology, 57*(4), 681–690.

24. Cox, C. R., Cooper, D. P., Vess, M., Arndt, J., Goldenberg, J. L., & Routledge, C. (2009). Bronze is beautiful but pale can be pretty: The effects of appearance standards and mortality salience on sun-tanning outcomes. *Health Psychology, 28*(6), 746.

25. Belmi, P., & Pfeffer, J. (2016). Power and death: Mortality salience increases power seeking while feeling powerful reduces death anxiety. *Journal of Applied Psychology, 101*(5), 702–720.

26. Roberts, T. A., Goldenberg, J. L., Power, C., & Pyszczynski, T. (2002). "Feminine protection": The effects of menstruation on attitudes towards women. *Psychology of Women Quarterly, 26*(2), 131–139. https://doi.org/10.1111/1471-6402.00051

27. McGregor, H. A., Lieberman, J. D., Greenberg, J., Solomon, S., Arndt, J., Simon, L., & Pyszczynski, T. (1998). Terror management and aggression: Evidence that mortality salience motivates aggression against worldview-threatening others. *Journal of Personality and Social Psychology, 74*(3), 590.

28. Frias, A., Watkins, P. C., Webber, A. C., & Froh, J. J. (2011). Death and gratitude: Death reflection enhances gratitude. *Journal of Positive Psychology, 6*(2), 154–162.

29. Kosloff, S., & Greenberg, J. (2009). Pearls in the desert: Death reminders provoke immediate derogation of extrinsic goals, but delayed inflation. *Journal of Experimental Social Psychology, 45*(1), 197–203.

30. Cozzolino, P. J., Staples, A. D., Meyers, L. S., & Samboceti, J. (2004). Greed, death, and values: From terror management to transcendence management theory. *Personality and Social Psychology Bulletin, 30*(3), 278–292.

31. Wade-Benzoni, K. A., Tost, L. P., Hernandez, M., & Larrick, R. P. (2012). It's only a matter of time: Death, legacies, and intergenerational decisions. *Psychological Science, 23*(7), 704–709. https://doi.org/10.1177/0956797612443967

32. Frias, A., Watkins, P., Webber, A., & Froh, J. (2011). Death and gratitude: Death reflection enhances gratitude. *Journal of Positive Psychology, 6*(2), 154–162. https://doi.org/10.1080/17439760.2011.558848

33. Vail, K. E., Juhl, J., Arndt, J., Vess, M., Routledge, C., & Rutjens, B. T. (2012). When death is good for life: Considering the positive trajectories of terror management. *Personality and Social Psychology Review, 16*(4), 303–329. https://doi.org/10.1177/1088868312440046

34. Jonas, E., Schimel, J., Greenberg, J., & Pyszczynski, T. (2002). The scrooge effect: Evidence that mortality salience increases prosocial attitudes and behavior. *Personality and Social Psychology Bulletin, 28*, 1342–1353. http://dx.doi.org/10.1177/014616702236834

35. Wade-Benzoni, K. A., Tost, L. P., Hernandez, M., & Larrick, R. P. (2012). It's only a matter of time: Death, legacies, and intergenerational decisions. *Psychological Science, 23*, 704–709. http://dx.doi.org/10.1177/0956797612443967

36. Belmi, P., & Pfeffer, J. (2016). Power and death: Mortality salience increases power seeking while feeling powerful reduces death anxiety. *Journal of Applied Psychology, 101*(5), 702–720. https://doi.org/10.1037/apl0000076

37. Peterson, C., & Seligman, M. E. P. (2004). *Character strengths and virtues.* Oxford University Press; American Psychological Association Press.

38. Oren, G., Shani, A., & Poria, Y. (2019). Mortality salience—shedding light on the dark experience. *Journal of Heritage Tourism, 14*(5–6), 574–578. https://doi.org/10.1080/1743873X.2019.1585438

39. Arndt, J., Routledge, C., & Goldenberg, J. L. (2006). Predicting proximal health responses to reminders of death: The influence of coping style and health optimism. *Psychology and Health, 21*(5), 593–614.

40. Boyd, P., Morris, K. L., & Goldenberg, J. L. (2017). Open to death: A moderating role of openness to experience in terror management. *Journal of Experimental Social Psychology, 71*, 117–127. https://doi.org/10.1016/j.jesp.2017.03.003

41. Harmon-Jones, E., Simon, L., Greenberg, J., Pyszczynski, T., Solomon, S., & McGregor, H. (1997). Terror management theory and self-esteem: Evidence that increased self-esteem reduced mortality salience effects. *Journal of Personality and Social Psychology, 72*, 24–36.

42. Kastenbaum, R. (2004). *On our way: The final passage through life and death.* University of California Press.

CHAPTER 5

1. Greyson, B. (1993). Varieties of near-death experience. *Psychiatry, 56*(4), 390–399.
2. Kuhl, D. (2002). *What dying people want: Practical wisdom for the end of life.* Public Affairs.
3. Tedeschi, R. G., & Calhoun, L. G. (2004). Posttraumatic growth: Conceptual foundations and empirical evidence. *Psychological Inquiry, 15*, 1–18.
4. Cole, B. S., & Pargament, K. I. (1999). Spiritual surrender: A paradoxical path to control. In W. R. Miller (Ed.), *Integrating spirituality into treatment: Resources for practitioners* (pp. 179–198). American Psychological Association.
5. Noyes, R. (2019). The human experience of death or, what can we learn from near-death experiences? In R. A. Kalish (Ed.), *The final transition* (pp. 51–60). Routledge.
6. Greyson, B. (2022). Persistence of attitude changes after near-death experiences: Do they fade over time? *Journal of Nervous and Mental Disease, 210*(9), 692–696.
7. Koo, M., Algoe, S. B., Wilson, T. D., & Gilbert, D. T. (2008). It's a wonderful life: Mentally subtracting positive events improves people's affective states, contrary to their affective forecasts. *Journal of Personality and Social Psychology, 95*(5), 1217–1224.
8. Josselson, R. (2008). *Irvin D. Yalom: On psychotherapy and the human condition.* Jorge Pinto Books.
9. Dickens, C. (1905). *A Christmas carol.* Victor.
10. Miller, W. (2004). The phenomenon of quantum change. *Journal of Clinical Psychology, 60*(5), 453–460. https://doi.org/10.1002/jclp.20000

CHAPTER 6

1. Saffrey, C., Summerville, A., & Roese, N. J. (2008). Praise for regret: People value regret above other negative emotions. *Motivation and Emotion, 32*(1), 46–54. https://doi.org/10.1007/s11031-008-9082-4
2. Leach, F. R., & Plaks, J. E. (2009). Regret for errors of commission and omission in the distant term versus near term: The role of level of abstraction. *Personality and Social Psychology Bulletin, 35*(2), 221–229.
3. Kedia, G., & Hilton, D. J. (2011). Hot as hell! The self-conscious nature of action regrets. *Journal of Experimental Social Psychology, 47*(2), 490–493.
4. Kedia, G., & Hilton, D. J. (2011). Hot as hell! The self-conscious nature of action regrets. *Journal of Experimental Social Psychology, 47*(2), 490–493.
5. Roese, N. J., & Summerville, A. (2005). What we regret most . . . and why. *Personality and Social Psychology Bulletin, 31*(9), 1273–1285.
6. Diener, E., & Seligman, M. E. (2002). Very happy people. *Psychological Science, 13*(1), 81–84.
7. King, L. A., & Hicks, J. A. (2007). Whatever happened to "what might have been"? Regrets, happiness, and maturity. *American Psychologist, 62*(7), 625–636.
8. Neimeyer, R. A., Currier, J. M., Coleman, R., Tomer, A., & Samuel, E. (2011). Confronting suffering and death at the end of life: The impact of religiosity,

psychosocial factors, and life regret among hospice patients. *Death Studies, 35*(9), 777–800.

9. Orenstein, G. A., & Lewis, L. (2023). Eriksons stages of psychosocial development. [Updated November 7, 2022]. In: *StatPearls* [Internet]. StatPearls Publishing. https://www.ncbi.nlm.nih.gov/books/NBK556096/

CHAPTER 7

1. Dunn, W. W. (2000). Habit: What's the brain got to do with it? *Occupational Therapy Journal of Research, 20*(1 suppl), 6S–20S.

2. Sinclair, M. (2011). Is habit "the fossilised residue of a spiritual activity"? Ravaisson, Bergson, Merleau-Ponty. *Journal of the British Society for Phenomenology, 42*(1), 33–52.

3. Avni-Babad, D., & Ritov, I. (2003). Routine and the perception of time. *Journal of Experimental Psychology: General, 132*(4), 543.

4. Avni-Babad, D., & Ritov, I. (2003). Routine and the perception of time. *Journal of Experimental Psychology: General, 132*(4), 543.

5. Ryan, R., & Deci, E. (2000). Self-determination theory and the facilitation of intrinsic motivation, social development, and well-being. *American Psychologist, 55*(1), 68–78. https://doi.org/10.1037/0003-066X.55.1.68

6. Nakamura, J., & Csikszentmihalyi, M. (2003). The construction of meaning through vital engagement. In C. Keyes & J. Haidt (Eds.), *Flourishing: Positive psychology and the life well-lived* (pp. 83–104). American Psychological Association. https://doi.org/10.1037/10594-004

7. Keshen, A. (2006). A new look at existential psychotherapy. *American Journal of Psychotherapy, 60*(3), 285–298.

8. Bench, S. W., & Lench, H. C. (2013). On the function of boredom. *Behavioral Sciences, 3*(3), 459–472.

9. Bagheri, L., & Milyavskaya, M. (2020). Novelty-variety as a candidate basic psychological need: New evidence across three studies. *Motivation and Emotion, 44*, 32–53.

10. González-Cutre, D., Sicilia, Á., Sierra, A., Ferriz, R., & Hagger, M. (2016). Understanding the need for novelty from the perspective of self-determination theory. *Personality and Individual Differences, 102*, 159–169. https://doi.org/10.1016/j.paid.2016.06.036

11. Kahneman, D., Diener, E., & Schwartz, N. (1999). *Well-being: Foundations of hedonic psychology*. Russell Sage Foundation.

12. González-Cutre, D., Romero-Elías, M., Jiménez-Loaisa, A., Beltrán-Carrillo, V. J., & Hagger, M. S. (2020). Testing the need for novelty as a candidate need in basic psychological needs theory. *Motivation and Emotion, 44*(2), 295–314.

13. Kashdan, T. B., & Silvia, P. J. (2009). Curiosity and interest: The benefits of thriving on novelty and challenge. In C. R. Snyder & S. J. Lopez (Eds.), *Oxford Handbook of Positive Psychology* (Vol. 2, pp. 367–374). Oxford University Press.

14. Gallagher, M. W., & Lopez, S. J. (2007). Curiosity and well-being. *Journal of Positive Psychology, 2*(4), 236–248.

15. Kashdan, T. B., Gallagher, M. W., Silvia, P. J., Winterstein, B. P., Breen, W. E., Terhar, D., & Steger, M. F. (2009). The curiosity and exploration inventory-II:

Development, factor structure, and psychometrics. *Journal of Research in Personality*, *43*(6), 987–998.

16. Oishi, S., & Westgate, E. C. (2022). A psychologically rich life: Beyond happiness and meaning. *Psychological Review*, *129*(4), 790.

CHAPTER 8

1. Ryan, R. M., & Frederick, C. (1997). On energy, personality, and health: Subjective vitality as a dynamic reflection of well-being. *Journal of Personality*, *65*(3), 529–565.

2. Uysal, R., Satici, S. A., Satici, B., & Akin, A. (2014). Subjective vitality as mediator and moderator of the relationship between life satisfaction and subjective happiness. *Educational Sciences: Theory and Practice*, *14*(2), 489–497.

3. Kark, R., & Carmeli, A. (2009). Alive and creating: The mediating role of vitality and aliveness in the relationship between psychological safety and creative work involvement. *Journal of Organizational Behavior: The International Journal of Industrial, Occupational and Organizational Psychology and Behavior*, *30*(6), 785–804.

4. Peterson, C., & Seligman, M. E. (2004). *Character strengths and virtues: A handbook and classification* (Vol. 1). Oxford University Press.

5. Cigna Healthcare. (2023). *Vitality: The next generation measure of health.* https://newsroom.cigna.com/the-state-of-vitality-in-the-united-states-chapter-1

6. Ryan, R. M., & Frederick, C. M. (1997). On energy, personality, and health: Subjective vitality as a dynamic reflection of well-being. *Journal of Personality*, *65*, 529–565.

7. Kemp, S. (2023, January 26). *Digital 2023: Global overview report.* DataReportal. https://datareportal.com/reports/digital-2023-global-overview-report

8. Statista. (2023, June). *Average daily time spent watching TV per capita in the United States from 2009 to 2022, by age group.* https://www.statista.com/statistics/411775/average-daily-time-watching-tv-us-by-age/

9. Veerman, J. L., Healy, G. N., Cobiac, L. J., Vos, T., Winkler, E. A., Owen, N., & Dunstan, D. W. (2012). Television viewing time and reduced life expectancy: A life table analysis. *British Journal of Sports Medicine*, *46*(13), 927–930.

10. Lebow, S. (2022, May 17). *Shifting patterns mean US adults are spending more time with media on entertainment devices.* Insider Intelligence. https://www.insiderintelligence.com/content/us-adults-spending-more-time-with-media

11. Akın, A. (2012). The relationships between internet addiction, subjective vitality, and subjective happiness. *Cyberpsychology, Behavior, and Social Networking*, *15*(8), 404–410.

12. Hunt, M. G., Marx, R., Lipson, C., & Young, J. (2018). No more FOMO: Limiting social media decreases loneliness and depression. *Journal of Social and Clinical Psychology*, *37*(10), 751–768.

13. Lebow, S. (2022, May 17). *Shifting patterns mean US adults are spending more time with media on entertainment devices.* Insider Intelligence. https://www.insiderintelligence.com/content/us-adults-spending-more-time-with-media

14. European Society of Cardiology. (2018, August 28). *Take a vacation—it could prolong your life.* https://www.escardio.org/The-ESC/Press-Office/Press-releases/Take-a-vacation-it-could-prolong-your-life

15. Killingsworth, M. A., Kahneman, D., & Mellers, B. (2023). Income and emotional well-being: A conflict resolved. *PNAS*, *120*(10), e2208661120. https://doi.org/10.1073/pnas.2208661120

16. Åkerstedt, T., Ghilotti, F., Grotta, A., Zhao, H., Adami, H. O., Trolle-Lagerros, Y., & Bellocco, R. (2019). Sleep duration and mortality—does weekend sleep matter? *Journal of Sleep Research*, *28*(1), e12712.

17. Alves, A. J., Viana, J. L., Cavalcante, S. L., Oliveira, N. L., Duarte, J. A., Mota, J., Oliveira, J., & Ribeiro, F. (2016). Physical activity in primary and secondary prevention of cardiovascular disease: Overview updated. *World Journal of Cardiology*, *8*(10), 575.

18. Ahmadi, M. N., Clare, P. J., Katzmarzyk, P. T., del Pozo Cruz, B., Lee, I. M., & Stamatakis, E. (2022). Vigorous physical activity, incident heart disease, and cancer: How little is enough? *European Heart Journal*, *43*(46), 4801–4814.

19. Li, S., Lear, S. A., Rangarajan, S., Hu, B., Yin, L., Bangdiwala, S. I., Alhabib, K. F., Rosengren, A., Gupta, R., Mony, P. K., Wielgosz, A., Rahman, O., Mazapuspavina, M. Y., Avezum, A., Oguz, A., Yeates, K., Lanas, F., Dans, A., Abat, M. E. ... & Yusuf, S. (2022). Association of sitting time with mortality and cardiovascular events in high-income, middle-income, and low-income countries. *JAMA Cardiology*, *7*(8), 796–807.

20. GBD 2017 Diet Collaborators. (2019, April 3). *Health effects of dietary risks in 195 countries, 1990–2017: A systematic analysis for the Global Burden of Disease Study 2017*. https://www.thelancet.com/journals/lancet/article/PIIS0140-6736(19)30041-8/fulltext

21. Harvard School of Public Health. (2017). *The importance of hydration*. https://www.hsph.harvard.edu/news/hsph-in-the-news/the-importance-of-hydration/#:~:text=Drinking%20enough%20water%20each%20day,quality%2C%20cognition%2C%20and%20mood

22. Christakis, N. A., & Fowler, J. H. (2013). Social contagion theory: Examining dynamic social networks and human behavior. *Statistics in Medicine*, *32*(4), 556–577.

23. Welzel, C., & Inglehart, R. (2010). Agency, values, and well-being: A human development model. *Social Indicators Research*, *97*, 43–63.

24. Prilleltensky, I. (2016). *The laughing guide to well-being: Using humor and science to become happier and healthier*. Rowman & Littlefield.

25. Holt-Lunstad, J., Smith, T. B., & Layton, J. B. (2010). Social relationships and mortality risk: A meta-analytic review. *PLoS Medicine*, *7*(7), e1000316.

26. Dutton, J. E. (2003) *Energize your workplace: How to create and sustain high-quality connections at work*. Jossey-Bass.

27. Cigna Healthcare. (2023). *Vitality: The next generation measure of health*. https://newsroom.cigna.com/the-state-of-vitality-in-the-united-states-chapter-1

28. Sianoja, M., Syrek, C. J., de Bloom, J., Korpela, K., & Kinnunen, U. (2018). Enhancing daily well-being at work through lunchtime park walks and relaxation exercises: Recovery experiences as mediators. *Journal of Occupational Health Psychology*, *23*(3), 428.

29. Kashdan, T. B., & Silvia, P. J. (2009). Curiosity and interest: The benefits of thriving on novelty and challenge. *Oxford Handbook of Positive Psychology*, *2*, 367–374.

30. Whillans, A. V., Weidman, A. C., & Dunn, E. W. (2016). Valuing time over money is associated with greater happiness. *Social Psychological and Personality Science, 7*(3), 213–222.

31. U.S. Bureau of Labor Statistics. (2022, August 22). *Men spent 5.6 hours per day in leisure and sports activities, women 4.9 hours, in 2021.* U.S. Department of Labor. https://www.bls.gov/opub/ted/2022/men-spent-5-6-hours-per-day-in-leisure -and-sports-activities-women-4-9-hours-in-2021.htm

32. Mansfield, L., Daykin, N., & Kay, T. (2020). Leisure and wellbeing. *Leisure Studies, 39*(1), 1–10.

33. Dweck, C. S. (2006). *Mindset: The new psychology of success.* Random House.

34. MacLeod, A. K., & Conway, C. (2005). Well-being and the anticipation of future positive experiences: The role of income, social networks, and planning ability. *Cognition & Emotion, 19*(3), 357–374.

35. McCullough, M. E. (2002). Savoring life, past and present: Explaining what hope and gratitude share in common. *Psychological Inquiry, 13*(4), 302–304.

CHAPTER 9

1. Frankl, V. E. (1985). *Man's search for meaning.* Simon and Schuster.

2. Baumeister, R. F., & Vohs, K. D. (2002). The pursuit of meaningfulness in life. *Handbook of Positive Psychology, 1,* 608–618.

3. Schnell, T. (2009). The sources of meaning and meaning in life questionnaire (SoMe): Relations to demographics and well-being. *Journal of Positive Psychology, 4*(6), 483–499. https://doi.org/10.1080/17439760903271074

4. Fredrickson, B. L., Grewen, K. M., Coffey, K. A., Algoe, S. B., Firestine, A. M., Arevalo, J. M., Ma, J., & Cole, S. W. (2013). A functional genomic perspective on human well-being. *Proceedings of the National Academy of Sciences, 110*(33), 13684–13689.

5. Gesser, G., Wong, P., & Reker, G. (1988). Death attitudes across the life-span: The development and validation of the death attitude profile (DAP). *Omega Journal of Death and Dying, 18*(2), 113–128. https://doi.org/10.2190/0DQB-7Q1E-2BER-H6YC

6. Routledge, C., & Juhl, J. (2010). When death thoughts lead to death fears: Mortality salience increases death anxiety for individuals who lack meaning in life. *Cognition and Emotion, 24*(5), 848–854. https://doi.org/10.1080/02699930902847144

7. Cohen, R., Bavishi, C., & Rozanski, A. (2016). Purpose in life and its relationship to all-cause mortality and cardiovascular events: A meta-analysis. *Psychosomatic Medicine, 78*(2), 122–133. https://doi.org/10.1097/PSY.0000000000000274

8. Lawton, R. N., Gramatki, I., Watt, W., & Fujiwara, D. (2021). Does volunteering make us happier, or are happier people more likely to volunteer? Addressing the problem of reverse causality when estimating the wellbeing impacts of volunteering. *Journal of Happiness Studies, 22*(2), 599–624.

9. Kumar, A., & Epley, N. (2023). A little good goes an unexpectedly long way: Underestimating the positive impact of kindness on recipients. *Journal of Experimental Psychology: General, 152*(1), 236–252.

10. Schlegel, R. J., Hicks, J. A., Arndt, J., & King, L. A. (2009). Thine own self: True self-concept accessibility and meaning in life. *Journal of Personality and Social Psychology, 96*(2), 473–490.

11. King, M. (2018). Working to address the loneliness epidemic: Perspective-taking, presence, and self-disclosure. *American Journal of Health Promotion, 32*(5), 1315–1317.

12. Prilleltensky, I., & Prilleltensky, O. (2021). *How people matter: Why it affects health, happiness, love, work, and society.* Cambridge University Press.

13. Garssen, B., Visser, A., & Pool, G. (2021). Does spirituality or religion positively affect mental health? Meta-analysis of longitudinal studies. *International Journal for the Psychology of Religion, 31*(1), 4–20.

14. Pew Research Center. (2015, November 3). *U.S. becoming less religious, Chapter 2: Religious practices and experiences.* https://www.pewresearch.org/religion/2015/11/03/chapter-2-religious-practices-and-experiences/

15. Bassett, J., & Bussard, M. (2018). Examining the complex relation among religion, morality, and death anxiety: Religion can be a source of comfort and concern regarding fears of death. *Omega Journal of Death and Dying.* https://doi.org/10.1177/0030222818819343

16. Nakamura, J., & Csikszentmihalyi, M. (2009). Flow theory and research. *Handbook of Positive Psychology, 195*, 206.

17. Calhoun, L. G., & Tedeschi, R. G. (Eds.). (2014). *Handbook of posttraumatic growth: Research and practice.* Routledge.

18. Rudd, M., Vohs, K. D., & Aaker, J. (2012). Awe expands people's perception of time, alters decision making, and enhances well-being. *Psychological Science, 23*(10), 1130–1136.

19. Yaden, D. B., Iwry, J., Slack, K. J., Eichstaedt, J. C., Zhao, Y., Vaillant, G. E., & Newberg, A. B. (2016). The overview effect: Awe and self-transcendent experience in space flight. *Psychology of Consciousness: Theory, Research, and Practice, 3*(1), 1–11.

20. Sturm, V. E., Datta, S., Roy, A. R. K., Sible, I. J., Kosik, E. L., Veziris, C. R., Chow, T. E., Morris, N. A., Neuhaus, J., Kramer, J. H., Miller, B. L., Holley, S. R., & Keltner, D. (2022). Big smile, small self: Awe walks promote prosocial positive emotions in older adults. *Emotion, 22*(5), 1044–1058.

21. Schnell, T. (2011). Individual differences in meaning-making: Considering the variety of sources of meaning, their density and diversity. *Personality and Individual Differences, 51*(5), 667–673. https://doi.org/10.1016/j.paid.2011.06.006

22. Shiba, K., Kubzansky, L. D., Williams, D. R., VanderWeele, T. J., & Kim, E. S. (2022). Purpose in life and 8-year mortality by gender and race/ethnicity among older adults in the US. *Preventive Medicine, 164*, 107310.

23. Alimujiang, A., Wiensch, A., Boss, J., Fleischer, N. L., Mondul, A. M., McLean, K., Mukherjee, B., & Pearce, C. L. (2019). Association between life purpose and mortality among US adults older than 50 years. *JAMA Network Open, 2*(5), e194270–e194270.

24. Pew Research Center. (2018, November 20). *Where Americans find meaning in life.* https://www.pewresearch.org/religion/2018/11/20/where-americans-find-meaning-in-life/

25. Schnell, T. (2009). The sources of meaning and meaning in life questionnaire (SoMe): Relations to demographics and well-being. *Journal of Positive Psychology, 4*(6), 483–499.

26. Nakamura, J., & Csikszentmihalyi, M. (2003). The construction of meaning through vital engagement. In C. Keyes and J. Haidt (Eds.), *Flourishing: Positive psychology and the life well-lived* (pp. 83–104). American Psychological Association. doi:10.1037/10594-004

27. Kretschmer, M., & Storm, L. (2018). The relationships of the five existential concerns with depression and existential thinking. *International Journal of Existential Psychology and Psychotherapy*, 7, 20.

28. Hoffman, I. Z. (1998). *Ritual and spontaneity in the psychoanalytic process: A dialectical-constructivist view*, p. 16. Analytic Press.

CHAPTER 10

1. Pink, D. H. (2019). *When: The scientific secrets of perfect timing.* Penguin.

2. Alter, A. L., & Hershfield, H. E. (2014). People search for meaning when they approach a new decade in chronological age. *Proceedings of the National Academy of Sciences*, 111(48), 17066–17070.

3. Turner, S. G., & Hooker, K. (2022). Are thoughts about the future associated with perceptions in the present? Optimism, possible selves, and self-perceptions of aging. *International Journal of Aging and Human Development*, 94(2), 123–137.

4. Levy, B. R., Slade, M. D., Kunkel, S. R., & Kasl, S. V. (2002). Longevity increased by positive self-perceptions of aging. *Journal of Personality and Social Psychology*, 83(2), 261.

5. Pew Research Center. (2009, June 9). *Growing old in America: Expectations vs. reality.* https://assets.pewresearch.org/wp-content/uploads/sites/3/2010/10/Getting-Old -in-America.pdf

6. Galfin, J. M., & Watkins, E. R. (2012). Construal level, rumination, and psychological distress in palliative care. *Psycho-Oncology*, 21(6), 680–683.

7. Carstensen, L. L., Isaacowitz, D. M., & Charles, S. T. (1999). Taking time seriously: A theory of socioemotional selectivity. *American Psychologist*, 54(3), 165.

8. Kasser, T., & Sheldon, K. M. (2009). Time affluence as a path toward personal happiness and ethical business practice: Empirical evidence from four studies. *Journal of Business Ethics*, 84, 243–255.

9. Whillans, A. V., Dunn, E. W., Smeets, P., Bekkers, R., & Norton, M. I. (2017). Buying time promotes happiness. *Proceedings of the National Academy of Sciences*, 114(32), 8523–8527.

10. Nawijn, J., Marchand, M. A., Veenhoven, R., & Vingerhoets, A. J. (2010). Vacationers happier, but most not happier after a holiday. *Applied Research in Quality of Life*, 5(1), 35–47.

CHAPTER 11

1. Heidegger, M. (1962). *Being and time* (J. Macquarrie & E. Robinson, Trans.). Harper and Row. (Original work published 1927)

2. Thoreau, H. D. (2009). *The journal of Henry David Thoreau, 1837–1861.* New York Review Books. (Original work published 1859)

3. Hemingway, E. (2002). *Death in the afternoon*, p. 100. Simon and Schuster.

INDEX

READER REVIEW

"THIS BOOK IS THE WORST.
JODI GETS READERS ALL JACKED
UP TO LIVE BEFORE THEY DIE —
WHICH GOES AGAINST MY BRAND
(AS A PURVEYOR OF DEATH). I
PREFER PEOPLE BORED AND LIFE-
LESS WHEN I COME KNOCKING.
THIS BOOK IS FAR TOO LIVELY +
MOTIVATING. HOW CAN WE
GET THIS BANNED?"

GRIM REAPER
GROUCHY READER

ABOUT THE AUTHOR

Jodi Wellman is a former corporate executive turned executive coach and keynote speaker. She has a master's degree in Applied Positive Psychology from the University of Pennsylvania, where she is an instructor in the master's program and a trainer in the world-renowned Penn Resilience Program. She is a Professional Certified Coach with the International Coach Federation and a Certified Professional Co-Active Coach with the Coaches Training Institute. She has coached and given talks for clients such as American Express, Fidelity, PwC, Royal Bank of Canada, BMW, and more and runs her own business, Four Thousand Mondays. Jodi's TEDx talk is called "How Death Can Bring You Back to Life" and is the fourteenth most-watched TEDx talk released in 2022 (out of 15,900). She lives in Palm Springs and Chicago with her husband and their cat, Andy.